# A Degree of Choice:
*Education After Eighteen*

Edited by JANET FINCH and MICHAEL RUSTIN

PENGUIN BOOKS

Penguin Books Ltd, Harmondsworth, Middlesex, England
Viking Penguin Inc., 40 West 23rd Street, New York, New York 10010, U.S.A.
Penguin Books Australia Ltd, Ringwood, Victoria, Australia
Penguin Books Canada Limited, 2801 John Street, Markham, Ontario, Canada L3R 1B4
Penguin Books (N.Z.) Ltd, 182–190 Wairau Road, Auckland 10, New Zealand

First published 1986

Typeset, printed and bound in Great Britain by
Hazell Watson & Viney Limited,
Member of the BPCC Group
Aylesbury, Bucks

# Contents

# Editorial Introduction

JANET FINCH

## Major Themes in the Book

This book is about what education after 18 *could* be like and also what it *should* be like if it were to become a coherent part of a social and economic policy which was both democratic and socialist. This means of course that we also have to consider what it *is* like now: our contributors have had to evaluate present provision in order to identify features which are valuable from their perspectives, and others which need to change. However, we have encouraged our contributors not to dwell too much upon the deficiencies of present provision, but to focus upon the kind of system which they would like to see. In that sense, this is essentially a visionary book. However, we do not attempt to elaborate a single blueprint for post-school education, and indeed there are some disagreements among contributors on specific issues. Nonetheless, there are common themes. This introduction is intended to draw out these and to offer the reader some signposts through the book.

Whatever their differences on specific issues, the contributors are all committed to what can best be characterized as the comprehensive principle in post-school education. This leads immediately to the question of the relationship between what presently is called 'higher' education and what is known as 'adult' or 'continuing' education. Of course there is a sense in which historically these sectors served different interests, as Rustin shows in his chapter. But the question for the future is whether the comprehensive principle in higher education implies that they must form a single, unified sector. Most of the contributors to this volume do see them as parts of a unified whole, although within that provision one would still be able to distinguish, for example, degree-level and non-degree-level work. This commitment to a policy which encompasses both 'higher' and 'adult' education leads to some difficulty with terminology. The term 'higher education' is neat and familiar, and is used sometimes in this book to refer to the whole sector. However, other contributors use the clumsier phrase 'post-school education' in the interests of accuracy, and to demonstrate their commitment to the comprehensive principle.

Commitment to the principle of comprehensive post-school provision leads to the two major sets of issues considered by contributors: what the principle means for potential participants, and what it means for institutions. First, so far as individuals are concerned, the broadening of recruitment well beyond those whom higher education now serves – especially through the principle of universal entitlement and the democratization of access which all this implies – is seen as the only basis upon which post-school education can legitimately make a claim for resources in any society which takes social justice seriously. Williamson's chapter sets out clearly the case against the present pattern of access, arguing that its élitist basis cannot be defended. Rustin argues that the notion of universal entitlement to post-school education builds upon the concept of citizenship rights, an important post-war commitment which has undergone various stages of re-definition and which ought now to be extended to encompass this particular right. This argument about universal entitlement is further enforced by White's personal account of the benefits which he derived from entering a degree course and then a post-graduate course as a mature student.

An important political development in relation to the principle of universal entitlement came in 1982, when the

Labour Party's Working Group on Post Eighteen Education produced its report.[1] This endorsed many of the principles which inform contributions to this volume: the comprehensive principle in post-18 education; the importance of 'continuing' education as well as 'higher' education as conventionally defined; the need to create an educational system which is open to all adults. The report's main specific proposal was that a future Labour government should introduce an 'adult education entitlement' of one year's education (taken full-time or in its part-time equivalent) to all people over 18, as of right. Thus, for the first time, a major political party has endorsed the principle of universal entitlement to post-school education, albeit at the minimal level of one year. We hope that contributions to this volume will serve to strengthen and promote the case for universal entitlement, which already has a foothold within the Labour Party.

A further important aspect of a comprehensive system is the need to ensure that individuals have a real possibility of taking up the right which they are being accorded in principle. This means ensuring that funding is available to support those who wish to take up their right to study, especially those who wish to study on a full-time basis. Cunningham's contribution, written from the perspective of a trade unionist, considers how entitlement to study might be negotiated as part of employment rights. Deem and Finch, however, while accepting this as potentially one very useful means of support, argue that the needs of women would not necessarily be met in this way and that alternative forms of student support would have to be available to cover people whose employment record does not entitle them to study leave. The whole question of student finance became politically significant during 1984, when the Secretary of State put the issue of loans firmly back on the agenda. Fulton's chapter surveys and discusses the issues highlighted in the subsequent debate about student finance.

Second, the comprehensive principle raises questions about the institutional organization of the post-school sector, which are addressed by a number of contributors. The most obvious of these is whether the comprehensive principle should be expressed within every institution offering post-school education, or rather within the system as a whole – in the latter case, leaving different institutions to specialize in different levels of work, much as they do at present. This issue is discussed in detail by Rustin, but there is no clear consensus between contributors on this matter, which is obviously important if our vision is to be translated into practical policy. The persistence of the binary line within the present system makes it clear that institutional change of a more radical kind would be strongly resisted. However, more modest steps which would facilitate the development of a system of linked institutions do seem more viable – indeed are already being taken. The principle of credit transfer between institutions, favoured in the Robbins Report but never seriously attempted at least in the university sector, is a vital step in this direction. It was reported in the summer of 1984 that agreement had been reached between certain colleges in London on both sides of the binary line to introduce a 'cafeteria' degree, which would enable students to take modules at different institutions. If successful, this certainly would be a modest step in the right direction.

Underlying this question of how the comprehensive principle should be given institutional expression is the tension which many people perceive between the principle of egalitarianism and the pursuit of excellence. Would more open, democratic access to degree-level courses mean that the content would have to be modified to accommodate a wider ability range? Would there be an expectation that academics should teach a range of courses, some of them below degree level, and would this blunt their capacity to advance their disciplines? How could the needs of research be protected within a system of universal entitlement? We cannot offer easy answers to these questions, but it is clear that the commitment of our contributors to the principle of widening access does not lead them to devalue those features of excellence within the British system of higher education which all would acknowledge. In more practical terms, the question concerns access to specific courses, and Rustin discusses strategies which could be adopted here.

A further issue underlying the discussions of the personal and institutional implications of the comprehensive principle is: what interests are served by the provision of post-school education, and what interests should be served? Unlike the Leverhulme Report on higher education, published in 1983,[2] which focuses principally upon the needs of the economy as the major justification for public funding of higher education, contributors to this volume envisage that a range of interests should be served by this provision, of which industrial needs are only one. In addition to the personal, intellectual and creative benefits which individuals derive from education, there could be substantial social and political benefits from the dissemination of intellectual tools more widely among citizens, and a strengthening of the democratic process if more people are able to participate in it more effectively. Along with a consideration of interests served by the present system, our contributors also raise questions of who controls higher education at the present time, and what processes of control would be appropriate to a more democratic system. Scott's chapter in particular is concerned with the tension between on the one hand maintaining the autonomy of educational system and especially its independence from government, and on the other hand the need for such a system to be democratically accountable.

The question of interests served by higher education in its present form also brings us back to the narrow population from which students are recruited and upon whom benefits are conferred. The narrowness of the class base of recruitment is spelled out by Williamson, and discussed by Rustin from a historical perspective. The base is narrow in other respects too, as Williamson makes clear. Admitting principally school-leavers creates a pattern of age recruitment which, among other things, disadvantages women, as Deem and Finch argue. The whole spirit of the comprehensive principle requires a quite different pattern of age recruitment, and the demographic changes of the next decade mean that the recruitment of more older students is likely to be a strategy which commends itself to many who work in higher education. Altering the gender balance of participation is an issue discussed by Williamson, by Deem and Finch, and by Rose in her chapter on science and technology. Williamson also identifies the issue of racial bias in participation, which is not taken up elsewhere – an omission of which we are very much aware.

Finally, the last four chapters are concerned with curriculum issues, and how the curriculum of a comprehensive post-school education could be developed. Schwarz argues that in a system of universal entitlement it would be even less viable than it is now to work within the boundaries of established disciplines, focusing his discussion on the development of cultural studies. Page and Lawrence review the curriculum of art and design, which has largely developed separately and only come into the mainstream of higher education relatively recently – a development which these authors regard as of uncertain value. This curriculum area, however, brings with it an alternative tradition which potentially provides a model upon which other developments could be based; for example, its emphasis on doing and making rather than on acquiring qualifications, the model of the student as the self-motivated, creative individual, and a desire not to press students into premature specialization. Shaw's chapter considers developments in social science in both teaching and research, and she argues for a changed relationship between the two. In her view research skills – in the broadest sense – should be at the core of the undergraduate curriculum, with the aim of giving students the capacity to formulate questions about the society in which they live and to find out about it systematically. Such a curriculum would play an important part in the democratization of knowledge. Finally, Rose's chapter discusses the development of science and technology, and links this with the very small numbers of women engaged in these areas at the present time. She argues not simply for bringing more women in, but for doing so as part of a process which would transform the content of scientific education and research, moving it away from predominantly serving commercial and military interests. Instead, she envisages science and technology which serves different and more complex interests such as those reflected in the concerns of the feminist and ecology movements.

The writing of this book has taken place over a period when the context in which education is provided itself has been changing. In general terms, the impact of public expenditure cuts is well known. But also, there have been specific changes introduced which clearly will have some impact on future developments in the sector, whatever government is in power. For example, the creation of the National Advisory Body for the local authority sector of higher education, while initially feared as a means of implementing expenditure cuts, seems if anything to have strengthened the sector *vis-à-vis* the universities, although financial controls have been stringent. N.A.B. has also confirmed the importance of research in polytechnics and colleges, rejecting the view that they should just be teaching institutions. Further, by 1985 several polytechnics had begun pressing to be renamed 'universities'. The character of the binary line is therefore already beginning to change somewhat, through the strengthening of the local authority sector. At the same time, certain changes in secondary schooling may have some impact on recruitment to higher education, especially measures to broaden the sixth-form curriculum, including the introduction of A/S-levels, which in the next few years may have the effect of creating different sixth-form routes into higher education. However, from our point of view, with our commitment to expanding the recruitment of older students (many of whom already do not enter higher education through the standard A-level route), this is less important than it would be if one continued to look to 18-year-olds as the main client group.

The last few years have also seen a series of shifts in the agenda of public debate about post-school education, some of which are reflected in contributions to this volume. For example, the idea of two-year degree courses was promoted by the Leverhulme Report and also considered by the C.N.A.A.

in 1983.[3] Following a series of very negative reactions to these proposals, this proposal seemed to be off the agenda, only to reappear at the end of 1984, associated with rumours that it was to be included in the planned Green Paper on higher education. The fluctuating fortunes of the two-year degree proposal is one illustration of the volatile nature of public and political debate about post-school education in recent years. Some of the parameters of that debate undoubtedly will be fixed by the publication of the government's Green Paper on higher education. Publication was expected in January 1985, after several delays, but was further postponed until the following summer, to include a review of student finance. We have therefore been unable to include any specific comment about the Green Paper in this volume, although we are bound to be addressing a number of issues raised by it.

## Background to the Writing of This Book

When cuts in the university budgets were implemented in the summer of 1981, a number of academics and others concerned with higher education came together in a group called the Campaign for Higher Education. Most of the contributors to this volume have been associated with that group in some way, and the ideas and proposals developed here owe much to the thinking of other members whose work is not specifically represented. We would like especially to acknowledge Professor Royden Harrison, whose contributions to our discussions greatly enriched our understanding of the historical context in which higher education has developed in Britain.

The underlying purpose of the Campaign group was three-fold, and the original thinking is still clearly reflected in the contributions to this book. First, although the cuts in universities provided the impetus for the group's formation, there was a strong commitment to uniting people concerned about the future of education across both sides of the binary line. In 1981 it was clear that many people in the university sector were tempted to the view that if the worst came to the worst in terms of government support for higher education, one could always argue that cuts should be concentrated in the inferior 'secondary modern' sector of polytechnics and colleges, leaving the superior 'grammar' stream of universities relatively intact. Members of the Campaign rejected both this grammar/secondary modern model of the binary system, and the view that the cuts should be concentrated in polytechnics, wishing instead of a divide-and-rule strategy to foster cooperation among interested parties across the whole of higher education.

Second, members of this group did not come together for the purpose of forming protectionist strategies which would merely defend the status quo in higher education against the ravages of the Treasury – the defence of jobs, for example, was seen as matter for trade unions, to which many were also actively committed. Rather, the formation of the group was seen as a way of developing a strategy for a more positive response to the cuts. It seemed that it might be possible to capitalize upon the changes engendered by the contraction to promote an alternative form of higher education for the future.

Third, and arising from this, the group hoped to be able to develop a vision for the future of higher education which would provide not only an alternative to defending the status quo, but also a different basis for making demands for higher education which might have a wider appeal. This rapidly came to be referred to as the 'socialist alternative' higher education. This book represents the attempt of various people to develop that vision. It is not intended to provide detailed proposals, although many of the contributions do have specific policy implications. Rather, all the contributors are committed to offering an alternative vision for what post-school education could be like, and what it needs to be like if it is to command wide support beyond those constituencies whose interests higher education hitherto has served. Many, but not all, contributors are members of the Labour Party and would look to a future Labour government to implement such proposals. But the case which this book makes is not party-political but socialist in the broadest sense, and seeks to make a case for post-school education which is popular rather than narrowly political in its appeal.

The editors would like to thank all the contributors to the volume for their cooperation in the process of producing it; and also the Socialist Society for inviting us to edit it as part of their series produced in conjunction with Penguin Books.

*Notes*

1 The Labour Party, *Education After Eighteen: Expansion with Change*, Labour Party, 1982.

2 Society for Research into Higher Education, *Excellence in Diversity: Towards a New Strategy for Higher Education*, S.R.H.E., 1983.

3 Council for National Academic Awards, *Future Development of CNAA's Academic Policies at Undergraduate Level*, C.N.A.A., 1983. The C.N.A.A. is the body which validates degree and diploma courses in the local authority sector of higher education.

# 1
# The Idea of the Popular University:
## *A Historical Perspective*

MICHAEL RUSTIN

This book explores the idea of a democratic and popular post-school educational system, in contrast to the élitist structures of 'higher education', by definition excluding the majority, that now exist in Britain. In this introductory chapter, I outline the case for such a system, in the framework of the extended rights of citizenship which have been the main benefit of political and social democracy. The concept of a popular post-school education system is contrasted with two antecedent historical types. The first of these is the aristocratic university, which was the dominant form in England until late in the nineteenth century, and has retained, through the example of Oxford and Cambridge, a significant influence on later developments. The second is the bourgeois or middle-class university, which has been numerically the dominant type of higher education in this century. The transition between these types can be summarized as the shift from the education of the sons of the well-born – the families of the aristocracy and gentry – to an education system which provides qualified and accredited labour power for the industrial and administrative bureaucracies of advanced capitalism, and also serves to reproduce the occupational and status advantages of its higher functionaries for a new generation. The desirable characteristics of a more universal and inclusive form of post-school education are then outlined, and policy measures suggested which could lead in this direction.

There is a long way to go to transform a system which now provides for only about 13 per cent of the post-18-year-old population into one which meets the needs of a majority. It is therefore more possible to write in concrete detail about what the educational system now does and does not do than it is to be accurate and specific about a transformed system. This chapter, and the book as a whole, should therefore be read as a programmatic sketch towards the future, not as a detailed blueprint.

## Education and Citizenship

In the post-Second-World-War period the idea of citizenship in Britain (and in some other advanced societies) has developed to encompass a number of universal social rights. Progress from a democratic socialist point of view can indeed be defined as the evolution of the concept of citizenship from its original political and juridical meanings to include certain economic and social entitlements. A minimal definition of political rights as the freedom from arbitrary interference was extended to allow rights of positive political participation, not universally achieved in Britain (in the form of equal voting rights for women) until as late as 1928. The state's role in providing material relief under various versions of the Poor Law became rationalized and universalized, as a result of the Beveridge Report of 1944 and ensuing legislation, as the concept of a minimum subsistence income available for all unable to maintain themselves by employment. The commitment to use the economic powers of government to maintain 'full employment' was the most important underpinning of this commitment to a sufficient material standard of life, in a way which was compatible with the operation of a market economy. In the same period, universal entitlement to free education from the ages of 5 to 15 was enacted in the 1944 Education Act, and entitlement to health care, free at the point of delivery, was established by the National Health Service Act of 1946. These forms of social provision have been extended in subsequent years, through government legislation and funding to improve the quality of housing, through extension of educational entitlements into the post-school age-group, and through action to provide access to cultural and environmental goods.

The case for such universal entitlements is that they provide the means of access to the fundamental conditions of life in society, without which individual liberty and citizenship become, for many, empty concepts. They establish a basis of minimal equality – the precondition of a just social order. Access to education is a particularly crucial entitlement, because of its role as a means to other goods. It is important that it should be 'free' because it determines so many life-opportunities for each generation. Education is best treated as a universal commitment by a society to its members, akin in the more impersonal way of rationalized societies to the commitment of a family towards its children. Since *some* educational process is almost by definition the key to development, and since all citizens should have an equal opportunity to fulfil their potential capacities, it follows that education should be equally available to all. Implicit ideas of this kind have already led to the creation of a more universalist and unified system of secondary education in Britain and most democratic societies. In Britain an important recent step was the requirement that local authorities submit plans for non-selective education from the 1960s onwards, and the substantial though uneven development of 'comprehensive' institutions which followed. Our argument follows this logic of comprehensive education into the post-school sphere. As the length of the educational process has been extended by occupational and other requirements, and as it becomes evident that both individuals and economic and social institutions will require education on a more lifelong basis, so it becomes appropriate and reasonable to argue not merely for universal education up to the age of 16, and for a minority of credential-holders beyond, but for a universal educational entitlement extending over 18 years and into adult life. This is the fundamental argument of this book.

The claims of universal forms of social provision have been subjected to determined attack by the Thatcher governments since 1979. The residual private sectors of both education and health care have become objects of favour by government, and public sector provision has been starved of resources, in the overt cause of greater efficiency but with a latent purpose of inducing better-off clients to turn to private provision and thus cumulatively alter the balance of political forces on which the public and private sectors depend. There seem likely to be no gains in efficiency from such transfers in educational and health from public to private sectors – rather the reverse – and there will be certain losses in fairness and in the relation of provision to need. A society in which basic access to needs of subsistence, health, and education depends on individuals' success in the market seems certain to become more unequal, more egoistical and also more oppressive and violent.

Especially in the current period of attacks on social services, and arguments for more competitive definitions of economic welfare, we think it is important to identify new steps in the possible advance towards a fuller concept of citizenship. Some 'practical utopianism' which can envisage how the future could be is vitally needed, to give confidence and substance to the idea of a 'long revolution' which can provide opportunity for creative lives not only for privileged minorities but for everyone. There is enough positive thinking in the post-school education system, and it remains a good enough experience for most of those who now gain access to it, for it to be an appropriate case study for such a sketch of a more hopeful future.

## The Evolution of the University: A Historical Outline

If socialist proposals are to be more than statements of hopeful preference, they need to be grounded in a view of historical development and the possibilities to which this gives rise. This need not imply an idea of historical inevitability, more of recognizing given limits. The institutional context in which policy decisions can be made is largely pre-established for each generation of policy-makers, and so are the intellectual traditions within which ruling definitions are constructed. It is thus important that we should understand the structures in order to grasp what specific limits on practice they have imposed, and what spaces for development they leave most open.

The account which follows can be, in an essay of this kind, no more than an outline intended to frame the later discussion of programme and policy. While it draws on an existing literature of historical and sociological research on higher education, it is not a work of original scholarship. It is, incidentally, a curious feature of British higher education that it has been so little the object of historical or sociological study, even though the raw materials for this lie so readily within academic reach. While this might be the outcome of a praiseworthy desire to explore more remote social fields, it is more likely to reflect the rarity with which occupants of donnish positions have chosen to examine critically their own role in society or that of their university institutions.

## Oxbridge and the Aristocratic University

Even though all but four universities in England date their existence from the later years of the nineteenth century, the origins of the university in medieval times remain extremely important to the formation and present-day shape of the British higher education system.

This is only one among many influences of a feudal class and status system in a society where there has not been a revolutionary overthrow of aristocratic power. Reverence for ancient tradition, attachment to inherited property and status over acquired wealth and power, and influential conceptions of established membership and corporate estate have continued to shape the élites of British society. They perhaps found some equivalents in the status boundaries and corporate qualities of earlier working-class life. The dominance of Oxford and Cambridge in British higher education, and in the recruitment of much of the British social élite, has been the main aspect of this aristocratic heritage in the university system, and explains both some of its characteristically exclusive features and some of its paternalist strengths.

One can contrast, following Halsey and Trow's account,[1] a 'traditional' and a 'modern' conception of the university in England, and suggest that they approximately correspond to aristocratic and bourgeois ideals. The contrast can be represented in tabular form as follows:

| Aristocratic | Bourgeois |
|---|---|
| antiquity | modernity |
| cosmopolitan | provincial |
| selective | open |
| humane education | vocational training |
| domesticity and intimacy (dense expressive culture) | impersonality; a 'culture of residence' not central to university experience (instrumental orientation) |

Oxford and Cambridge, for centuries the only universities in England, developed as medieval institutions under the control of the church and landed aristocracy, and were tied by relations of patronage and dependence to these centres of power and wealth. The rise of universities in medieval Europe was made possible, however, by the development of cities, by better communications, and by institutional rivalries – between the papacy and secular powers, for example – which allowed some space for the development of independent learning and some institutional autonomy. The development of more centralized state bureaucracies, in the sixteenth and seventeenth centuries, which depended on higher levels of literacy and especially on legal knowledge and skills, and the religious resurgence and controversies associated with the Reformation, provided further stimulus for the development of autonomy in university education out of the direct control of church or state. Renaissance ideas of humanism, associated with more rationalized forms of administration, international exchange, and the more open culture of cities, provided a cultural matrix within which separate institutions of learning and teaching could develop. While universities have always depended substantially on exchange with the dominant institutions and classes of the societies in which they exist, nevertheless they have since their first foundation usually been able to claim some autonomy within these ruling systems of power. The concept of the aristocratic university should not imply the narrow reduction of the medieval and Renaissance university to a direct expression of landed or ecclesiastical power. A peak in the development and autonomy of the university was achieved in England in the period between 1580 and 1670. Oxford and Cambridge had gained indirectly or directly through the dissolution of the monasteries, and through the increased demand for educated officials to serve the growing state and national church bureaucracies. Economic expansion also made resources available for wider layers of the gentry to educate their sons (it should be emphasized that until the twentieth century universities were exclusively a male monopoly). The Reformation and the rise of Puritanism also produced a much wider commitment to literacy, to learning, and to science, and the religious controversies of the seventeenth century were vigorously pursued and represented within the universities. Thomas Hobbes famously argued that the Civil War had been a malign product of the subversive ideas generated in Oxford. The more democratic climate of this period, and the divisions in the ruling élite which made this possible, meant that many sons of the poorer gentry were able to enter university.

There had been a medieval tradition of powerful clerics sponsoring poor students as a means of educating a 'stable' of loyal and capable functionaries, and of secular landowning families sending poorer men to college as companions and servants to their sons, free education being made available in return. It has been suggested that at the highest point of influence of these democratic and puritan ideas, a larger proportion of 18-year-olds were in university in England than again occurred until 1900. It is possible to see the seventeenth-century period of social revolution as much a forerunner of modern radicalism in university education as in other spheres.[2]

After the Restoration of 1660 much of the intellectual openness and complexity of this earlier period was lost. The exclusion of Dissenters from the universities cut off the major source of religious controversy and debate and also ensured that much of the development of natural sciences and technologies took place in separate institutions – the Royal Society, provincial scientific societies, the Dissenting Academies – and not in the ancient universities. It was a matter of deliberate landed class policy to ensure that Oxford and Cambridge should not again become centres of controversy and disaffection: Thatcherite conservatives are not the first to have recognized that university education can be a source of unwanted questioning of the status quo. The universities, like the established church, became more worldly, relaxed, and conforming. Unlike in Scotland, where the University of Edinburgh became the centre of a high culture of the Enlightenment, Oxford and Cambridge drifted out of the forefront of speculative inquiry.

While Oxford and Cambridge have always been highly complex institutions, responsive in virtue of their central cultural location to a plurality of social pressures, nevertheless their medieval and aristocratic origins have remained important to their modern character. This might have been less the case had their development not been arrested by the Restoration and the imposition of a clerical and philistine traditionalism during the eighteenth century. They were devoted to providing an education in a ruling class culture (which could take many different forms both within and between epochs) rather than to the development of 'useful knowledge', until the twentieth century. They were always closely linked to the centres of national political power. The central importance given to classical education served to mark a boundary between the cultural world of the university-educated, and everyone else. While classics could provide a discourse within which various intellectual and ideological outlooks could be formulated (for example, a humane Hellenistic liberalism as well as an identification with imperial Rome), one of the main effects of the entry prerequisite of Latin was to exclude the lower orders from access to the university.

From the middle of the nineteenth century, Oxford and Cambridge became subjected to criticism for their intellectual backwardness and traditionalism and faced competition from the newer and more 'utilitarian' foundation of the University of London and later some provincial universities. The contemporary processes of rationalization and modernization of the civil service, of the armed forces, the rise of public education, and the growth of the modern professions of law and medicine, produced a new demand for educated and certificated manpower. The development of the modern examination system, and the broadening of the curriculum under the influence of figures such as Jowett, began the accommodation of Oxford and Cambridge to a more rational bourgeois order. In the twentieth century these universities have succeeded in putting themselves at the forefront of scientific studies, and been the locus of radical middle-class movements (roughly – scientific empiricism) in humanities disciplines such as English Literature, Philosophy and History. They have sought, with success, to add to an ascribed superiority derived from their monopoly situation, an *achieved* superiority of intellectual merit. Their social prestige, superior endowment, and privileged access to subsequent élite positions have allowed them to retain a position at the apex of the English system of educational stratification, despite an expansion by approximately twenty times the number of students receiving degree-level education at any one time, in the period since 1900.

This successful transformation of an inherited order of wealth, status and power into an institution able to compete in the more modern currencies of instrumental performance has many parallels in British society. Recruitment to top positions in leading companies, to positions of political leadership (radicalized more by the Thatcherite revolution of the self-made middle-class than by previous Labour governments), to the administrative class of the civil service, and to senior professional positions in the law, armed forces and medicine, shows a similar pattern of retention by the upper and upper-middle class of distinct 'hereditary' advantages even in institutions where competent performance has become a necessary condition of advancement. The outcome has been a symbiosis of aristocratic and bourgeois values, which at its topmost levels retains many attributes – rural, anti-intellectual, status-conscious, exclusive – deriving from the older heritage.

The processes of modernization and adaptation of the ancient universities continue today. Women have recently been admitted to the majority of what were formerly men's colleges. Separate Oxbridge entrance exams are being radically simplified or by-passed to make access less restricted and to protect the universities from more radical egalitarian demands. The requirement of Latin as a condition of entry has also recently been eroded, for similar reasons. But the model of a tutorial and college-based system which emphasizes the sponsored induction into a privileged way of life, more than the acquisition of useful knowledge, remains dominant, and has had a wide influence over British higher and consequently also secondary education. (The present writer and his fellow first-year entrants were advised on their first evening in their Oxford College – admittedly many years ago – that if they had come only with study in mind they would have been better advised to have attended the University of Reading, down the river.) Entry remains heavily skewed towards the upper classes, and the output of graduates is even more strongly directed towards élite positions in society than it is upper-class in origin. The ancient universities retain a model of collegial self-government, on the model of an aristocratic oligarchy, that is also distinct from the more hierarchical and rational-bureaucratic model of the faculty or department-based redbrick universities. These descendants of medieval corporate bodies are more difficult to enter, but confer a greater quality of status and larger rights of membership on those who do, than more bureaucratized and less privileged institutions.

The aristocratic model of the university remains able to impress new generations of students and visitors with a remarkable depth of culture. Its buildings symbolize its cloistered and collegial character. They encode complex ideas of social boundary, representing both a fundamental continuity of conception from their medieval origins, and of precise idiosyncrasy and variation within a controlling tradition. The relationship of Oxford and Cambridge is of a stylized rivalry between two institutions which are both contrasted and yet symmetrical in their dominant position and connections with numerous centres of power and prestige. The sociologically most striking attribute of undergraduate culture in these institutions is the way in which so many activities are connected, in the minds of participants and in fact, with the corresponding spheres of influence – politics, journalism, scholarship – in the wider society. The prestige of these institutions, and the disproportionate share of financial and scholarly resources which they still secure, are a powerful instance of the continuing influence of aristocratic ideals and inherited wealth and power in British life.

## The Bourgeois University: Its Development

The second major phase in the evolution of the British higher education system came with the development of what we shall describe as the middle-class or bourgeois university during the nineteenth and twentieth centuries. This development was surprisingly late: in 1850 there were still only four universities in England (Oxford, Cambridge, Durham and London), and the first three of these (and King's College, London) were still dominated by the Anglican church. Only ten universities had received charters in England by 1900. Science had mostly developed from the seventeenth century, in institutions outside the universities. The technologies associated with the industrial revolution had been developed by craftsmen, inventors, and entrepreneurs, closely associated with the manufacturing areas of the country and with religious Dissent – far from the concerns of the ancient universities. The modern social sciences of economics and sociology had been initiated in Scottish universities in the late eighteenth century, with their more European and rationalist outlook, and not in England. But from the mid-century, reforms were slowly instituted which set the pattern for the contemporary university system.

The University of London was given its charter in 1836, but it was only in the 1870s and 1880s that the industrial cities of provincial England instituted their own university colleges. These emerged from the movement of Mechanics Institutes, on the side of 'useful knowledge', and also from the 'humane learning' tradition of the Oxford and Cambridge extension movements. Colleges of science were built in Leeds in 1874, in Newcastle in 1871, in Bristol in 1882. Owen's College, Manchester, became the first constituent college of Victoria University in 1882, and was joined by Liverpool in 1884 and Leeds in 1887. University colleges in Nottingham, Southampton, Exeter, Leicester and Hull prepared students for the external examinations of the University of London until after the Second World War, when they obtained their own charters.[3] (The University of London provided a similar external facility for British overseas territories in Africa, the Caribbean and elsewhere.) The development of the 'redbrick' universities is thus very late. With the partial exception of London University, the development of 'modern' or 'redbrick' universities in England and Wales coincides not with the first phase of industrial capitalism, but with the second. The expansion in the role of the state, and the emergence of modern professions and bureaucracies, are the preconditions for the significant growth of higher education in the twentieth century. The 'bourgeois university', as we shall call it, is a phenomenon of advanced and not early industrial capitalism.

The provincial universities had a distinctive orientation to useful knowledge – notably the natural sciences and technology – in contrast to the classicism and humanism of the ancient universities. They maintained a more middle-class and local recruitment, in contrast to the predominantly upper-class and national recruitment of Oxford and Cambridge. They were more secular institutions from the first. They became committed to the 'production' of knowledge, and especially scientific knowledge, as one of their major functions, rather than merely to the perpetuation and elaboration of a traditional classical or humanist culture. Academic 'subjects', and the professorships and departments which formed to develop research and teaching in them, became the most powerful organizational structures in the London and red-brick universities, whereas in Oxford and Cambridge the multi-disciplinary college with its implicit commitment to a more unified and universal idea of knowledge and culture remained dominant, despite the parallel development of separate faculties and major scientific laboratories. The idea of the university as a 'knowledge factory',[4] funded in part by the state because of the unpredictable and long-term nature of the returns of investment in ideas, was influenced by the example of rival industrial nations, notably Germany, which was perceived to be overtaking Britain as an economic and military power. Industrialization in Germany, taking place during the second half of the nineteenth century, involved a closer and more deliberate linkage between industrial companies and academic institutions.[5] Research, for example in the chemical industry, was recognized from an early stage to be a crucial element in industrial success. Business had a similarly greater effect on the development of academic institutions in the United States, whereas in England the gentlemanly ruling circles continued in their disdain for industry and trade. Even professional education in law and medicine took place, during the nineteenth century, outside the universities themselves. Anxieties about national economic competitiveness returned in the 1960s as powerful motivating forces for the 'bourgeois modernization' of the university system, producing in the post-Robbins period demands for business, technological and vocational education in contrast to the classical humanist curriculum. Nevertheless, the development of the 'bourgeois' university in England was constrained by the influence of the pre-existing aristocratic model. Oxford and Cambridge were reformed by pressures within and without (following the Parliamentary Commissions of 1850), and their 'modernization' preceded and kept pace with the development of the new institutions. They broadened their subject-base, and strengthened their investment in the pure sciences. As government began to take a more active role in the funding of scientific and medical research, especially during the following World Wars, Oxford and Cambridge were able to claim a leading position in these fields. Their established international position was also of great importance in sustaining their claims to intellectual leadership. While their recruitment remained biased towards the public schools and thus the upper class, they became increasingly competitive and meritocratic. Membership of the upper social classes now provided privileged access to the top institutions in part in less direct ways, through the superior *educational* preparation which was provided in the best schools. The leading public schools also reformed themselves from within in a meritocratic direction: academic ability became increasingly one condition of access to them, in a competition which took place largely within the upper class. The top strata of the public and grammar schools (with their predominantly upper- and middle-class populations, respectively) joined in a competition for Oxford and Cambridge entry (and for their prestigious scholarships) whose implicit other side was the downgrading of other universities to second-choice status. The products of Oxbridge came to fill a disproportionate number of teaching posts in other universities, whose incumbents often retained their attachment and loyalty to their universities of origin. Surveys over twenty years have continued to report that British academics value Oxbridge college fellowships above all other posts they might attain. The liberalism of the ancient universities has also been broad enough to allow some representation to some of the leading figures of the intellectual left in each generation. The intention of this has perhaps been to ensure the intellectual engagement of the 'dominant ideology' with alternative and oppositional conceptions. Marxism, for example, was subject to sustained liberal critique in the post-war period, and the effect of this was to reinforce predominantly empirical and ethical approaches as the orthodoxies of British social science until the late 1960s. But a secondary consequence of this liberal incorporation of academic dissent has been to protect these privileged institutions from attack by oppositional intellectuals, in periods of more general radical pressure. Egalitarian reform of Oxford and Cambridge, though logical, considering the key role of Oxbridge in the recruitment of British élites, has not so far been part of the programme of the British left.

The consequence of this pattern of development of the English university has been a compromise between 'aristocratic' and 'bourgeois' principles which has many other parallels in the British class system. The 'traditionalist' ideal of the university, summarized on page 22, has remained dominant despite an enormous expansion in the number of students – less in the number of institutions – in the twentieth century. Universities have aimed to maintain the qualities of a cultured corporate life in contrast to the idea of an open and accessible multi-versity.[6] Their scale is generally small, by American or Continental standards. Even the University of London has reproduced a kind of college system, now being rationalized under economic pressure. The new universities established in the 1960s represented an attempt to update and modernize the Oxbridge ideal of an education for general culture, rather than any democratic new departure. They were characteristically sited in historic centres like Norwich, Warwick, York and Lancaster, rather than in industrial towns. Part-time and evening education has been a marginal element in university work: the separation of 'extension' classes from the main teaching system, and their irrelevance to the major examination and certification process, only emphasize that the main commitments of the university are to full-time students and research. British higher education has thus remained a system of 'sponsored' rather than 'contest' mobility, in Ralph H. Turner's[7] lucid terms. It has been able to reproduce the traditional pattern of residential provision and intensive teaching for those few who gain entry to the system, in contrast to the more open and competitive entry, but less supportive forms of pedagogy, of the American and Continental systems. There is a smaller proportion of entrants to degree courses in Britain, even after the expansion of the 'public sector', than in most comparably advanced countries. But the length of time taken to graduate is less, and the proportion of successful graduates to entrants is much higher.

## The Bourgeois University: Maturity

Universities characteristically depend on institutions external to them in society, for resources and perhaps protection, but if they are to be centres for free intellectual inquiry they also have to achieve some significant autonomy and insulation from external pressure. The idea of a university as a distinctive institution is compromised by excessively direct administrative, ideological, or corporate control. The education and research programmes carried out or directly sponsored by parties, governments, or corporations, effective as they may be, are distinct from the pluralist idea of a university to which the contributors to this book probably all subscribe. If a university is *only* one or other set of these programmes, then a university it ceases to be. Universities in different epochs and societies are shaped by different kinds of external institutional pressure (there is no such thing as a 'pure' or wholly autonomous university). But they seem to flourish best where external pressures on them are limited, or when the sources of these pressures are divided among themselves, as in seventeenth-century England.

The middle-class university can and will be sharply criticized in this book for what it does not do. But it seems that this model of higher education has achieved a 'mature' state of realization in Britain in the post-war period. It has been a characteristic product of mixed economy capitalism, and of a complex class compromise. Higher education, as a form of long-term investment both for individuals and for institutions, was able to gain substantial financial and political support from the state. Yet the state has mostly refrained from direct control of educational and research programmes. Instead, it has established and maintained the conditions for a kind of free market in education and research (weighted like other markets in favour of those already possessing the relevant kinds of power and resources). Governments of both main parties have allocated increased funds to students (through a generous system of grants for fees and maintenance), directly to universities (through the University Grants Committee), and for research purposes through the Research Councils (again operated as semi-autonomous quangos). In this system, market forces were able to make themselves felt through the ultimate occupational recruitment of students and the consequent shift in subject-demand for college places, and also through a measure of direct funding of selected institutions and research. Changes in the balance of power within the mixed economy and political system were reflected in the university system by changing demand for its intellectual and human products. As the public sector and especially the services of the Welfare State grew, so the associated new professors and their related academic disciplines (especially the social sciences) were able to expand disproportionately. When political anxiety about Britain's technological or industrial competitiveness grew strong, governments acted to redress the balance in favour of these sectors by the formation of business schools, the 'technological universities' and the regional management centres.

While the university system was thus made indirectly responsive to market forces, its development also involved a compromise favourable to older-established élites which preserved much of its traditionalist character. Given generous resources by the central government, universities could turn their backs on private industry or the municipalities as potentially interfering sources of revenue. A gentleman's agreement with government left them free to manage their own affairs through the U.G.C. The dominant position of Oxford and Cambridge in the university system, and the recruitment of so much of the political and civil service establishment from their graduates, were probably the essential preconditions of this cosy arrangement. But the pattern has been similar to the state's relations to other professions in Britain, such as medicine and law, where the state has increased economic support to their élites and their practising and training institutions while on the whole refraining from subjecting them to centralized bureaucratic control. The universities thus remained committed to the humanistic ideals of pure knowledge, education, and culture, and the dons came to aspire to the status of a professional estate, whose position was sustained by a number of unique rights. 'Tenure', while given legitimacy by the liberal norms of academic freedom, actually more closely resembles a feudal entitlement of lifelong income and status, and the system of quinquennial grants (while it existed) also insulated the university corporation from direct economic pressures. Even the concept of the non-repayable student grant belongs to this family of concepts, as a kind of right (subject only to the minimal conditions of physical attendance and the survival of annual examinations) to temporary and junior membership of this estate. A particular instance of this implicit preoccupation with élite social membership (to which Ernest Gellner[8] first drew attention) was in the domination of the discipline of philosophy in the 1950s and 1960s by the 'ordinary language philosophy' of Wittgenstein and Austin (Cambridge and Oxford figures, respectively). In this approach, consistency with presumed canons of everyday (actually senior common-room) linguistic usage became a criterion of philosophical truth, and the wider universe of systematic ideas was completely excluded from consideration. Other countries' bourgeois university systems, such as those of Germany, the United States, or France, though developed during the same stage of bureaucratic capitalism, showed rather different and less distant relationships between higher education institutions and business and administrative practice. Technology, applied science, and the administrative and behavioural sciences were less slow to develop in these societies where the industrial virtues were more highly valued.

The maturity of the bourgeois university has, however, rested firmly on the interests of a particular social class. Pierre Bourdieu[9] has pointed out how the bureaucratization of the commercial and industrial corporation has transformed the importance of education for the middle classes. Control in the modern organization is exercised through the command of abstract procedures (of measurement, specialized technology, and symbolic manipulation) and not by the force of personality and will as in the earlier days of industrial capitalism. The smooth and not the rough now rule. (There are exceptions.) While inherited financial capital remains important in determining ultimate economic power, 'cultural capital' has assumed a new importance as the number of independent entrepreneurs has declined, and as the middle classes have become dependent on, and exercise their claims to resources and power through, employment in large organizations.

Educational credentials have become a key currency in the competition for life-chances. For employers, they signify a certain level of competence, and, at the higher levels, of prior socialization into managerial and professional attitudes. For potential employees they offer some passport to privileged occupational positions. The growth of state bureaucracies from the late nineteenth century onwards has been similar in its effects to the bureaucratization of the private corporation, in creating an increasing demand for certified manpower. The modernization of the higher civil service, with its examination-based, predominantly Oxbridge entry, occurred at the beginning of the modernization and expansion of the universities. The education in classical culture that was most valued as a qualification for élite positions in the British civil service approximates in fact to a 'pure type' of Weber's idea of bureaucratic recruitment.

For the middle classes, access to the higher education system is now thus a crucial means of acquisition and transmission of cultural capital, vital if each new generation is to maintain and/or increase its advantages in competition with other social strata. The very full use being made of higher education by the children of the salaried middle class, and the much smaller use made of it by the members of lower-middle-class and working-class families, is a major factor in reproducing their relative opportunities. The culture of the middle class (especially the 'new middle class' concerned with technical and symbolic skills) is closely connected to the functional importance for them of education in their struggle for position. The relative 'closure'[10] of the middle-class university, and of the higher education system more widely, is thus far from being a historical accident.

The survival of the idea of university education as an induction to a culture and a way of life is an index of the aspiration of the British middle-class to status values associated with an earlier élite. University education thus maps on to previous patterns of status distinction so notoriously marked in British life. Experience of higher education becomes one of many distinctions between the quality and the popular, which appear for example in the stratification of accents, the national press, broadcasting channels, and the arts and sports. These status aspirations then reinforce the universities' aloofness from industrial and commercial life.[11]

The evidence for the 'maturity' of this system rests in part on its approaching 'saturation' of the potential student population it draws from the 'service class'.[12] It is now normative for children from these upper social strata who have the capacity to take a degree to do so. Part of the current crisis of higher education has been caused by the exhaustion of this source of recruitment and expansion (the recruitment of girls being the one sector where middle-class recruitment continues to increase) combined with a decline in the number of 18-year-olds in the population at large. The narrowness of the social base of higher education has also left it relatively unpopular, and ill-supported when faced with political attacks from the right.

The middle-class university can be defined by the fact that

its population of students is drawn not chiefly from the propertied classes but from the children of professional, salaried and white-collar workers, for whom education is vital to advancement in the labour market. Because of the high cost and delayed return to higher education, an element of state funding has been crucial to this development, which has been typical of the 'middle-class Welfare State' in post-war Britain. Even in more capitalist societies where grant-aid for students is more limited, such as the United States, substantial government expenditures have nevertheless gone to the universities, which have mostly by no means had to fend for themselves in the free market. Because of the formal openness of the British higher education system to those qualified, and the support of student grants, considerable numbers (though a small proportion) of the children of manual workers have also benefited from it. There was a sense in Britain in the 1960s, through the emergence into cultural visibility of young working-class people in many spheres – films, theatre, rock music, writing – that the post-war educational reforms *were* bringing about considerable social mobility. The phenomenon of the 'scholarship boy' delayed the recognition that the university system remained *proportionately* as exclusive as it had ever been.

Another aspect of positive correspondence between the higher education system and the modern mixed economy has been in the role of the universities as key institutions in the 'knowledge industry', which is one of the major dynamic forces of modern capitalism. Funded largely by the state because of the indirect and long-term returns from investment in 'fundamental' knowledge, universities were able to encourage their own internal division of academic labour into subject-specialisms. These could establish their knowledge-base, and their particular relationship to professions and fields of work external to them. An example from the humanities is the successful 'modernization' of the teaching of English literature from the 1920s, and its adaptation as a central 'humanistic' element in the curriculum of the expanding school system.[13] This was led in England by an intellectual grouping around F. R. Leavis, whose ideology was quite specifically middle-class and meritocratic (though much else besides), and some of whose members have subsequently played some part in the neo-conservative educational backlash and defence of 'standards' in the 1970s. The reproduction of the specific stratum of university teachers and researchers (certified initially by their high class of degree) was always one purpose of the university curriculum, even though this emphasis works to the disadvantage of the less academically adept and committed students.

The role of the universities in the generation of knowledge was a product both of their late stage of development, in relation to the corporate economy and the institutions of government, and of more specifically English factors. The developing scale of production and administration created a need for the organized gestation of knowledge. Academic disciplines, especially in the sciences, function like a form of collective or corporate production. The pattern of 'normal science' described by T. S. Kuhn[14] in his *Structure of Scientific Revolutions* as taking place in a planned and corporate way in well-capitalized scientific laboratories bears the same relationship to individual scientific discovery as the 'oligopolistic competition' of corporations bears to the perfect competition of small producers in industrial markets. The small-scale entrepreneurial capitalist, the inventor, and the individual scientist are alike figures of an earlier period of capitalism, where the modern university and industrial corporation are contemporaries of the twentieth century. This may also explain the limits to the 'liberalism' and free-thinking of the university, noted by Peter Scott in a later chapter. Instead of a 'free market' of ideas, in which independent writers and intellectuals compete, there are instead many specialized markets, each requiring, as the normal condition of entry, membership of a producer-corporation (a laboratory or department) which can achieve state and corporate funding for its work. The social sciences and other 'controversial' fields become unpopular with their academic peers because they 'spoil the market' for the others. The peculiar English feature is the priority given to 'pure' as opposed to applied science, and the 'hands-off' relationship which the universities have been able to achieve for their knowledge-generating role with the external providers of funds. The quasi-autonomous research councils after the Second World War institutionalized this arrangement. The present government's attacks on the former S.S.R.C., its preference for 'customer–contractor' relationships, and the pressure for the universities to rely on independent (i.e. free market) funding, indicate the unpopularity of this autonomist élite model among some Conservative and business circles. But the direct funding of research by central government departments, though less visible than the Research Councils, has long been an important component of the total research budget. The long time-lags and uncertainties involved in the production of fundamental knowledge in fact make the role of state funding, and a measure of institutional autonomy, positively functional for this activity. The plurality and independence of the university, as it has been defined above, remains an important precondition of its contribution to the advancement of knowledge in modern mixed capitalist societies, just as it has been in the past.

The definitive charter of the bourgeois university was formulated in the Robbins Report of 1963. The most radical Robbins proposal was that places should be provided for all those school-leavers who wished to enter higher education and who were qualified to do so. This formulation brilliantly succeeded in making an entitlement appear universal which was in fact highly partial and selective. A particular credential-holding class was thus, as Marx might have said, able to represent itself as a universal class. 'Qualifying' meant succeeding in examinations (by this time highly bureaucratized through G.C.E. Ordinary and Advanced level syllabuses and examinations) which had mainly been devised in response to the requirements of the academic and similar professions, and which most working-class children would never even enter.

Robbins argued for a universal and relatively homogeneous

conception of higher education, thus marking out the graduate as a distinct and uniform proto-estate. A university degree was to be of standard worth: its internal honours classifications were also intended to reflect comparable standards across the country. The segregation of abilities signified earlier by grammar-school selection was thus further ratified, with a more highly selected population, by university selection and graduation.

The Robbins Report endorsed the relationship between the universities and the wider society which had evolved in the post-war period. Robbins was suspicious of manpower planning and proposed to allow student demand to determine subject-provision. The effect of this consistent application of market theory (in contrast to Robbins's more *dirigiste* Conservative successors) was to allow only an indirect link between occupational 'demand' factors, and educational 'supply'. Universities thus remained neutral in relation to competing demands for their output. Where demand came chiefly from the public sector, as in the decade following the Report, so the universities could follow it. The universities thus served a mixed economy whose 'mix' could and did vary.

Robbins's recommendation was for the maintenance of a unitary university system, rather than for any separate-tier expansion of the kind that was to follow with the development of the 'binary system'. (This was one of the few Robbins recommendations that the succeeding Labour government did not follow.) The combination of the inherited advantages of Oxbridge and other leading institutions, with an open competition among students for places in the most admired institutions, and among universities for the best qualified students, ensured the continuation of a national hierarchy of prestige. But the competition was to be within a fixed estate of universities, all requiring the same minimum academic entrance qualifications. Indeed academic definitions were imposed, following Robbins, on one important kind of institution – the colleges of art – formerly free of them, a move which revealed the impulse of rationalizing credentialism that lay behind these reforms. The teacher training colleges were also incorporated into the universities (the Robbins proposal) or the C.N.A.A. system.

None of the possible means of making the university system more equal or pluralist in character were considered. It was thought radical enough by the standards of the time to be recommending higher education for all who could reach A-level standard. A collectivist version of 'levelling' might have required the deliberate sharing out of the best-qualified students, to erode some of the privileged position of Oxbridge and certain other institutions. This was the policy for secondary schooling later adopted by some education authorities following the comprehensive reforms, in the decision to 'band' children and insist on a 'balanced entry' to all schools in an area. A more liberal version of democratization would have allowed a more variable definition of a university degree, and greater autonomy and freedom of entry for institutions who might wish to award them. This is the basis on which the much more inclusive and open system of post-school education has been developed in the United States.[15] In England, however (Scotland is slightly more egalitarian), the unitary standards of a middle-class estate, still under upper-class leadership, were to prevail. It can be seen in retrospect that the recommendations of the Robbins Report (even in its exemplary scientific methodology) represented the high point of a middle-class credentialist university system.

The Binary Policy after 1964:
An 'Expanded Middle-class Model'

The Robbins Report's ideal of the meritocratic university provided the intellectual foundation for the subsequent expansion of higher education, and its cardinal principle of providing places to meet the demand of all qualified entrants has not yet been abandoned. (What *has* happened is that cuts in university grants have held down the number of university places, and forced many university applicants to accept places in non-university institutions.) But the Labour government of 1964–70 gave priority to expansion outside the university sector, through what became known following Anthony Crosland's Woolwich speech of 1965 as the 'binary system'. Thirty institutions were designated as polytechnics, and these, unlike the universities, were to remain under the control of elected local authorities though with the greater part of funding coming from central government. The Council for National Academic Awards was set up as the national degree-awarding institution for the non-university sector. In addition to the thirty polytechnics, funding was provided for many other local authority colleges to expand their advanced (i.e. degree-level) work. (There is now advanced work in over a hundred.) Unlike the 'new universities' established by the previous Conservative government, the 'new polytechnics' were invariably created by amalgamation or upgrading from existing regional or other local authority colleges. They were usually situated not in 'green field sites' on the edges of historic cities, but in the middle of industrial towns – in Coventry, not Warwick; Preston, not Lancaster. Unlike some of their Robbins-designated forerunners, the 'technological universities', they have stayed put. (Whereas the University of Surrey has moved from Battersea to Guildford, and Brunel University from Acton to Uxbridge.)

The 'binary policy' represented a significant departure from the university model, in the direction of a limited opening-up of higher education to a wider population. The new 'advanced further education' institutions did not share the distinctive English university values of antiquity, cosmopolitanism, humane education, selectivity, or corporate life. On the contrary, their origins mostly lay in local colleges offering 'useful knowledge' often on a part-time and certainly not residential basis. They were not given the resources or locations which would encourage aspirations in traditionalist directions. Providing higher education at a lower unit cost was supposed to be one of the advantages of the local authority sector over the universities. The new institutions were also distinctively educational rather than knowledge-producing institutions. They began with a small research base, and staff who were mostly either very junior and inexperienced, or, at the senior levels, formed by the old technical college-teaching ethos. While research was subsequently encouraged as a prerequisite for honours-level degree teaching, funds have never been made available to enable the public sector to compete in research terms with the universities.

The 'public sector' was encouraged (until recent years) to respond to the market of student demand in a more flexible and entrepreneurial way than the universities. The polytechnics were given a managerialist administrative structure at their foundation, within resource allocation in the hands of hierarchical directorates rather than collegial academic boards. There was scope in the early days for entrepreneurial directors to determine distinctive educational policies for their institutions. While the polytechnics were formally accountable to local authority education committees, their funding came largely from central government, and this was in the early days fairly freely provided in response to projections of increased student demand. This effective separation between the sources of political control and the ultimate sources of revenue increased the freedom of action of polytechnic managements, who were helped by the inexperience of many local authorities in controlling institutions of these kinds. The 'capping' of the pool (which set a fixed and lowering ceiling to expenditures) and the establishment of the National Advisory Body (which now determines recruitment by institution and subject-area for the public sector, like the U.G.C.) by the Thatcher government has deliberately shut these doors. In their managerial organization and incentive to follow student demand, therefore, the new polytechnic institutions (and the colleges and institutes of higher education which have followed them along this road) were encouraged to operate in a more market-oriented and less traditional spirit. The object has been to provide, in short, the expanded education that students and society seemed to want, without the traditional trimmings.

There was encouragement, too, of the ideology of 'useful knowledge' and vocationalism, which was part of the rationale for the binary divide. Sandwich courses and programmes related to occupational needs – in business, social and health studies, for example – have been an important element of growth, and part-time courses remain a much larger proportion of the local authority than the university sector. The idea of encouraging higher educational expansion in existing local institutions which already enjoyed a tradition of part-time and vocational teaching was intended to lead to a more practically-related and open form of education.[16] This was a break with the Robbins preference for an expanded university system. The combination of utilitarianism (vocational needs, urban sites, etc.) with an encouragement of a wider social recruitment was characteristic of the Wilsonian compromise between a 'technological revolution' (the interests and values of the industrial middle-classes, especially the new echelons of skilled workers and technicians) and Labour's egalitarian commitment to advancement of the working class and under-privileged.

The 'public sector' *has* achieved a broader social intake than the university system, though it seems to have done more to repair educational than social disadvantage. It has a significantly higher proportion of older entrants, often without formal qualification, in contrast to the mainly 18- or 19-year-old A-level entry of most university departments. The current evidence suggests that this has been more an opening of the system to students with limited educational attainments or making a late choice of higher education, than to the economically or socially disadvantaged. The proportion of sons and daughters of working-class families entering higher education seems not to have been much altered by the rise of the 'public sector'. It is even possible that the loss of the intense sponsorship of a minority of working-class boys through grammar school selection has cancelled out the benefits of the formally more open comprehensive school system, so far as access to higher education is concerned. It seems likely that the main effect of the expansion of the public sector has been to supply the manpower needs for lower professional and junior managerial or administrative occupations for which degrees have become a relevant qualification. Since public sector institutions generally require somewhat lower entrance qualifications than universities, and enjoy less social prestige, it seems likely that their graduates find themselves on average at a disadvantage in competing with those of the universities for jobs offering the best prospects of income and status. They may also graduate with lower and more realistic job aspirations.

While the local authority sector has achieved some measure of democratization of post-school education, it has failed so far to become more than a less privileged variant of the 'middle-class university'. It constitutes an extended version of this system, but not a distinct 'popular' alternative to it. It is necessary to identify the administrative mechanisms and cultural constraints which have inhibited a more open-ended development, which incidentally pre-date the Thatcherite period of resource limitation.

The main constraint on the public sector has been the priority given to the reproduction of the three-year full-time honours degree as the standard form of higher education. The establishment of the C.N.A.A. and its obligation to ensure comparability with the standards of university degrees, and the requirement of the same minimum entry requirements (of two A- and three O-levels at G.C.E.) encouraged the colleges to follow the pre-existing patterns of university education. The need to gain accreditation for degree courses from C.N.A.A. panels which were initially dominated by university teachers, and of course the prior formation at universities of most of the first generation of public sector staff, ensured the reproduction of the university degree, even single honours specialization, as the largest element of the public sector curriculum. In some respects the system became more and not less restrictive. The opportunities for students with one A-level pass – especially women – have probably been diminished by the replacement of teacher certificate courses by arts and social science degrees as teacher education has contracted and colleges closed or amalgamated. In art and design education, academic requirements have been raised in a probably misplaced desire to achieve academic recognition for education in the visual arts. (This issue is discussed in more detail in a later chapter.) A policy decision which had particularly restrictive consequences was the requirement that entry to the new Diploma in Higher Education courses (in part a replacement for declining teacher training) would be based on two A-levels rather than one. By this rule the opportunity to use the Dip. H.E. to attract a new kind of entrant into the higher education system was for the time being wasted.

Financial arrangements have also worked in favour of the recruitment of 'conventional' degree students and against other kinds of programmes. There has been little encouragement for the development of courses of different lengths and kinds, either for colleges or students. Mandatory grants have been available only for degree courses or the new Dip. H.E. courses, and discretionary grants have been in increasingly short supply. An evening-only degree is funded at one fifth the scale per student of a full-time course, thus giving colleges every discouragement from offering evening and part-time programmes. The tacit implication of these various procedures is that the main task of the public sector colleges, whatever the Department of Education may say, is to provide full-time degree courses to students holding qualifications which are formally comparable to those of university students, though in practice at the lower end of the range required for entry to universities.

In these circumstances the public sector is able to do relatively little to redress the failings of the secondary system with regard to the achievement of working-class children, and the children of disadvantaged ethnic minorities. The fact that student grants are available to 18-year-old college entrants with A-levels, but not to 16- to 18-year-olds engaged in acquiring these qualifications, bears particularly severely on working-class aspirations. Since the assumption of working-class, but not of middle-class, families is that children will be financially independent or at least able to make some contribution to the household from the age of 16, the absence of a grant from 16 is a major discouragement, and does much to explain the discrepancy between middle-class and working-class participation in 16+ and 18+ education. The introduction of the Youth Training Scheme has made this even more anomalous: financial support from 16 is now available for more or less everything except A-level studies. Nothing could more clearly signal that academic education is not intended for the children of the working class.

Other institutions have tried to break with or provide an alternative to the exclusiveness of the middle-class university. Some of these, such as Northern College and Ruskin College, have had to operate on the margin of the system, though having a key role over many years in the education of adult trade union members. But perhaps the largest and most important experiment has been that other child of the Wilson government, the Open University. This has shown a combination of *both* innovation and inclusiveness, *and* conservatism, which is quite similar to that of the polytechnic sector. The Open University has pioneered techniques of distance learning, via the media of print, television and radio broadcasting, and has shown that it is possible to provide higher education at much lower unit costs than on the traditional model. (Those who want to see a mass, popular post-school education system have to pay attention to such economic factors, and must avoid the temptation of demanding on egalitarian grounds that every institution, especially their own, must enjoy the material and environmental standards of Oxbridge. Such a demand implies contraction, not expansion, in student numbers.) It has also shown that mature students without normal degree entrance qualifications can achieve standards comparable to those of conventional students – an important refutation of the idea that degree-level studies depend on continuous full-time education from 5 to 18. Partly because of the understandable democratic commitments of its staff, the Open University has been sometimes able to pioneer more radical course material than conventional

programmes, and has often, through its distinctive specialization in written and broadcast course-preparation, been
able to provide the highest standard of course material
available anywhere in higher education. Some of its summer
school programmes also show an impressive quality of innovative activity-learning methods.

But in other respects the Open University remains conventional. It, too, has been obliged to compete in the currency of
the honours degree, and has adopted, partly because of its
distance-learning techniques, a model of educational *transmission* which is in some ways more hierarchical than many
conventional face-to-face programmes. An Open University
course has to be learned and 'played back' – there is often
little scope for students' own appropriation, research activity,
practical work, or problem-solving. The particular opportunity of the part-time course to relate academic work to the
student's day-to-day immersion in the non-academic world
of work, home or neighbourhood, is rarely taken. Though the
Open University is now being criticized for alleged political
radicalism and bias, we can note that in fact it has most often
played safe – it has probably had no choice – and has *not*
sought to use its incomparable access to audiences for broadcast and print to stimulate public controversy or debate. In a
more democratic culture than ours, an institution such as the
Open University could be a force for popular education not
only in the sense of providing *courses*, but in providing
informed material and expert discussion on every conceivable
matter of social and scientific interest. With the Open University as well as the 'public sector', the licence to experiment
within the boundaries of the honours degree course has been
granted on the tacit condition of attempting very little outside
these limits.

Despite these limitations, there have been significant gains
from these post-Robbins developments of public-sector higher
education. There have been increased opportunities – for
previously unsuccessful and excluded students, especially
mature students and women returning to study after child-
rearing. The priority given to teaching in the public sector

colleges has given rise to a somewhat different structure of organization, at the lower levels, than that typical of the universities. Where Oxbridge is still college-based, and red-brick universities are organized by subject-departments headed usually by professors with a major research record (with variants of elective chairmanship mostly in the social sciences), the key unit of organization in the polytechnics has been the degree course. The course and the course team responsible for it usually forms the basis of departments, not research output. The external validation of courses by the C.N.A.A., by documentation and formal hearing, has also given a cooperative character to course development in the public sector, since it is the unified scheme rather than its individual subject-units which have been the main object of external evaluation. Knowledge has thus tended to become the shared property of the course team rather than privately owned by the subject-specialist. This has encouraged a greater attention to educational coherence and teaching method in the public sector, and has brought about some shift, to use Basil Bernstein's terms,[17] from 'collection' to 'integrated' educational codes. The dependence of the polytechnics on their teaching staffs to produce courses which would meet C.N.A.A. criteria and attract students has also given teaching teams scope to innovate in subject-areas and teaching methods. They acquired some of the powers of a 'technostructure'[18] in the new institutions. Project-based assessment, modular programmes, sandwich courses, and new kinds of integrated courses in areas such as business studies, cultural studies, and self-designed 'independent study' courses have been developed in some number. While the technological and new universities were also the sources (in some cases the original sources) of many such initiatives, the environment of the public sector has probably been more open in general than that of the universities to innovations at the undergraduate teaching level. There were many advantages for educational radicals in beginning afresh rather than under the weight of existing academic hierarchies, and this should be an important consideration in planning further enlargement of the system.

Conservative Retrenchment after 1979

The democratization of post-school education brought about by the post-Robbins expansion of the universities, and by the development of a 'public sector' of almost comparable size, was a limited one. It is because the system still *does* cater overwhelmingly for the children of the middle classes that the Thatcher government's policies towards it have so far been relatively cautious. Expenditure on higher education has been substantially cut, but nevertheless the number of students has continued to increase in response mainly to a demographic peak in the number of 18-year-olds. It seems that the government has not wished to be seen to be responsible for qualified entrants being excluded from degree courses, and this has so far placed limits on how far its attacks on the system could go.

The government has increased its centralized control over the system, and set out to reduce its more leftward-leaning and egalitarian sectors. Both universities, through the U.G.C., and the public sector, through the National Advisory Body, have been placed under tighter centralized control. These bodies now determine the allocation of funds both to institutions and subject-areas. The manner in which the government's own preferences for subject-areas have been translated into positive recommendations by supposedly autonomous committees has been an object-lesson in the limitations of informal means of self-regulation when these are subjected to strong government pressure. Peter Scott's chapter, 'Autonomy to Accountability', argues for the possible advantages of a more formal and publicly accountable arrangement. While some of the pressures for centralization have simply been for cost-effectiveness (not without some justification after years of relatively easy funding), it has also had the purpose of changing the subject-balance away from the arts and social sciences by the allocation of subject-quotas to universities and public-sector colleges. Often, as in the treatment of sociology, and in the ministerial intervention in the internal affairs of particular colleges, it has been based on little more than ideological prejudice. It has been surprising that a market-oriented government has shown so little confidence in the power of the ultimate employment market to allocate students efficiently to courses which provide the highest return to them. Instead the government has resorted to a kind of educational manpower planning which has had almost no empirical basis. The intention (also evident in the government's strategy for research funding) has been to attack those areas of higher education least sympathetic to the business ethic, and which tend to sustain the values and intellectual basis of the Welfare State.

But in other respects the Thatcherite higher education programme has been by no means well adapted to the needs of business. The compromise described above as characteristic of the British system (between an aristocratic and a middle-class conception of the university) has been reinforced by the government's methods of educational policy-making. The University Grants Committee, given the effective power to administer the cuts, chose mainly to enforce traditional élitist standards, not intervene on behalf of the needs of business and industry. The institutions most committed to technology and 'useful knowledge', the new technological universities, fared spectacularly badly in losses to their budget and student numbers. Whereas arts and sciences also generally suffered, the most important criterion of allocation was claims to 'academic excellence' (measured by external research funding and A-level scores) which are one of the most distasteful expressions of the universities' self-regard. It was a case of the privileged looking after their own. In the public sector there is similarly some evidence that the National Advisory Body has sought, as regulatory agencies usually do, to carry its most powerful constituency with it. Here the most favoured institutions have been the larger polytechnics, and the most disadvantaged the smaller non-polytechnic colleges.

The Thatcher government may still be considering more radical measures to bring the higher education system closer to the market place, via student loans instead of grants, and by encouraging more direct (corporate) funding for universities. These ideas may yet come to something. But while it has established much stronger means of administrative and financial control over higher education, it seems to have preferred in their exercise a compromise with the coalition of interests committed to the post-Robbins system. The interest of the middle classes in a state-funded system seems too strong to be challenged. The government has found an accommodation with the donnish counterparts of a traditional upper social stratum with which in other fields (the higher civil service, for example) it has been in ideological conflict. It has preferred to keep the traditional academic élite as allies in its sharp attacks on the more egalitarian and radical subject-areas, rather than to push them into opposition by criticizing their aloofness from business or their dependence on state funds. Surprisingly, perhaps, the fundamental structures of the post-Robbins higher education system remain intact.

## Towards Comprehensive Post-school Education

The present system of higher education *appears* to provide opportunities for all – at least for those who leave school as late as 18 – by making possible grant-aided entry to degree courses to all those achieving specified minimum qualifications. It makes a certain kind of educational career 'open to the talents' in the true spirit of bourgeois liberalism. The *appearance* of universality, even though the facts indicate that these advantages are enjoyed by only about 13 per cent of the most relevant age-group – is a potent means of making privilege invisible, as in the corresponding case of opportunities *apparently* available to all in a 'free' labour market.

This illusion of equal opportunity and choice is achieved through the ruling definition of what counts as post-school education and its instruments of public funding and entitlement to student grants. The concept of 'higher' education, and the restricted rights of access which attach to it (minimum entry requirements for degree courses, etc.), ensure that the greater part of post-school education is available only to the small minority who achieve academic success in the school and further education system. Financial aid and grant support outside this 'higher' system is in scant supply, though to be sure there have been adult education, training opportunities (T.O.P.S.) and adult literacy programmes funded at a vastly inferior level which do touch the potential needs. Full-time education for those over 18 is in effect confined to academic higher education: life-stage is conflated with educational level. The first prerequisite of a popular and democratic system is therefore to think in terms of *post-school* education, and to abandon an exclusive preoccupation with those forms of post-18 education now defined as 'higher'. The conventional terminology of higher and lower is now a block to thinking about democratic education.

Fundamental to this book is the argument for an extended educational entitlement, for the ideal of post-school education for all. This is no more than a natural extension of the principle of universal secondary education, once it becomes recognized that personal and educational development is a lifelong process, and that technical and economic change already require the 'continuing education' and 'retraining' of most skilled workers more than once in their adult lives. It is possible to repair the failings of the educational experience of childhood for many people, and this function alone would provide an almost infinite clientele for a more comprehensive post-school system. The limits to the expansion of such a system should only be those of available economic resources, and the skills and capacities needed to develop appropriate programmes on a large scale. There is probably no economic justification in terms of the return on investment for the present balance of provision for academically high-qualified post-18-year-olds, *vis-à-vis* the less well-qualified. Evidence suggests that Britain is more deficient, in comparison with competing nations, in its resources of skilled labour below graduate level, than in its graduate output. For this reason the Labour Party's current commitment to give its greatest priority to education from 16 to 18, to increase the average level of education of school-leavers even at the relative expense of the most educationally successful, is justified. The existence of high levels of unemployment further suggests the good sense of increasing educational provision for adults. One obvious contribution to the problem of unemployment would be to fund more full-time and part-time study, and to mobilize the massive under-used human resources for both its provision and enjoyment. The fundamental principle which should underpin such an extended provision is the idea of a universal post-school educational entitlement, which was first proposed by Oliver Fulton and then taken up by the Labour Party in its 1982 policy document for post-18 education. This idea is basic to the thinking of this book.

The expansion of post-school educational opportunities should be conceived both as a widening of opportunities to participate in the existing system, and the creation of new forms of provision for those whom the present academic modes of higher education are unlikely to benefit. Means of improving access to the present system have already been widely discussed. The introduction of educational maintenance allowances for those engaged in full-time study from 16 to 18 would be one important means of increasing working-class participation in education. The high drop-out rate of academically-talented working-class children has long been the most glaring failure of the ideal of equality of educational opportunity. The goal of improving standards in the schools, to which the present government attaches some importance, will also be helped by improving children's opportunities after 16. Performance in schools is affected by the prospective relevance of studies to future livelihoods as well as by the factors of prior parental education and occupation. The Labour Party's proposals for a universal concept of education and training from 16 to 18, with the same grant entitlements whatever form of education is undertaken, would meet this problem, and would have important knock-on effects for demand for post-school education. This proposal, incidentally, would do little more than bring Britain into line with the post-16 education and training provisions of other advanced Western European states such as West Germany

Its institutional support came chiefly from the state, acting on behalf of a 'mixed economy' of private and welfare sectors, and sensitive to the interests of middle-class as much as working-class voters.

In this book we argue for a more open system of education for adults, adapted in subject-area and 'level' to the interests and capacities of students, but allowing flexible transfer across curriculum boundaries. There are (and have always been) great differences within universities between the basic levels of work of most undergraduate education and the most advanced forms of research. The university system of the United States combines such a 'comprehensive' range of first-degree teaching with the highest levels of intellectual work. There is no reason therefore why a comprehensive system should be the enemy of the 'standards' or the vital 'knowledge-generating' functions of the university or polytechnic.

But it would be an insufficient reform of the present system merely to create a new 'tier' of tertiary colleges which leave the existing institutions unaltered. Such a system would be all too similar to the 'tripartite' model of secondary education established in 1944, with the new 'tertiary colleges' in the role of secondary moderns. Just as the 'binary system' allowed some popular extension of higher education at the price of leaving the dominant system of educational stratification unchallenged, so the mere creation of a new sector for less academic courses would reinforce the existing hierarchies.

It is therefore vital that the idea of the popular university should obtain some institutional and cultural recognition, as the comprehensive ideal has obtained through the reorganization of secondary education. One cannot expect the whole of the present system to be transformed in a day. It would be dangerous to the credibility and potential support for an expanded post-school system not to be sensitive to the concerns for the existing high-quality forms of work. But there needs to be some scope created for experimentation and variety in the organization of post-school education, so that more democratic structures can be initiated.

One proposal worth considering would be to bring all of

post-school education under elective regional control, preferably through the creation of elective regional authorities with many functions, but alternatively through the setting-up of tertiary education boards by nomination from local authorities and other professionally-interested parties. Tertiary education institutions have a natural catchment area larger than a county or borough, but need greater local accountability and diversity of approach than is compatible with central government control. Central government should establish a general framework of educational entitlement, and the funding provision for it. It could then, on the lines of the earlier comprehensive secondary reorganization, invite each regional tertiary authority to submit a scheme for comprehensive post-school education in its region. All areas should be required to implement a universal post-18 entitlement, and to introduce the new kinds of provision that would follow. But they could choose different institutional patterns for it. Some more radical authorities might choose unified institutions, linking regional universities, polytechnics, and 'third sector' adult colleges and programmes in a single network. There would be scope for integrating facilities, and for constructing unified new campuses to give a spatial and symbolic existence to the new democratic conception. More conservative authorities would leave existing institutions as they are, and would develop new provision in quite separate colleges. Another pattern might be to integrate the first stages of post-school education, and specialize at post-graduate level. The advantage of allowing regional diversity is that new conceptions should be tested out, and the strengths of the existing models of higher education – generally high standards of teaching, for example – could be absorbed into the practice of a broader system. There is too little experience and political support to justify a unitary pattern for the whole country at this stage, and to attempt this might only mobilize conservative anxieties against the whole idea of universal adult provision.

There is a conflict of principles between desirable autonomy at the individual institutional level, which is vital to academic and educational freedom, and the necessity for centrally established rules to bring about equal opportunities. One solution to this dilemma would be to channel only a proportion of the funding for each kind of institution through regional authorities, leaving other funding to come from central government, student fees, or local authorities. This would ensure that colleges remained subject to a pluralist environment, and thus retained choice over their own development. But a more vigorous competition between regions in support of their own institutions would be valuable in breaking down the dominant status-hierarchy of British higher education, which is a legacy both of the aristocratic university and of over-centralized government. It would be beneficial if the concentration of so-called 'excellence' in the leading and especially ancient universities were lessened. There would be more benefits than costs to educational standards if there were a dispersion of the highest-achieving students and teachers over a wide number of institutions. The present 'creaming' of talent (inefficient as it is)[20] is at a high cost to the majority of institutions. Just as it has been necessary for educational authorities to limit the concentration of the most capable children in particular secondary schools, so it is desirable to bring about some more equal or random allocation of students at tertiary level. This might be encouraged even by preferential funding for students attending regional institutions, or by a regionalized system of first-degree entry. The élite structure of British higher education is also a major support of the continuing domination of British society by closed élites. A more democratic society will also require a more open and plural form of recruitment to top positions. For these reasons it is clear that a reduction in the importance of private-sector education should also be part of a democratic educational strategy.

Another means of challenging the existing status-hierarchy would be to remove Oxford and Cambridge from the field of first-degree education altogether, and make them exclusively institutions for research, postgraduate and continuing education. This might achieve a greater measure of equality among institutions engaged in first-degree education, while not sacrificing too many of the distinctive qualities of the ancient universities. It might be a better use of the unparalleled cultural resources of the two ancient university towns and their colleges to make them available to adult students for periods of continuing or advanced education, than to a super-privileged population of 18-year-olds. There are real conflicts of principle between the idea of comprehensive provision and the inequalities of funding and standards of provision that now exist. Some interference with hallowed liberal freedoms will have to be contemplated, with due consideration of the costs involved, if progress towards a less exclusive and hierarchical system is to be achieved.

The greatest emphasis has been given in this chapter to provision for those hitherto excluded from post-school education, since this is the respect in which the British system is most clearly exclusive and élitist. The provision of continuing or recurrent education for individuals who may already have higher education qualifications, and the wider cultural role of the colleges in the community, need also to be developed. A post-school education system is already impoverished by being mainly a chronological conveyor-belt extension of schooling, because of the lack of life-experience of its beneficiaries. A proportion of post-school funding should be available for short-term periods of full-time or part-time study in later life. This might be a case where a supported student loan scheme (which would treat educational leave as a human capital cost to be spread out over several years) would have less inequitable disadvantages than it has for immediately post-school education. There might be grounds for distinguishing between an initial entitlement, funded by grant, and additional education, funded by loan.

The development of recurrent education on a short-term basis could also be a way of ensuring the broader use of the capital resources now invested in higher education, and of making the colleges more open to the community. The summer courses being developed by some universities and polytechnics (and in some cases, such as the Open University, in ways that are integral to their main teaching programmes) are a pattern that should be more widely used in continuing education or paid educational leave programmes. Even the development of more leisure-oriented and touristic activity-holiday courses are a step in the direction of openness.

The purpose should be to encourage a closer relationship between higher education institutions and the lives of the majority. While it is difficult to justify providing the highest standards of amenity in a university which caters for only a small minority of school-leavers, it would be a different matter if colleges' resources were accessible to their surrounding communities. The pattern that many schools and further education colleges follow of 'doubling' as evening institutes is also relevant for colleges. Programmes in the performing and visual arts, music, and sports and physical education are not luxuries if colleges come to be natural centres for these pursuits for their areas. An element of regional funding might be a catalyst and force for such developments.

Our earlier analysis suggested that the university had in its main stages of development been subject to the pressures of dominant interests and institutions in its external society, while nevertheless in favourable conditions achieving a vital independence and freedom of its own. The university system will not achieve a democratic and popular stage of development without the weight of popular interests and the institutions which represent them becoming stronger. This is not an argument against pluralism, but rather for the greater influence of working-class and popular agencies, among others, in the determination of post-school education. Certainly reforms will not be achieved if they are left to the dons.

The democratic model of the university must also extend to the funding and uses of knowledge. At present the external funding of research (teachers have some freedom to pursue their own interests too) is divided between government and private corporations (with military and defence purposes taking a disproportionate share of expenditure). Research should be more substantially funded also by local authorities and trade unions, in the latter case in pursuit of a more positive conception of industrial democracy. Voluntary and political organizations should also have access to the knowledge-generating process. There should be Oxfam and National Union of Mineworkers fellowships, as well as posts or projects funded by I.C.I. or the Medical Research Council. Some element of matched funding or tax relief should be provided by a radical government in order to encourage a more diverse and productive intellectual culture, as part of a broader democratic and pluralist policy for science and the arts. Social movements and communities should know that the intellectual resources of society are available to them, as well as to the interests of business and the central government bureaucracies. As Raymond Williams has pointed out, the neglect of cultural policy has been one of the major failings of Labour governments in the past, contributing to their loss of morale and initiative. The amount of theoretical attention that cultural issues have received from radicals in the past twenty years – in the development of movements for popular social history or women's writing as well as in critical intellectual work – should preclude any further neglect of a practical politics of culture by any Labour or radical government. The democratic case is that universities and polytechnics should be the centres of adult education, research and culture for a whole society. This aspiration is contained in their very names. It should be the historical mission of socialism to make such universal goals a contemporary reality.

## Notes

1 A. H. Halsey and M. Trow, *The British Academics*, Faber, 1971, contains a useful outline history of the British university system and an account of the distinctively 'English Idea of the University' which has shaped its modern development. A shorter summary account is given in A. H. Halsey's chapter on 'Higher Education' in A. H. Halsey (ed.), *Trends in British Society since 1900*, Macmillan, 1972. The Robbins Committee Report and Appendices, *Higher Education*, Cmd. 2154, 1963, was the fullest source on the universities up to that date.

2 An account of Oxford and Cambridge in the seventeenth century is given in L. Stone, 'The Educational Revolution in England 1560–1640', *Past and Present*, No. 28, July 1964. More detailed research on Oxford and Cambridge up to the early nineteenth century is reported in L. Stone (ed.), *The University in Society*, Vol. 1, Princeton University Press, 1974.

3 This summary is largely taken from Halsey and Trow, op. cit., and Halsey, op. cit.

4 A more recent historical outline which gives emphasis to the importance of the universities' later role in generating knowledge through research is in Peter Scott, *The Crisis of the Universities*, Croom Helm, 1984.

5 This development in late nineteenth-century Germany is briefly discussed in K. Borchardt, 'The Industrial Revolution in Germany 1700–1914', in C. Cipolla (ed.), *Fontana Economic History of Europe*, Vol. 4, Fontana–Collins, 1973.

6 The phrase 'multi-versity' comes from Clark Kerr, *The Uses of the University*, Harper & Row, 1966. 'The idea of the Multi-Versity is a city of infinite variety . . .'

7 R. H. Turner, 'Modes of Social Ascent through Education', repr. in J. Floud, A. H. Halsey and C. A. Anderson (eds.), *Education, Economy and Society*, Free Press, 1961.

8 In E. Gellner, *Words and Things*, Routledge (repr.), 1979.

9 P. Bourdieu and L. Boltanski, 'Changes in Social Structure and Changes in the Demand for Education', in S. Giner and M. S. Archer (eds.), *Contemporary Europe: Social Structure and Cultural Patterns*, Routledge, 1978. Also see P. Bourdieu and J. Passeron, *Reproduction in Education, Society, and Culture*, Sage, 1977.

10 On the useful concept of 'social closure' more generally see F. Parkin, *Marxism and Class Theory: a Bourgeois Critique*, Tavistock, 1979, especially chapters 4 and 5.

11 Martin Wiener, *English Culture and the Decline of the Industrial Spirit 1850–1980*, Cambridge University Press, 1981, discusses this anti-industrial bias of English culture more generally.

12 This idea of 'saturation' is discussed in A. H. Halsey *et al.*, *Origins and Destinations*, Clarendon Press, 1980.

13 This development of English studies is discussed in F. Mulhern, *The Moment of Scrutiny*, New Left Books, 1979.

14 T. S. Kuhn, *The Structure of Scientific Revolutions*, University of Chicago Press, 1970.

15 The advantages of the American system are discussed in M.

Trow, 'Binary Dilemmas; an American View', in *Higher Education Review*, Vol. 2, No. 1, 1969.

16  There is a judicious summary of the outcome of the 'public sector' post-binary expansion in P. Scott, op. cit.

17  B. Bernstein, 'The Classification and Framing of Educational Knowledge', in *Class, Codes, and Control*, Vol. 3, Routledge, 1976.

18  This phrase comes from J. K. Galbraith, *The New Industrial State*, Penguin, 1968.

19  A concept of social justice based on respect for the autonomy of such separate spheres of value has been developed by M. Walzer in *Spheres of Justice: A Defence of Pluralism and Equality*, Martin Robertson, 1983.

20  The recent revelation of the unreasonably small mark-differences between the A-level achievement grades which universities use to choose students undermines the recent claims by universities to justify 'excellence' by their quality of student intake.

# 2
# Who Has Access?

BILL WILLIAMSON

There are about 500,000 students enrolled in full-time higher education in Britain and a further 200,000 are doing it the hard way part-time. Since the early 1960s these numbers have increased by over 130 per cent. Full-time enrolments in higher education have increased much faster than part-time ones. The period of the 1960s was one of expansion in higher education with an annual growth rate of about 8 per cent. The 1970s saw a marked slowdown in the rate of growth but a steady expansion in numbers. For demographic reasons the number of 18-year-olds from which higher education will recruit most of its intake will increase up until 1985/6 and then begin a steady decline throughout the 80s and 90s.

Higher education in this country is therefore faced with a series of daunting challenges. For quite apart from the policies of the present Conservative government to control public expenditure and rein in the financing of higher education – policies which severely threaten it and the scaffold of educational opportunity it supports – the long-term demographic trends point to a need to rethink policies on admissions and recruitment. Higher education is now poised either to nose-dive, sacrificed at the altar of a miserably myopic monetarism which recognizes frugality as its only virtue and strident élitism as its only social goal, or to diversify creatively and open up opportunities where none previously existed and meet the real challenges of the remainder of this century.

Which way it goes is not a matter, however, of birth rates. It is essentially one of vision and political commitment, of daring to imagine that things could be different and being prepared to do something about it.

Higher education costs the country a lot of money; how it develops is vital to the future economic and cultural life of this society. It is very proper therefore to ask about who gets it and who does not. The sad truth at the moment is that behind an ideological smokescreen of fatalism – that things are as they are and cannot be otherwise – and such a shrunken view of learning that equates current provision with excellence and current admissions policies with a defence of standards, we have a higher education system which reinforces rigidly a class system which itself is the root cause of the inequalities and economic malaise of this society. The challenge for socialists is not to defend what we have got in the face of Tory assaults; it is to transform higher education into something very different.

## The Value and Meaning of Higher Education

The question of who gets what from higher education must be seen in a broader context of the advantages higher education can confer on individuals and the contribution it makes to society. That is on the one hand. On the other the disadvantages of being denied higher education have to be weighed, and in such a way which acknowledges the growing complexity of modern society and the direct linkages of knowledge and power, which are strengthened relentlessly through progress in science and technology and through changes in the organization of production and in the growth of the institutions of the modern state.

The advantages of higher education to individuals are well-known and can be easily measured; they include higher lifetime earnings, better promotion prospects, job security and social status. For those who accept their higher education in the spirit in which many of their teachers claim to offer it, it brings, too, access to knowledge and culture and an improved quality of life. Society benefits too in this way of looking at things. It gets a trained labour force, scientists, engineers, doctors, lawyers, teachers and the rest – people on whom we all depend and who will make the economic wheels turn. Whether in reality the rewards are quite like this is, of course, a much more open question.

The disadvantages of being denied even that which is currently on offer are, however, enormous and unequivocal. It is a feature of modern capitalist societies (and socialist ones, too, although in different ways) that power follows the logic of increasing centralization – in the state, in big business, even in supra-national institutions – so that at the centre of society there is tight control and increasingly unaccountable decision-making. At the periphery there is growing powerlessness and de-politicization and, for working-class people in particular, a growing vulnerability to impersonal forces for which their traditional institutions, trade unions, the Labour Party or their councils, provide little real defence.

How to make sense in the 1980s and 1990s of the tightening bands of knowledge and power which lie behind these profound changes of social structure and then to break them is the real challenge to socialists. And the quality of education, particularly higher education and the character of its presence and distribution in society, is right at the heart of the matter. It is no longer sufficient to pursue those essentially liberal hopes that the expansion of higher education and the widening of opportunities is the way to a new Jerusalem. That policy has clearly failed, and we are no longer in any case in a situation where economic growth can finance a 1960s-type expansion. The politics of decline is setting the parameters within which we must work. It is actually irrelevant now simply to demand a greater share of a shrinking cake; we must demand and build something else. In any case, if the present government lasts its full term the institutions of higher education themselves will be so far from being capable of supporting socialist policies – rampant élitism in the universities, resource starvation and demoralization in the public sector – that we had better begin now planning their replacement.

Who, then, benefits? It is not a straightforward question to answer, but once we have cut through the cant of political propaganda and the clever complexities of counting procedures, and, above all else, through the metaphysical pathos of those who think the best brains are already in the system and the pool of real ability already pumped dry, a clear conclusion stands out. Higher education in this country is deeply inegalitarian. It reflects the class structure of society denying opportunities to working-class people and favouring those from a middle-class background.

Real privilege of the sort rooted in great wealth and the public schools still retains its grip on the most prestigious institutions of higher education. Somewhat subdued by the fast-receding demands of the 1960s and early 1970s for greater opportunities in education, academic privilege is reasserting itself in arguments about standards, cutbacks, choice and freedom, and among students themselves there is a growing self-confidence in élitism and a return to the lifestyles of an earlier age, when the universities were more authentically finishing schools for the sons of the bourgeoisie.

For their sisters, higher education was always too much to hope for. And for working-class girls it remains out of bounds. George Bernard Shaw once described universities as places containing 'a rowdy rabble of half emancipated school children and unemancipated pedants'. The evidence remains that older people still do not get their fair share of what is on offer. And to be black is to suffer in addition the injuries of discrimination on grounds of race. It does not help either to live north of the Trent or to have gone to an ordinary comprehensive school. Socialists have, in the past, dared to imagine that it might be otherwise. The awful truth is that much has remained the same but the packaging is different.

That, of course, is a contentious summary of a complex position and I must turn now to the facts. These must be approached with care from four different directions. First they must be seen through time in relation to changes in the social structure of the society and in particular to patterns of social inequality. Second, they must be seen in relation to demographic trends, to changes in the age and sex composition of the population and the size of different age groups. Third, just to make sure that the British case can be seen in perspective, data on access for this country must be compared with other modern industrial societies. Finally, the data must be judged in terms of the country's changing needs for manpower and training and for the needs of individuals for personal development and greater control over their lives. For these things, too, are at the heart of class inequalities.

## Social Inequality and Access to Higher Education

The Robbins Committee Report on Higher Education in 1963 summarized the evidence on social class background and entry to higher education in the following way:

> The proportion of middle class children who reach degree level courses is eight times as high as the proportion from working class homes, and even in grammar schools it is twice as high . . . the difference in grammar schools is not chiefly due to lower intelligence, but rather to early leaving. However, it is not only in these schools that the wastage of ability is higher among manual working class children. There is much evidence to show that, before the age of 11 and in later years, the influence of environment is such that differences in measured ability between social classes progressively widen as children grow up.[1]

This report provided the arguments to justify a massive expansion in the provision of university places throughout the 1960s, and I quote from it to establish a benchmark against which to measure the progress to a more equal structure of opportunity in the course of the last twenty years. It is worth noting, too, that patterns of access to higher education cannot be discussed in isolation from what is going on in schools, of which more later.

In 1981 a further study was completed as part of the

Leverhulme programme of study into higher education which established the following data on the social background of full-time students between 1961 and 1977.

Table 1  *Age Participation Rates for full-time students by social class: 1961/2 and c. 1977 : Great Britain*

Percentage distributions assumed in (B)

| Class | c. 1961 (A) | c. 1977 (B) | Universities | Advanced further education | 18-yr-olds |
|---|---|---|---|---|---|
| I | 45 | 42.6 | 20.9 | 13.3 | 5.3 |
| II | 19 | 25.4 | 41.2 | 36.7 | 19.6 |
| IIIN | 10 | 21.2 | 14.7 | 18.9 | 9.7 |
| Middle | 19.5 | 26.9 | 76.8 | 68.9 | 34.7 |
| IIIM | 4 | 5.6 | 16.6 | 20.0 | 40.2 |
| IV | | 4.7 | 5.2 | 8.9 | 17.8 |
| V | 2 | 2.8 | 1.2 | 2.2 | 7.3 |
| Working | 3.2 | 5.0 | 23.0 | 31.1 | 65.3 |
| All | 7.5 | 12.7 | 99.8 | 100 | 100 |
| | | N= | 65340 | 39460 | 831000 |

Source:
(A) *Higher Education* (1963), App. 1, pp. 39–40, based on survey of 20/21-year-olds.
(B) U.C.C.A. *Statistical Supplements*, 1978–9, Table E5 for universities in 1977. Advanced further education estimated from Table 2.17(7), (9), (10) (above). 18-year-olds: *Census 1971. Household Composition* Table 46, aged 10–14. Oliver Fulton (ed.), *Access to Higher Education*, 1981. Table 2.18.

The Age Participation Rate measures the number of young entrants into higher education as a proportion of the size of the relevant 18-year-old age group. This figure can then be broken down by social class background. What Table 1 shows is that the A.P.R. has increased from 7.5 per cent to 12.7 per cent. These are overall figures. Looked at a little more closely, it can be seen that the rates for young people from different social class backgrounds are very different. Middle-class young people accounted for 19.5 per cent of full-time students in 1961 and 26.9 per cent in 1977. This is a percentage increase of nearly 40. In contrast, students from a working-class background – 3.2 per cent in 1961 and 5.0 per cent in 1977 –

increased their share by just over 56 per cent. While the rate of increase in the participation rate for working-class people was higher than that for middle-class students, the latter group has a much higher representation overall. In any case the two student populations come from cohorts which are markedly different in the population at large. Sixty-five per cent of 18-year-olds stem from a working-class background but they represent only 23 per cent of those who are students in the universities. This contrasts sharply with the figures for students from a middle-class background.

Another way of looking at this can be seen in Table 2, which compares successful candidates who have entered university by their social origin.

Table 2 *Percentage of acceptances to university by social class 1979–83*

|  | | 1979 | 1980 | 1981 | 1982 | 1983 |
|---|---|---|---|---|---|---|
| 1 | Professional occupations | 21.9 | 22.3 | 24.5 | 23.9(7.0) | 23.5 |
| 2 | Intermediate occupations | 42.3 | 47.8 | 48.9 | 49.0(22.0) | 48.4 |
| 3 | Skilled occupations non-manual | 13.4 | 10.4 | 9.1 | 9.1(10.0) | 8.7 |
| 4 | Skilled occupations manual | 16.3 | 14.0 | 12.3 | 12.2(38.0) | 12.4 |
| 5 | Partly skilled occupations | 5.0 | 4.4 | 4.2 | 4.9(18.0) | 18.0 |
| 6 | Unskilled occupations | 1.0 | 1.0 | 1.0 | 0.9(6.0) | 1.1 |
|  | Total | 100 | 100 | 100 | 100 | 100 |

Figures in brackets are percentage of total 1982 18-year-old G.B. population.

*Source:*
U.C.C.A. *Statistical Supplements.*

It illustrates that students entering university are drawn overwhelmingly from the higher occupational groups of this society. If these results are compared to those for earlier years, it can be shown that the relative chances of young people from different backgrounds gaining access have changed only slightly, and then in favour of those groups already well off.[2]

Research by Halsey, Heath and Ridge at the University of Oxford[3] has shown in addition that, at least for men, the relative chances of people from different social class backgrounds gaining access to university have remained remarkably stable throughout the greater part of the century. Such is the cul-de-sac into which liberal expansion has led us. The costs to the Exchequer of the post-Robbins expansion of higher education in this country were borne by all taxpayers (probably more so in the case of working-class taxpayers given that we have a regressive system of taxation in this country), but the balance of reward, like much else in this society, favoured those who were already better off. The expansion of the public sector of higher education after 1965 with the polytechnics has not altered the overall picture in any substantial way. There is some evidence to suggest that this expansion was beneficial to working-class students in that they are more likely to join the public sector. But even within this sector, degree-level courses tend to recruit students from the higher socio-economic groups.

Such statistics rouse the hackles of socialists. And so they should. But there are people who accept them as signalling the inevitable and even desirable. And the policies of the present government – cutting back on university places, cost-cutting exercises through the National Advisory Body for the public sector, the active discussion of student loans as a way of financing the system – amount to a serious erosion of the Robbins principle of 1963 that all those qualified for and seeking places in higher education should find them. Socialists defending higher education have therefore to find a coherent answer to working-class supporters who, in the face of such observations, might ask, 'So what?' Is the argument about equality to be left where it has languished, with the claim that working people should have a great share of the places in higher education? They have been asked by successive postwar governments to finance that dream but have reaped few rewards from their investment.

Against the Tory onslaught, socialist policies must stress first the losses which this society as a whole and thousands of individuals have sustained as a result of inequalities, and how many more in the future will be denied what would be well within their capabilities to complete. Professors Halsey[4] and Edwards[5] have separately shown that there is a substantial wastage of ability among working-class children in the educational system of this country. Halsey has calculated that for most of the 1970s at least 7,000 boys each year could have gained A-level passes had they stayed on at school to take the exams; in the 1960s the figure was an annual rate of 30,000 and in the 1950s about 40,000. And Ted Edwards has calculated that the cutbacks in university education implemented by the present government will result in the destruction of university hopes for upwards of 40,000 students within the space of two years, students who will be predominantly from a working-class background. Given the demographic quirk of higher fertility rates among professional and managerial families and growing expectations from such people for higher education, the social exclusiveness of the universities and polytechnics will increase dramatically.

But it is not only individuals who will lose; as a society we are failing properly to develop the talents our people possess, and that is a policy of socio-economic suicide. And higher education itself is the poorer for it, incapable as it will be of drawing on a wider pool of experience and interest to challenge its orthodoxies and test its structures. For as several others in their contributions to this book have shown, what is actually on offer as an education in many departments and faculties of our higher education system is but a pale shadow of what intellect at full stretch should look like, and the élitism of the system, its insulation in significant areas from what is going on in the society and economy, has stilted the development of the system as a whole and weakened it intellectually.

## Population Trends and Higher Education

Three groups of people have encountered additional barriers to higher education in addition to those of class. Women, older people and black people have been denied opportunities in a system which remains predominantly male, white and young. Changes in the size of the population of 18-year-olds throughout the second half of the 1980s and into the 1990s offer opportunities within existing resources to increase massively the size of the student population and shift the balance of its social, sexual, age and racial composition.

In 1979 the Department of Education and Science issued a green paper, *Higher Education in the 1990s,*[6] which drew out the implications of falling fertility rates for the undergraduate population of this country. The report showed that there would be a marked tailing off after the mid-1980s in the size of the 18-year-old age-group which would leave considerable spare capacity in the system. Closures and cutbacks with redundancy among staff were one way of dealing with the problem, i.e. by pruning the system to meet the size of the younger age-group. But the report envisaged several other different possibilities, one of which was that of increasing the numbers of mature students in the system, particularly those from a working-class background. If the participation of women could be further increased then, it was argued, there would be no need and certainly little point in contracting the system.

There were many obstacles to the effective implementation of these ideas. Even if Jim Callaghan's Labour government had survived the 'winter of discontent' and the general election which followed it, the institutional and ideological obstacles to implementing the famous 'Model E' would have been formidable. But the opportunities, at least in so far as numbers of students determine them, are still open. The tragedy now is that the system is being cut back much faster than it needs to be cut. The effect is that some groups, particularly women, who were beginning to breach the walls of higher education in a significant way, will be thwarted.

The most recent figures on the size of the student population throughout the 1980s and 1990s are not so pessimistic as were those of *Higher Education in the 1990s*. They predict a student population in the 1990s of between 562,000 and 533,000, nearly 40,000 more than in 1980. The reason for this growth, given an absolute fall in the number of 18-year-olds, is a small rise in the age participation rate, and a parallel rise, fuelled perhaps by unemployment, of qualified candidates actually going on into higher education.[7] But these figures could be a serious underestimate. It may be true that the qualified participation rate will increase by only 3 or 4 per cent over the remainder of the decade (i.e. from 85.7 per cent in 1980 to 89.0 per cent in 1990) and on a lower estimate it could be even less than this. But it could equally well be the case that more young people could be persuaded to stay on to higher education. The recent report of the University Grants Committee, *A Strategy for Higher Education into the 1990s*,[8] underlined the conclusion from several recent studies of student numbers that: 'Demand will not diminish in the early 1990s just because there are fewer 18-year-olds available to meet it.' In any case, figures being discussed could quite easily under-represent the participation of some groups, particularly women. The Robbins Report predictions of twenty-two years ago were a considerable underestimate of the numbers who came in to higher education. Present-day projections could well suffer the same fate.

Take the participation of women in universities. Their share of university places is set out in Table 3 (overleaf). This shows a steady increase in the taking up of university places by women. And this itself reflects trends in the school system, with girls being more prepared to stay on at school and pursue A-level qualifications. But it would be naïve to imagine that this is the reserve pool of recruits for the future. Given the overall fall in the size of the 18-year-old age-group, the increase in the proportion of female students will only steady the overall decline.

For working-class women the chances of a place in higher

Table 3 *Percentage of full-time students in universities in Great Britain 1971–2/1981–2*

|          | Men  | Women |
|----------|------|-------|
| 1971–2   | 70.3 | 29.7  |
| 1976–7   | 66.0 | 34.0  |
| 1977–8   | 65.4 | 34.6  |
| 1978–9   | 64.6 | 35.4  |
| 1979–80  | 63.4 | 36.6  |
| 1980–81  | 62.4 | 37.6  |
| 1981–2   | 61.6 | 38.4  |

Source:
Adapted from Table 2, *University Statistics 1981–2* (Vol. 1, *Students and Staff*), University Statistical Record published by the University Grants Committee.

education have perhaps even deteriorated. Table 4 is adapted from the data in John Farrant's paper for the Leverhulme inquiry into higher education.[9] It indicates that while the proportion of women accepted by British universities has increased during the past quarter century, the proportion of women entering university from a working-class background has actually declined slightly.

Table 4 *Women, class and university entrance 1956–80*

|                          | University entrance |        |      |        |
|--------------------------|---------------------|--------|------|--------|
|                          | 1956                |        | 1980 |        |
|                          | Male                | Female | Male | Female |
| From working-class homes | 26.8                | 19.1   | 20.1 | 18.5   |
| All candidates           | 70.6                | 29.2   | 59.4 | 40.6   |

Source:
Adapted from J. H. Farrant, 'Trends in Admission', in O. Fulton (ed.), *Access to Higher Education*, Society for Research into Higher Education, 1981, Table 2.19, p. 87.

Why this should be the case is a question going right to the heart of the sexual division of labour of this society, to our attitudes towards women and their intellectual development, in families, schools and places of work. It is connected to the way in which women are denied opportunities of employment and of promotion in the occupations for which higher education has become a necessity. And it is about the role models and adult identities which are held out to women to achieve. In personal terms it is about the character of relationships between men and women in our society and the kinds of competence and confidence these relationships nurture.

What socialists have to examine are the ways in which the institutions of higher education of this country discourage women and whether changes need to be made in methods of recruitment, course organization, curriculum content and teaching methods to accommodate the different needs of women and the problems they encounter in the normal patterns of work, unemployment and family life. For socialists who are committed to the widening of educational opportunities for working-class people, it would be quite wrong to demand only that the doors of higher education be opened wider. The people who have benefited from that policy are more likely to have come from a middle-class background. Different options must be explored and encouraged if more women from a working-class background are to taste the fruits of it. (See the paper by Rosemary Deem and Janet Finch in this volume.) The general point to be stressed is that it is not possible to conceive of ways of increasing access to higher education to those who have been denied the opportunity without thinking of ways to change higher education itself.

The same point can be illustrated differently in the case of older people, another group under-represented in the present system and to whose needs the system responds very badly. It is a group, of course, which contains those hundreds of thousands of people who could have completed a higher education successfully but who never got the chance to do so. And they are people whose presence in higher education could be such a creative one.

The proportion of initial entrants into higher education in Great Britain aged 21 and over has increased from 16.8 per cent in 1966 to 24.0 per cent in 1980.[10] If the number of over-25-year-olds is examined the situation is much worse. For obvious family, occupational and financial reasons, it is likely that those over 25 are less prepared to enter higher education.

In the case of men the proportion from this age-group doing so has declined slightly since the early 1970s (from 3.2 per cent to 3.0 per cent) and for women it has increased a little (1.3 per cent to 2.7 per cent).

Such figures are, however, difficult to interpret, since the size of the pool of appropriately qualified adult potential candidates is not really known. A recent report from the D.E.S. has, however, calculated the mature entry rate for the period 1970 to 1981 and suggested provisional figures for the current academic year. The mature entry rate measures the proportion of people aged over 21 or 25 who were appropriately qualified at the age of 18 to enter higher education but did not do so, but who have subsequently applied to do so. For both the 21–24 age-group and the over 25s the mature entry rate has decreased over the decade and is poised to decrease even further.[11] The figures are fractional in any case but that they are so small – 0.2 per cent – is really very worrying and a sad measure of the opportunities which are effectively made available to people to develop their education further.

To come from a working-class background, to be female and to be over 25 years of age are three serious handicaps to anyone seeking higher education in this country. To be black is another. West Indian and Asian children in this country seem to perform differently from one another at school, with Asians doing significantly better than West Indians and perhaps, too, than their age-group as a whole. But as Alan Little and Diana Robbins have pointed out, 'Black and brown British young people are markedly under-represented in higher education.'[12]

The roots of this go deep into the colonial history of this society and the racial discrimination which is woven into the normal routines of the way many of our social institutions function. There is political ambivalence, too, about discriminating positively in favour of the disadvantaged, particularly when they happen, too, as many do, to be black. The disadvantages to which black people are vulnerable are well known. That they have a cumulative impact on educational life-chances is also something we can grasp. The problems of black people underline how important it is to think about higher education in the wider context of how schools operate and of how, in their turn, schools can be supported or undermined by the way in which housing markets and labour markets function.

Higher education cannot be expected to transform the life-chances of black people. But it does have a role to play. At a minimum we should, as a society, expect institutions of higher education to examine themselves carefully to see whether there is anything in the way they carry on their work which discourages black people from entering them. But as part of a socialist commitment to the full development of all human beings we should expect more than this; we should expect universities and other places of higher education to reflect in their teaching and research the backgrounds and interests of the different ethnic groups of this society and to be sufficiently flexible to be influenced by them. Once more it is not simply a question of deflecting the issue back to the schools or to families, for higher education itself is implicated in how people come to value themselves and map out their futures. A system of higher education culturally and intellectually accessible only to a narrow range of people cannot be defended.

There is a further inequality worth mentioning which overlaps those already discussed, the variation in access which is related to region of the country. It is an important variation because it shows too what scope there is for boosting the access of some young people to higher education within the framework of existing arrangements. Table 5 (overleaf) illustrates the extent of variation between the regions.

The table shows that with the exceptions of Wales and the North West, all other regions apart from those of Greater London and the South East fall below the national average in terms of entry into higher education. Crude data on regional differences would cause a statistician to take fits since they are influenced by many factors not at first apparent, and the most important of these is class. The regions in the Midlands and the North contain a far higher proportion of industrial workers

Table 5 *Indices of Age Participation Rates: by region (England and Wales=100)*

| (A) | (B) | (C) | (D) | (E) | (F) |
|---|---|---|---|---|---|
| *England* | | | | | |
| North | 75 | 84 | 86 | 79 | 89 |
| Yorks and Humberside | 85 | 93 | 92 | 83 | 89 |
| North West | 101 | 104 | 106 | 104 | 94 |
| East Midlands | 89 | 90 | 88 | 82 | 92 |
| West Midlands | 93 | 87 | 90 | 83 | 92 |
| East Anglia | 81 | 87 | 84 | 89 | 100 |
| Greater London | 122 | 109 | 107 | 97 | 105 |
| Other South East | 111 | 107 | 110 | 128 | 116 |
| South West | 97 | 102 | 97 | 101 | 106 |
| *Wales* | 106 | 114 | 110 | 106 | 93 |
| *England and Wales* | 100 | 100 | 100 | 100 | 100 |
| (percentage of age group) | (18.4) | (19.1) | (10.9) | (8.5) | |
| *Scotland* | | | | 126 | 92 |

(A) Standard regions (small changes in definition in 1974 have been ignored).

(B) Proportion of 16- to 18-year-olds in school or on full-time G.C.E./C.S.E. courses in F.E. colleges, 1977/8.

(C) Unweighted means of proportion of average of 18- and 19-year-olds taking up new L.E.A. awards or entering initial teacher training, 1975/6–1977/8.

(D) As (C), but excluding award-holders in F.E. colleges.

(E) Candidates accepted for university entrance, 1979: rates per 1,000 18-year-olds.

(F) Predicted Age Participation Rate, on the basis of distribution of household heads by social class.

*Source:*
(B) D.E.S., SB 15/79. (C), (D), SE, 5. (E) U.C.C.A. *Statistical Supplements*, 1978–9, Table F4. D.E.S., SB 2/H1/1981. O.P.C.S., *Population estimates 1979. Annual estimates of the population of Scotland 1979.* (F) *Census 1971, Household composition*, Table 41 (heads of all households by social class by region; 18-year-olds assumed to be distributed by social class similarly). Age Participation Rates as for c. 1977 in Table 2.18 above.

Adapted from J. H. Farrant, 'Trends in Admission', in O. Fulton (ed.), *Access to Higher Education*, Society for Research into Higher Education, 1981.

than those of the South East. But what is interesting about Table 5 is that it shows too what the regional participation rates should be when known variations in social class composition of the population are taken into account. Scotland, Wales and the North West clearly do much better than might be expected on the basis of their social class make-up; the North and East Anglia are doing rather worse than we might expect. The reasons for this go back to even deeper variations in levels of financial support to schools, local policies in education and academic traditions. One way of reading the differences between actual and expected performance, however, is that they indicate that a lot can be done even within present frameworks of provision to increase participation rates.

International Comparisons

There is a mood in Britain, particularly among the defenders of the existing system, of fatalism, a belief that the world is as it is and cannot be otherwise. It is bolstered by arguments about pools of ability and educational standards. In the early 1960s, when the Robbins Committee urged a major expansion in higher education, there were stridently insulting cries from right-wing quarters that 'more would mean worse'. Under the guise of economic necessity these arguments are reappearing, deployed to justify cutbacks in higher education which are being made to get government spending down. International comparisons with other major industrial societies show on the other hand that there can be no educational reasons for doing so and that on manpower grounds the current policies of the Tory government are self-contradictory.

Britain enrols a much lower proportion of its young people in higher education than almost any other European society. Table 6 gives some indication of this.

Table 6 *Annual entry into higher education as percentage of relevant age group,\* 1970 and 1976*

Ratio new entrants to population percentage

|  | 1970 | 1976 | percentage change 1970–76 |
|---|---|---|---|
| U.S.A. | 46.2 | 42.8 | −3.4 |
| Japan | 24.0 | 39.2 | +15.2 |
| Australia | 18.4 | 37.7 | +19.3 |
| Denmark | 27.2 | 36.8 | +9.6 |
| Belgium | 29.6 | 33.9 | +4.3 |
| Spain | 26.7 | 31.5 | +4.8 |
| Canada | 28.9 | 30.9 | +2.0 |
| Italy | 24.4 | 30.6 | +6.2 |
| France | 26.3 | 27.7 | +1.4 |
| Finland | 19.0 | 26.0 | +7.0 |
| Netherlands | 18.2 | 25.5 | +7.3 |
| U.K. | 20.4 | 21.8 | +1.4 |
| West Germany | 16.0 | 19.2 | +3.2 |
| Austria | 15.7 | 18.6 | +2.9 |

\*Relevant age group is the population (divided by number of years) in the range covering at least 70 per cent of new entrants.

*Note:* The figures refer to full-time students with the exception of the following countries, for which it is not possible to distinguish between full-time and part-time students: Australia, Denmark, Finland, U.S.A.

*Source:*
O.E.C.D.
From National Economic Development Council, *Education and Industry*, 1982.

In its campaign guide to candidates for the 1983 general election, Conservative Central Office put this gloss on the problem:

> 12.9 per cent of those aged 18–20 were enrolled in higher education in 1981–2. This is a lower percentage than in some other countries. But there is no reason to suppose that this puts us at a disadvantage: it merely means that our students are better qualified for higher education, and more able to make proper use of it. As Mr William Waldegrave, Parliamentary Undersecretary of State for Higher Education, said: 'we are, of course, more

rigorous than many countries about what we allow to be called degree-level work.'[13]

If international comparisons are made in such a way that part-time enrolments can be taken into account, the picture for Britain is not quite so bleak. The Organization for European Co-operation and Development (O.E.C.D.) have a formula for doing this, and on this basis the participation rates for new enrolments are as follows: Federal Republic of Germany, 19.2 per cent; U.S.A., 42.8 per cent; France, 27.7 per cent; Japan, 39.2 per cent.[14] The figure for Britain is 31.0 per cent. What remains true for Britain and Europe as a whole, however, is that part-time higher education is much less prestigious than its full-time counterpart and is more concerned with vocational courses and sub-degree work.

Whatever gloss is put on the figures it remains true, as a recent report from the National Economic Development Office pointed out, that 'the U.K. participation rate in higher education is low amongst O.E.C.D. countries. Expressed in terms of relevant age groups the U.K. has a participation rate in higher education about half to two thirds of that of many major O.E.C.D. countries. The increase in participation between 1970 and 1976 is also one of the lowest, implying a worsening relative position.'[15]

But the far more serious point is that the attitude which the above quotation from Conservative Central Office reflects is a deeply entrenched one in British higher education. It is based on a misplaced national pride and a totally unexamined assumption about the quality of higher education here and particularly in the universities.

British universities and their counterparts in the public sector of higher education pride themselves on the quality of their degrees, and academics are quick to defend academic standards. They have, however, over the years avoided a careful inspection of what these standards really are and why, to be defended, they require the universities to be so delicately selective in their intake. What really is the intellectual mettle of a manager with a lower second-class honours degree in

English or History? What skills have they acquired or refined in advance of those they started with? And what are the grounds for belief that English Literature can be studied appropriately in exclusive little seminars of people without much experience of the world beyond their own exclusive schools? It is not a question which lends itself to precise measurement, for it is about the value placed on different kinds of academic work. But it is a well-known, if unproven, fact of academic life that in the arts and humanities and social sciences some students can coast along relying on wit, question-spotting and cramming for exams, and pass through the 'blasphemous baptism' of the degree ceremony secure in the knowledge that although they might not know much, they have won that prized ticket for which the whole of their secondary education and that of their less fortunate peers has been totally distorted. And it is not just in the humanities and social sciences that these questions need to be asked. Even the present government is concerned with the quantity and quality of the scientific and technological training which takes place in British higher education and the way it does not meet the needs of British industry.

Class inequalities in higher education are, in fact, woven into its very fabric, into how students are selected, the way they are trained, the way they are financed and assessed and the way, according to culturally dominant notions of ability and worth, they are distributed across faculties and among institutions. And behind the respectable façades of academic life there is the long-term decline of the British economy relative to its major industrial competitors; and the two are connected. Recent research by Prais and Wagner of the National Institute of Economic and Social Research, comparing vocational training in Britain and the Federal Republic of Germany, showed Britain to be far behind in vocational training in a number of important trades.[16] They emphasized 'that the very much larger proportion of the German workforce attaining vocational qualifications has done so at standards which are generally as high as, and perhaps on the whole a little higher than, those attained by the smaller proportion in Britain'.[17]

It is the case, then, that in Britain there are serious short-comings in the way people are educated and trained, in that those who are in the system receive a training not well suited to the needs of industry. But it is also the case that we neglect to develop the abilities of a very large number of people. A report in 1981 from the National Economic Development Office, which had reviewed industrial policies among Britain's main (and more successful) industrial competitors, underlined a serious aspect of this, namely that 'any major expansion in many of the faster growing high technology areas would run into a crippling lack of skill infrastructure very rapidly'.[18]

The mechanisms of this society, which function to exclude a very high proportion of young people from higher education and debar their elders from it too, not only unjustifiably limit individual rights to education and personal development but act as well to hold back the economic political development of the country. International comparison which shows up the British case in such a poor light underlines the fact that a great deal of change and improvement is possible and that com-placency here is dangerous.

## Socialist Policies for Higher Education

A socialist strategy for higher education should clearly announce support for the values of equality and social justice, of academic freedom, disinterested scholarship and the pursuit of truth. It should aim to defend academic standards in the sense that those who receive higher education should acquire a respect for logical discussion, precise observation and careful research. It should be defined, too, in relation to the develop-ment of qualities of mind and feeling which any civilized society should regard as the end of education.

But none of this presupposes the forms of higher education we have at present. The separation of science and the arts, of studying from working, of research from teaching and of those being educated from the majority of people who are not, is not a system defensible on any of the intellectual criteria it itself would claim to represent.

Higher education cannot be discussed apart from the system of secondary education on which it feeds. Here, too, deep-seated inequalities of a cumulatively damaging kind exist and must be rooted out, and the case for doing so is not just an economic one. Given the tightening bonds between knowledge and power in this society, not to be educated and to be denied opportunities for further re-education is to be denied the ability to participate effectively and creatively in the political life of the society. For this reason we cannot be complacent about how well schools are performing or adapting to the changes in the society and the economy which are going on around them.

In higher education the lesson has to be learned that the post-Robbins expansion of the system without structural changes to it did not breach the bastions of social inequality. Further expansion, in any case, is not a serious option. Socialists face the much more difficult task of working out creative policies of change in the context of declining numbers in the 18-year-old age-group and shrinking resources.

The Labour Party has made a good start on this. Discussions have taken place of a comprehensive system of tertiary education for the 16- to 19-year-old age-group.[19] And in the document *Education after 18; Expansion with Change*,[20] several ways of diversifying higher education and broadening access to it were canvassed; these include an adult educational entitlement for one year's further education either full-time or part-time, the replacement of the present A-level system of admissions requirements with one much broader, and a progressive movement towards the elimination of the binary line in higher education. It envisaged reform in university government, student financial support and a national council for the development of adult and continuing education. It recognized the importance of discussions with the trade unions about paid educational leave for workers with the ultimate aim of a universal right to education after the age of 18.

Ideas like these deserve the support of socialists; but with this qualification, that they cannot be left as manifesto proposals for the future. Support must be mobilized for them here and now, and they must be refined in the course of political struggle. The development of alternatives to the present system will depend upon the support of people who have been denied access to it. It is not a matter of M.P.s breathing fire at ministers or of conference resolutions. It is above all a matter of building up a commitment to change which through the ballot box becomes a mandate.

It was an article of faith for Aneurin Bevan that the tragedy of the British working man was the poverty of his imagination and that it was not the responsibility of Labour politicians to pander to the aspirations fuelled by capitalism. Their job was rather to give definition to new values. That, in essence, is a problem of the imagination, of a vision of a better society. It remains the most urgent practical problem that we face. And we can face up to it now. The discussions upon which a refined imagination will depend can be catalysed wherever socialists are and can act; in local authorities, in trade unions, in advisory bodies, on the boards of governors of schools and colleges and university courts. And if they are under-represented they can seek to rectify it. For socialists working in education and in vocational education, their job is to fight for socialist ideals in the course of their daily work. At each level and point in the political organization of this society, socialists must cultivate support for their ideas. From their political representatives in Parliament and local authorities, socialists have a right to expect careful forward planning. The aim should be to build up a dense network of educational opportunities which facilitates a growth in the educational participation of those currently denied access to what even the present system can offer. And for those in Parliament who will guide the education policy of a future Labour government, there is an urgent need to plan the financial framework of higher education in a way which rewards those institutions which are prepared creatively to overcome the deficiencies of the present system and meet the needs of a much more diverse student body.

There is no other way ahead; to be practical we have to be visionaries. Our task is not to defend higher education as we know it, but to change it.

## Notes

1 Robbins Report, *Committee on Higher Education*, H.M.S.O., 1963, Cmnd. 2154, Appendix 1, p. 46.

2 See E. G. Edwards and I. J. Roberts, 'British Higher Education: long term trends in student enrolment', *Higher Education Review* 12(2), 1980.

3 A. H. Halsey, A. F. Heath and J. M. Ridge, *Origins and Destinations: family class and education in modern Britain*, Oxford University Press, 1980.

4 ibid.

5 E. G. Edwards, *Higher Education for Everyone*, Spokesman Books, 1982.

6 Department of Education and Science, *Higher Education in the 1990s*, D.E.S., 1979.

7 Department of Education and Science, *Report on Education: No. 100. Demand for Higher Education in Great Britain 1984–2000*, D.E.S., 1984.

8 University Grants Committee, *A Strategy for Higher Education into the 1990s*, H.M.S.O., 1984.

9 J. Farrant, 'Trends in Admissions', Ch. 2 of O. Fulton (ed.), *Access to Higher Education*, Society for Research into Higher Education. Programme of Study into the Future of Higher Education, 1981 (Leverhulme).

10 Alan Woodley, 'Age Bias', in D. Warren Piper (ed.), *Is Higher Education Fair?*, Society for Research into Higher Education, 1981.

11 Department of Education and Science, *Report on Education: No. 99. Future Demand for Higher Education in Great Britain*, D.E.S., 1983.

12 A. Little and D. Robbins, 'Race Bias', in D. Warren Piper (ed.), *Is Higher Education Fair?*, Society for Research into Higher Education, 1981, p. 57.

13 *Campaign Guide*, Conservative Party, 1982, p. 211.

14 Department of Education and Science, *Report on Education: No. 99*.

15 National Economic Development Council, *Education and Industry*, National Economic Development Office, 1982, p. 15.

16 S. J. Prais and K. Wagner, *Some Political Aspects of Human Capital*

*Investment: Training Standards in Five Occupations in Britain and Germany*, Discussion Paper No. 56, National Institute of Economic and Social Research, 1983.

17 ibid., p. 46.

18 National Economic Development Council, *Industrial Policies in Europe. A Study of Policies Pursued in European Countries and the EEC and their Implications for the U.K.*, National Economic Development Office, 1981, p. 7.

19 *16–19 Learning for Life*, Labour Party, 1981.

20 *Education After 18: Expansion with Change*, Labour Party, 1982.

# 3
# Student Finance

OLIVER FULTON

## Introduction

There is a utopian vision of future participation in higher
education which has inspired the Left for many years, as
Michael Rustin shows in Chapter 1. Generally, it has three
interlocking elements. Numbers will be high, making the
opportunity of degree-level study not only a right but virtually an expectation of citizenship in an economically
advanced democratic society. Access will be unbiased, with
exclusion only for those with no taste for the higher learning
or the careers for which it prepares – and perhaps also
(depending on your view of meritocracy) for those without
the intellectual capacity, generously defined, to benefit. And
as befits a right of citizenship, participation will be cost-free,
with no means tests to tie young (or older) adults to the
purse-strings of arbitrarily stingy or impoverished parents.
It is an admirable vision, to which many British socialists
have stayed devoted for longer, perhaps, than those anywhere
else in the world. In the perspective of twenty years ago, the
post-Robbins euphoria when economic growth made everything possible (and such a programme would anyway be self-
financing by leading in due course to greater economic
growth), it seemed not only attractive but perfectly reasonable.

In the mid-1980s, however, it looks less realistic – at least in the short or medium term. We are little nearer mass, let alone universal, access than we were in 1970; class and ethnic biases are probably worse, and gender and age biases little better – on the most generous interpretation. The real cost to students has risen sharply, and it is generally believed that this not only penalizes students themselves but also helps to depress participation and bias access. What is to be done? Voices from the past are clear enough: increase financial support, and things will begin to improve once again. But is this right? There are now many good reasons for thinking that a very different policy is needed.

## The Present System

Let us begin by looking hard at the present undergraduate student support system and especially its effects. The mandatory grant system pays the full amount of a modest tuition (set at an arbitrary rate – see below) for all eligible students, and provides a maintenance allowance which is means-tested by reference to parents' or (in the case of some mature students) spouse's income. Eligibility in turn depends on two elements: the course – which must be an approved course of 'higher' education, taken *full-time*; and the student – who must be a British resident who has not previously received a similar grant. These regulations, apparently common-sensical enough, have turned out to lead to a series of unforeseen and undesirable consequences.

First, the system is 'mandatory' and has been so since the recommendations of the Anderson Report were adopted in 1962. It is quite right that eligible students should be entitled to equal treatment regardless of where in the U.K. they happened to live before starting their courses. Unfortunately, this entitlement to a grant means that, in the accounting jargon of the mid-1980s, expenditure on grants is 'volume-based' and not 'cash-limited': if demand rises, central government expenditure must rise (as it did by an unforecast £75m in 1981/2). This is not popular with the Treasury – and not only under Conservative governments. The result is constant pressure not only to reduce the real value of the grant, but also to restrict demand by restricting the supply of places. It is true that this has been resisted by the public sector of higher education and that universities have succumbed to it largely for other, if no less discreditable reasons; but the downward pressure is there and is unlikely to go away. Without it, it would be far easier to squeeze in extra students with the same staff and fixed costs. Those who wish to keep a large per-capita subsidy need to be aware that they are giving a powerful weapon to the opponents of broader participation.

Second, the fee element. In recent years this has fluctuated from less than 5 per cent to well over 20 per cent of the estimated true cost per student. It may seem a trivial distinction how much of an institution's income arrives in a direct grant and how much in per-capita fees, since it all comes ultimately from the government's education budget. But in fact it is not trivial, not only to the Treasury for the reason given above, but also to the institution. One does not have to be an uncritical devotee of market forces to see that potential students who bring a cheque for 20 or 30 per cent of their costs in their hands can strengthen those within colleges and universities who wish to expand the supply of places, whereas a purely nominal fee gives more decision-making power, and especially the power to limit access, to the centre of the institution or its government-appointed controllers. Those who believe in strong central control for higher education need to face up to the dangers of that control in the wrong hands: the *Conservative* government *halved* the fee in 1982/3 (after the 'overshoot' in student numbers of 1981/2), and replaced the shortfall with an increased direct grant to institutions – precisely in order to reduce the temptation of responding to 'market forces' by taking in more students in the public sector.

Third, means-tested maintenance grants. Again, most governments – and certainly both major political parties – have reduced the real value of the 'full' grant, a process which seems to be accelerating. The present means test, aside from leaving most young students dependent on their parents' (unenforceable) generosity, is in any case inadequate to avoid all cases of hardship. An alarmingly high proportion of students is not in receipt of the full parental contribution, generally because their parents are not unwilling but unable to provide it. Aside from the hardship to individuals, which can be considerable, the prospect must surely be a deterrent to some doubtful applicants. One result, as surveys by the N.U.S. and the D.E.S. showed in 1984, is that we already have a *de facto* loan scheme, but administered by the major banks at normal overdraft rates, and subject to their acceptance of individuals as suitable commercial risks. This last point is bound to discriminate against certain classes of student whose prospects of high earnings bank managers may question – for instance older students in general, married women re-entrants in particular and those in unfashionable subjects with poor employment prospects. The obvious conclusion is that we need to increase the grant to more generous levels and abolish the means test – and this, understandably, is the aim of the N.U.S. If, as seems likely, this is not achievable – nor, as I have already argued, necessarily desirable – the alternative of a well-designed, centrally run or monitored loan scheme as a supplement to a basic grant could at least protect student finance from its present arbitrary and potentially discriminatory nature.

As for the eligibility criteria, it is here that perhaps the worst difficulties arise. When the present system was invented, part-time students were a small minority, and it seemed reasonable and equitable that those who, it was thought, would still be at work should not be given any support beyond a fee subsidy. But the Open University's research has demonstrated that there are plenty of potential part-time students for whom even apparently moderate costs are a very serious deterrent, and there seems no good reason (beyond the extra cost to the Treasury) why part-time students should not be supported at least pro rata on the same basis as full-time – i.e. with maintenance as well as fee support, means-tested if necessary. Similarly with the type of course for which grants are available: 'advanced' or 'degree-level' courses may have been a clearly defined category in 1962, but the growth of 'non-advanced' further education, continuing education, credit transfer, etc., and the sheer variety of courses on offer, have made nonsense of the simple concept of 'level', as others in this book have argued. And finally, every admissions and welfare officer knows of cases of genuine hardship created by the restriction on the number of degree-level courses one person may take. There is an almost unanswerable case, therefore, for widening the scope of the mandatory award system by removing most if not all of the present restrictions on eligibility.

But all of these proposals will involve significant increases in expenditure. They will compete with other more or less desirable candidates for extra resources within and outside education and, if successful, give greater hostages to fortune in greater resistance to expansion. Rather than tinkering with, or expanding, a (theoretically) generous system of support which was invented when fewer than 6 per cent of 18-year-olds made use of it, to cope with an uptake which we hope will far exceed that figure (and even now, if we included part-time students, we would be talking of up to five times as many in proportion to the 18-year-old age cohort), should we not start again from the beginning?

## First Principles

The fundamental questions have to do with equity and expansion. Unfortunately there are several of them and their answers are not always either obvious or reconcilable with each other. I take it as axiomatic that the supply of higher education is too limited, that there is a 'pool' of more or less latent demand which should be met; and that any scheme of finance should not only not restrict present levels of access but should encourage expansion. It is often claimed that any reductions in the maintenance grant will immediately reduce demand and that introducing loans would certainly do so. The evidence, such as it is, is not so clear. There is no easily visible relationship between the quite striking fluctuations in the growth of the participation rate from 1963 onwards and the level of student grants: as a whole, participation by younger students at least seems much more strongly affected by perceptions of the labour market. In other words, three years' potential hardship seems to weigh less heavily than the hope of many more years in which to benefit. Changing to a less generous system, especially if it were more rational, more equitable, and *more* generous to other kinds of student, would not necessarily depress demand. Whether loans in themselves would provide an extra deterrent is a separate question, to which I shall return below.

But if the tendency of recent years to spread the Treasury's jealously guarded butter more thinly has not noticeably reduced the total number of students, it does not follow that it has had no effects at all. We know lamentably little about participation in the public sector, but we do know that the distribution of *university* students by parents' occupations has changed, with working-class participation showing a marked relative decline, sharpened since the cuts of 1981. There are plenty of competing explanations of greater or less plausibility, including the loss of grammar schools as channels of 'sponsored mobility' for the favoured few, the reduction of the working-class pool by the growth of lower white-collar occupations, or, more positively, the growth of a democratic, non-élitist alternative in the public sector. None of these carry instant conviction in the absence of hard evidence, and one must at least consider the possibility that slow erosion of the present grant system is partly responsible. Surveys in Sweden confirm that while most middle-class students will persist in their choice of higher education without much attention to the level of financial support, working-class students are, understandably, much more likely to be deterred by high costs. Presumably a sensitively designed progressive means test ought to have the opposite effect; but the income 'floor' beyond which parents are assessed a contribution is in fact now set low enough to catch many people in manual jobs, even in households with only one wage-earner. We do not have the information on which to judge, but we may certainly suspect that British grants are no longer high enough to attract so many potential first-generation students.

Another aspect of the equity debate has already been mentioned: the difference between 'higher' and other forms of post-compulsory education. The argument is both direct and indirect. In its direct form, there is little justification other than tradition for the distinction in financing between non-advanced' courses – predominantly vocational or preparatory – and 'advanced' courses – academic or higher level. The value system which the distinction reveals has little to commend it in principle; and it is clear that the effect can be directly discriminatory. But it also discriminates indirectly. However generously students on degree courses may be funded, this is little use if the courses they need to take first, in order to obtain their entry qualifications, carry no maintenance grants. There is plenty of research evidence, here and overseas, to show that the crucial decision for young people, and the one where finance plays the greatest part, is that taken not at 17+ but at 15+. The Labour government's Education Bill of 1979 included proposals for modest means-tested Education Maintenance Allowances (E.M.A.s) for 16- to 19-year-olds who stayed in full-time education after the minimum school-leaving age – something that some local authorities had already pioneered, though fewer are still offering them today. The proposal was dropped by the new government. The absence of E.M.A.s, set against the free availability of Y.T.S. with its allowance, and other state benefits for those out of work and *not* in full-time education, provides a positive disincentive to anyone without families well able to support them. Nor is the problem confined to 16- to 19-year-olds: only a few 'special access' courses for adults and those given by adult residential colleges carry maintenance grants. These distinctions are unjustifiable by reference to any principle.

A third aspect, however, is more complex. Now that it is clearer, first, that the financial return to most young people who 'invest' in higher education is still positive – and probably increasingly so as unemployment bites harder on unqualified school-leavers – and secondly that the 1960s' hopes of greater equality in access to higher education have not been fulfilled, it has become steadily easier to see the state's financial support for students as a regressive transfer of resources – from the uneducated majority to the educated minority, and from the broad mass of taxpayers to an unrepresentative élite who can mostly expect high incomes for the rest of their lives once they graduate. The fact that it was a Conservative Secretary of State, Sir Keith Joseph, who used these arguments in the autumn of 1984 to justify an attempt to reduce subsidies to students from the richest families, need not invalidate them – as his half-defeat at the hands of his own party made clear. In strict equity such a system could not be justified, on its own terms, though a utilitarian might approve it if its benefits outweighed its costs.

These benefits are said to include the promotion of the other main purposes of higher education – e.g. the creation and transmission of knowledge and culture through research and teaching, and the provision of an adequate supply of educated talent for the labour market. Whether the overall size and hence the output of the higher education system would be seriously damaged by a different system of financial support is, I have already argued, open to doubt. If, in particular, we were to institute a system whereby those who benefit most were asked to repay part of their subsidy in due course, it is still not clear that this would act as a deterrent. The counter-argument is that a progressive tax system should take care of the problem. Higher earners contribute more taxes according to their higher means, and education, like health and other services, should be provided at no cost, according to needs. Whether access to higher education, like that to health care, is best treated as an essential right of citizenship from which the whole society benefits, or as a personal investment (or consumption), like transport, for which individuals may reasonably be asked to pay part of the cost, is perhaps a question to leave to political philosophers. Moreover, the answer might well be different if instead of a minority's privilege, leading to a considerable relative advantage in the labour market, higher education were widened to something close to universal access. Meanwhile, there can be little disagreement that under the present tax and grant regulations and at present levels of participation both the individual benefits, and the costs to others, are high, while the social benefits are less clear – and might well be as large or larger under a different system. There is a reasonable case for arguing that *part* of the cost should be repayable by the individual through a loan system.

## Possibilities for the Future

We need a system which spreads grants more widely by encouraging greater participation and reducing biases in recruitment. In addition, it should not subsidize the present or future wealthy; it should be easy to administer; it should not create inefficiency in higher education (for example by compelling students to drop out frequently to earn their own fees and expenses); and it should not create an incentive to governments, or to institutions, to restrict expansion. This is a tall order.

One partial solution would be to make a determined effort to separate essential living expenses from the *additional* costs which people incur by undertaking post-compulsory education. The present absurdities, by which the employment, through the M.S.C., rewards 16-year-olds for *not* continuing in formal education, and the social security system rewards people who restrict their formal education to a limited number of hours per week, cannot be defended. A revised social security system which gave uniformly administered, needs-based allowances indiscriminately to all those not in paid employment, including everyone in education and training, would avoid the worst distortions of the present system. It would have the considerable added advantage of removing a large element from the education budget where it does not rightly belong. (The present system counts the whole cost of student grants as education expenditure, with no allowance for savings in the costs of supporting unemployed people which would otherwise fall on other departments.) This basic support could be provided regardless of the number of years a person had been a student, since as far as possible, it would be neutral between different forms of education, training or unemployment.

Beyond this, however, there are considerable further costs to be met. Although this is not the place for a general discussion of higher education finance, the system of subsidizing fees through block grants to institutions is obviously right. Even if all students were fully reimbursed, full-cost fees would effectively create a private system of post-compulsory education which is thoroughly undesirable. On the other hand, a purely nominal fee gives institutions little or no incentive to respond to students' changing needs. By providing a nearly unconditional grant, it strengthens the hands of staff who wish to restrict access – a very substantial number in higher education, as a *Times Higher Education Supplement*/MORI poll showed in early 1985. The alternative of more direct government intervention through increasing direct control of institutions is not cost-free and gives hostage to unsympathetic governments. A fee of around 30 per cent of 'full cost' (which could still be cross-subsidized within institutions, or directly subsidized in particular subjects if governments wished) was suggested by the Robbins Committee and still seems sensible.

This would leave the social security aided student to find both a non-trivial sum for fees and also all the other expenses of studying, both direct costs and the costs of travelling or living away from home. There is a strong case for financing these through a *mixture* of *grants* and *loans*, to recognize and symbolize the benefits which both society and the individual derive from education after 16.

First there should, I believe, be a clearly identified educational 'entitlement', in the form of a grant to cover fees and basic expenses, which (1) can start at 16 but can be taken, in whole or in part, at any age; (2) is not restricted to particular courses or levels of study; and (3) is available pro rata for full-time or part-time study. The amount of grant would need to be carefully worked out, but it should be high enough, in combination with the proposed social security reform, to leave a 16- to 18-year-old living at home and studying full-time with no extra expense. I have suggested elsewhere that it might be for a total of four years full-time or their equivalent, so as to cover up to two years at the present higher education level, on the assumption that this would lead to much greater participation than at present in a widened range of courses as alternatives to the present honours degree. However, the length and conditions, as well as the value, would need to be reviewed from time to time as different kinds of course become available and participation levels change. As I argued earlier, the equity case against full support for all students depends on their being a minority who have received a relatively substantial advantage in life-chances over most of those whose taxes support them. If participation became near-universal – as is already in sight with 16-year-olds if we include Y.T.S. – one would expect the state to pay the full cost.

The remainder of a student's costs (which might normally include the cost of residence if they studied away from home) would be covered by a publicly controlled and publicly subsidized loan scheme. I have already described the arguments in principle, but we need to be clear about the practical arguments, for and against. First, the alleged deterrent effect. There is no evidence from experience in Canada, Sweden or the United States, reviewed by Maureen Woodhall in 1982,[1] that loans in themselves are any more of a deterrent than other forms of student finance to groups such as working-class children or young women in those countries. Indeed, if they provide funds which would otherwise not be available, they help to encourage participation. There is no reason to suppose the effects would be different in the U.K., unless the potential burden was seen as very high or very risky. A system such as that proposed here, which used loans to top up social security and entitlement payments, would not generate massive debts, and it would in any case be reasonable for the state to subsidize interest payments at least until the borrower had finished studying, as is done elsewhere. The best way to deal with the risk is to ensure that repayments are graduated according to income, so that anyone on low wages or who is unemployed would not have to keep up their full repayment – something that would be needed anyway to avoid unnecessary defaults. The simplest way to achieve this would be to collect repayments through the income tax system, with a small additional percentage to be added on to the standard rates of tax. This system would have the attraction of not deterring older students, who might otherwise be unsure about their prospects of paying off a fixed loan in a shorter space of time. (Many of these, it might be hoped, would in any case benefit from the expansion of Paid Educational Leave proposed by Michael Cunningham in Chapter 5, and so not need to depend on loans.)

The other main objection to loan schemes is that they will not decrease government expenditure for a considerable time and may in fact increase it. It would certainly be essential that loans should be freely available without means tests or other restrictions to anyone who wants them, which would increase the immediate outlay substantially. And if, as I have suggested, an entitlement only covered four years post-16 there would presumably be a very substantial demand from those in their third year of a degree course – and subsequently, if postgraduate courses were included, as they should be. However, if this were a serious political problem it should be possible to include the commercial banks in the scheme with the right form of government guarantees and interest subsidies; in any case, although the outlay from the Treasury would be heavy in the short term, overseas experience shows that the return can build up to 25 per cent or more of the cost in the long run, freeing funds for use elsewhere.

Essentially, the idea of loan finance is neutral: it is possible to devise schemes which can range from the highly progressive to the highly restrictive. Fear of the most restrictive versions should not discourage us from trying to develop a combined system, using social security, entitlement grants and loans, which would satisfy the broad aims outlined above and reflect reasonably fairly the balance of advantages which accrue both to society and to the individual from participation in higher education.

*Note*

1 M. Woodhall, *Student Loans: Lessons from Recent International Experience*, Policy Studies Institute, 1982.

# 4
# Education Is Ordinary:
## *A Biographical Account*

ALAN WHITE

> I wish, first, that we should recognize that education is ordinary: that it is, before everything else, the process of giving to the ordinary members of a society its full common meanings, and the skills that will enable them to amend these meanings, in the light of their personal and common experience. If we start from that, we can get rid of the remaining restrictions, and make the necessary changes.[1]

I have just been reading the article from which the above quotation is taken. It is a warm, rich, human evocation of one man's feelings generated by the transforming power of a 'liberal' education. It is also a plea for those in control of the destiny of society to realize that education – and culture – is ordinary, and should be made open and accessible to all who wish to make use of it. It contains a number of practical and realizable – if, at times, vague – suggestions as to how such a state could be brought about. It was published a quarter of a century ago. To the vast majority of academics its message of open access must seem like a voice from another time. With the waters of Thatcherism washing over the gunnels of the sinking university system, the name of the game is damage containment.

The atmosphere in the universities now is one in which the voices arguing for moves to make education more ordinary – among which I number my own – are lost in the thunder of academics personing the barricades of 'academic standards' and 'centres of excellence'. And yet ... we do have to have standards, and excellence *is* a fine one to aim for. When this seemingly endless era of cultural destruction comes to a close, as it must, we will have a golden opportunity to re-define the aims and goals of the education system. It would make no sense only to rebuild the edifice in its old style. The post-war consensus has been broken for good. We either build alternative explanations, alternative meanings, or we yield the ground to the opposition. I would like to offer some suggestions as to what such an edifice would look like. They are born of my personal and, I think reasonably common, experience. But first some biography.

Education is ordinary. I was born in 1952 in a place called Leytonstone in the East End of London. It is one of the many areas on the outer edges of the city that act as a cordon sanitaire between the decaying working-class inner city, and the semi-detached middle-class commuter land of the suburbs. The term 'respectable working class' could almost have been coined to describe the families of the majority of my (secondary modern) school friends. In as much as anywhere is ordinary, Leytonstone was an ordinary place to be born in.

My own family was on that uneasy and shifting border line between the classes. My father had a skilled white-collar job with British Road Services. My mother came from a large Edwardian family of fourteen brothers and sisters. The matriarch of this horde was a kindly woman who had married below her station to the son of a dock worker. Her father – who had refused to have anything to do with the couple until, too ill to resist, he was taken to their house to die – moved to London from rural Berkshire in 1893 and worked his way up to head gardener at the Royal Infant Orphan Asylum, Woodford. It was my grandmother, I think, who was responsible for introducing into the family some of the crucial attributes for a working-class individual on the upward path. These include the ability to respect those placed in authority above you, to keep still and not make a fuss, and – at times – a desperate over-identification with some of the central values of the English middle class. To be fair, it also included respect for 'knowledge' (I am told my grandmother knew the names of all the English kings and queens), the desire to 'get on' (not in itself a bad thing as long as we *all* get there), and that intriguing tickle at the back of the brain that some call a 'social conscience'. However, just as the parvenus that we had the potential to become will take a coffee-table book and lay it on the table, with no idea of its relationship to other texts, so 'knowledge', 'getting on', and a 'social conscience' were kept rotating in that timeless never-never-land that only the working class seems to inhabit. To be precise I am here referring to phrases like 'It will all come out in the wash', 'A hundred years from now it won't matter', and 'There is always someone worse off than you.' On one level these are just ways of getting through the day, ways of filling the time. On another, and much more serious level, they do 'unbend the springs of action', they take working-class experience and place it in a timeless, changeless world, where the daily perception of a world in change is nullified and emasculated. So, my grandmother's knowledge of the kings and queens was just that, a list of names. Getting on is achieved – for some – with no thought to what the cost may be in terms of happiness, fellowship and love. A social conscience is kept on the tight lead of historical specificity. (My mother when visiting my brother in Jamaica was appalled at the conditions that his weekday, live-in, house servant had. 'I wouldn't keep a dog in a room like that,' she said. Yet she seemed to be taken in by his argument that if it wasn't for my brother the servant wouldn't have a job.)

Education is ordinary, and my early life gave me an ordinary view of the world that a later education would turn into the stuff of which book chapters are made. But what about my *real* education? I must admit that all that I learnt at my secondary modern school has since escaped me. I know what I didn't learn. I didn't learn to expect that I would go to university, or get a 'good' job (a careers person once told me that I should forget about working in a library as most workers in libraries are women and men don't like working under women), or that knowledge about the world is one of the tools by which one can start to change it. So, leaving school at 16 with one

O-level, I went to work as a shop assistant in a camping, sports and fishing-tackle shop. And there I might have stayed had it not been for certain personal events which led me to change my group of friends, from those who had been at the secondary modern school with me, to others who had gone to the local grammar. Most of them were about to go off to some magical and alien place called a university where, on my visits, I would experience feelings that I would later find laid bare in Hardy's *Jude the Obscure*. I think it was around this time that I began to put as much distance as I could between myself and my working-class background. Looking back I can see that I deliberately introduced foreign phrases into my speech, or references to writers or books that I considered 'intellectual'. I even, oh shame! began to cross my sevens in the Continental style. I did not then see my cultural background as a source of strength. It was something to be ashamed of and to keep quiet about. *Inter nos* (old habits die hard), this can be one of the worst effects of changing one's class position. I shall return to this point later.

After five years I left the shop and went to work in a children's home. This was a quite natural move at the time, as I'd spent a lot of my evenings working in two local youth clubs. After eighteen months in the home I decided that this was what I wanted to do as a career. There was only one problem. If you want to 'get on' in the social services you really need a Certificate of Qualification in Social Work (C.Q.S.W.). If you want to get a place on the C.Q.S.W. course you need more than one O-level. So, without much thought for the future, I gave up my job and paid a visit to my local technical college to find out about taking enough O- and A-levels to get me on to a C.Q.S.W. At the Tec, I met someone who was a tutor on a one-year course designed to 'feed' people into the C.Q.S.W. This course gave people who had neither the qualifications nor the experience to gain a place on the social work course, three days a week at college studying for G.C.E.s and two days in a social work placement. I got a place on the course. I even got a discretionary grant – remember those?

By definition most of the people on that course were like me. Mature (i.e. over 24), with few, if any, qualifications, and a desire to change the direction of their lives. I suppose you could say that we were highly motivated, although I'm never quite sure what that term means. I suspect that it was invented by academics who want to feel that mature students who come to their course must place a very high value on it as they have given up a full-time job to come. Certainly the drop-out rate was low, and we did keep turning up for the lectures. But then they were paying us a grant, and that beats working any day.

What I remember most about the course is the feeling of companionship that we had. Of course we were still competing with each other for grades – and for the attention of the tutors – but there was a feeling that we were learning with each other. It does seem that the further up the academic structure one moves the more knowledge comes to be seen as something which is to be hoarded, and which is uniquely individual. This turning of public property into private commodity is one of the strongest institutional impulses working against changing education into something which is ordinary. For it seems to me that while we have a system under which only the few can do well (well=a degree first, or two-one), how can it be ordinary? This is particularly a problem for a discipline such as sociology, which sees part of its task as being the creation of a critical awareness of social processes within the minds of its students. Such reflexive ways of thinking do not lend themselves well to traditional methods of examination. Or, to put it another way, the traditional methods of examination do not tell you much about the success or failure of the attempts to create such a way of thinking.

Education is ordinary; yet some very ordinary skills are not taught. As I approached the end of this one-year course my A-level sociology lecturer asked me if I had thought about doing a degree in sociology. My reaction was to say that degrees are for clever people and not for the likes of me (despite now having a degree I still sometimes suspect this to be the case). However, convinced by him that I 'had it in me', I obtained an U.C.C.A. form and filled it in. If there is anyone out there who is thinking of doing the same, a word of advice. Filling in an U.C.C.A. form is not an ordinary event. It requires some knowledge of the pecking order in which the universities are ranked. (Some experience with pools coupons might also come in handy.) The problem is that if you should happen to put one university after another which the first university considers itself superior to, there is a tendency for professional jealousy to show itself. This is not to say that it happens all the time and, of course, qualifications and experience also count. But it does happen, and mature students – as I was – should get some help in filling the form in. I didn't, and I think that goes some way towards explaining why Keele University was the only one of the five which I listed to offer me an interview, and later a place.

Universities, of course, are not the only places where one can study for a degree. The polytechnic system was created in the 1960s to meet the growing demand for degree places, and to provide courses which contained a greater practical element than the typical university course. The academic apartheid system of 'separate but equal' development was to be maintained by the Council for National Academic Awards (C.N.A.A.), ensuring parity between polytechnic and university degrees. Starved of resources at the best of times, operating in the shadow of their bigger brothers, polytechnics tend to feel that they have a permanent need to justify their position. Yet perhaps here, if anywhere, education could be more ordinary.

I applied to a number of polytechnics and was offered a place on the Sociology with Professional Studies B.A. course at North East London Polytechnic. As it meant being able to stay living in the same place and not having to go through the trauma of making new friends, I took the offer. The degree is taught in a building called Livingstone House, in Stratford, in the East End of London. Let me tell you something about its location. No dreaming spires, no ducks on the pond and no scenes from *Brideshead Revisited*. The main A11 trunk road out of London is about 100 yards from the front door. To the right of the building is a steel containers factory, at the back a North

Thames Gas depot. No one came to Livingstone House for the scenery.

Now let me tell you about my reactions to the degree. It is hard now for me to think myself back to 1976 and experience the feelings that I had during the first few months of my degree course. I think they were something like . . . Help! I can't cope! What do you mean you want an essay that's longer than a side and a half! Read a whole book! . . . etc. But then, at some point during the first year, came the soft explosion in the head as suddenly I began to see that all the things we were talking about were not happening somewhere else to someone else; but here, and to me. It may have been while reading Richard Hoggart's *The Uses of Literacy*, when I became aware that the activities of the working-class family from which he came (allowing for the shift in time and place) bore a striking resemblance to the activities of my own family. And that his feelings of being uprooted from his cultural background and placed in an edgy, uneasy relationship to his peers was exactly what I was feeling. This was *real*. I felt as if sociology was a way of thinking that would enable me to make some sense of what had happened to me. This is surely what Raymond Williams is talking about in the extract I have placed at the head of this chapter. My ordinary experience was being taken and transformed by the common fund of meanings of others who had taken the same path before me. Through Hoggart's eyes I could see that my family were not lacking in 'Culture' because they didn't read the *Observer*, or listen to classical music, or watch the 'right' programmes on TV; they had a *different* culture.

Was the degree course at N.E.L.P. ordinary? Well, having spent some time since in a university sociology department, I think it would be true to say that the attitudes of the members of staff in the two institutions are different. Whether that means that the members of the department at N.E.L.P. had a more 'ordinary' (and just let me remind you what I mean by ordinary – 'the process of giving to ordinary members of a society its full common meanings, and the skills that will enable them to amend these meanings . . .') approach is hard to say. One of the problems which face me when I try to answer that question is that at N.E.L.P. I was learning the skills that I am putting into use now. Also, at N.E.L.P. I did not have much chance to 'look behind the scenes' and break through the façade of unity that most institutions like to present. With those two qualifications taken into account, I think it would be fair to say that at the polytechnic the main focus of concern of the staff was on the students and on methods of teaching. While at the university their primary allegiance is to the more abstract concept of the 'discipline'. Given the historical conditions that have produced the two institutions this is not altogether surprising. The universities have tended to define themselves as places of research first and teaching second, where questions concerning the application of knowledge can get overlooked. Equally, polytechnics have seen themselves as providers of a practical education, geared more to the demands of the job market. Perhaps the most that can be said is that at this point in the growth of the British education system polytechnics have the greater potential to produce a more ordinary curriculum.

Education is ordinary *but* you pay a price. In the film version of *Educating Rita* there is a scene in which Rita goes to a party at her Open University tutor's house. Arriving on the doorstep she can see the middle-class people in the front room making the kind of social small-talk that they do at such gatherings. Rita hesitates, and decides that she does not belong at such a place. She would be a fish out of water. She hurries back to the pub where her husband, mother and various relations (note the extended family) are singing what Rita describes as 'one of those stupid songs on the jukebox'. Rita joins in, thinking that this is the place where she can at least appear to be at home, when she notices that her mother is crying. When Rita asks her why, her mother says, 'Because there must be something better to do than this.'

Leaving aside Willy Russell's implicit assumption that the working class actually don't have a very high cultural standard, I think that this scene captures very well the dilemma in which a number of working-class students find themselves. Rita no longer feels at home in the world that she knew, nor does she feel at home in the world she is coming to know. But she does feel that she knows of 'something better to do', and she knows that the price she may well have to pay to 'do' it is to sunder the ties that she has with her old world. Education may enable us to take our experience out of the day-to-day, one-damn-thing-after-another level of perception. But the tragedy seems to be that as soon as this happens we become incapable of speaking to the people from whom we came.

For myself, I discovered that the class from which I came, and from which I had been trying to put as much distance as possible, had a history and a tradition that could be seen as a source of strength, not of shame. On a personal level this led me to start doing research into my own family tree and to trace the way my family, on my father's side, had moved around in nineteenth-century Buckinghamshire looking for work. I also discovered that one of my ancestors had been wounded in the Crimean War and had received an Army pension. Sociology taught me to make the connection between my personal biography and wider social movements. My ancestors had a part in making history. WOW! Coming from the working class was not so bad after all. Others in the world of academic life found it hard to agree. I can still remember the look of bemused surprise on the face of one professor when, while attending an interview for a Ph.D. place, I told him that I had worked in a shop for five years. Worse still, I remember the deep feeling of anger at a senior member of staff in another university when, also at a postgraduate interview, he made me feel like some jumped-up oik from a polytechnic who should know his place (which was not in his department).

During the course of my four years at N.E.L.P. I came to realize that I had no desire to go back into the social services. Therefore, instead of taking a C.Q.S.W. option in my third year, I opted for a research course. This involved a five-month placement somewhere 'doing' research. I had to choose where to go and what to do. Being a sociologist, I decided to base my decision on firm rational grounds. The 'person with whom I was having a relationship' was doing her degree at Sheffield University. Why not go there? I did, and spent a very happy five months researching the nature of the industrial middle class in mid-nineteenth-century Sheffield.

Then finals, and out into the big wide world. But not in my case, for being unable to secure funding for a postgraduate degree, I went back to the Sociology Department at N.E.L.P. to work as a research assistant. In my second year of trying for a postgraduate place I was offered two, both with money (moral, don't give up). I took one of the offers and am now coming to the end of three years' research extending the work on Sheffield which I did as an undergraduate. I feel that I have done well. I know that I have been lucky and that some people (quite rightly) will feel that I have not got much to moan about. Eight years' study at the taxpayer's expense is a luxury which sometimes embarrasses me. I feel that most of my contemporaries at school could have done just as well as me if they had had the chance. I am sure that if I had stayed in the camping shop and now found myself reading this I would think, 'What's the bugger got to complain about?' Let me make it clear that despite all its faults and problems I would not want to stop anybody from studying for a degree. In the institutional spaces that the degree creates there is room to run, jump and roll on your back, in the sheer rapture of being able to 'stretch' your mind. It is wonderful.

Education is ordinary, but trying to say what the democratic college of the future might be like is an extra-ordinarily difficult thing to do. In some ways it is much easier to say what it won't be like; no gender/race/class bias in its intake and subject matter, greater access for materially disadvantaged groups (i.e. single parents), no treatment of knowledge as a commodity to be hoarded for future exchange in the market place of examination grades, etc. However, bear with me and I will try and say what I think it might be like.

What is the point of education? One possible answer to that question is that the point of education is to get a good job. It would be naïve to deny that having qualifications helps in the job market. However, such a narrowly utilitarian conception is – I feel – against the spirit of the college of the future. What then *should* education be about? I can only speak from experience about the social sciences, but in my view these disciplines should be about giving people the confidence and the expertise to exert greater control over their lives. At one end of the spectrum this means showing people how to fill in forms, open bank accounts, deal with officials, etc. The other end is harder to define. It is about showing people that things happen for a reason, that there is not just one way of looking at the world, that decisions can be questioned and, perhaps most important, that they have the potential to do almost anything they want to do.

For more concrete suggestions I refer the reader to the other chapters in this book.

*Note*

1 Raymond Williams, 'Culture is Ordinary', in Norman Mackenzie (ed.), *Conviction*, MacGibbon & Kee, 1959.

# 5
# Paid Educational Leave

MICHAEL CUNNINGHAM

Much of this book is devoted to increasing, extending and varying access to further and higher education. The articles concentrate on actual and potential students taking up a variety of vocational and non-vocational courses. Reference is made to rights to education after the age of 18. I would like to speak for, and about, those people whose lives are completely untouched by the debate – people for whom the whole business is remote or inaccessible because education costs too much money, or takes up too much time, or 'is not for the likes of us' – or is just plain irrelevant. In this chapter I will be focusing on this group for the most part, although, as we shall see, the negotiating of time off work for courses leading to vocational qualifications might also be planned in the same way.

For this alienated group, vocational courses typically lead to management and/or middle-class jobs, and they have a cynical view of the declining number and applicability of traditional apprenticeships and of the questionable usefulness of new technology training, and they look at such government schemes as Y.T.S. with great disillusionment. Non-vocational courses carry an even more overtly class message – indeed, by far the most substantial working-class take-up of this kind of education is in shop steward education. We must beware of sliding into a debate which ignores a staggering lack of interest in further education by a substantial proportion of the population. These disenfranchised can be counted in millions.

Tertiary education does not even *look* attractive: academics and students appear to lead charmed lives earning untold sums of money and doing very little work. This can be seen most sharply in the opinions of those who actually work in universities and polys: these same well-paid academics now occupy positions of great importance in the power-structure of the university or poly, and manual workers also have to clear up after the students – and are appalled at their inconsiderateness. My experience as a trade union official shows me that these same manual workers also look at their own pay rates, the massive pay differentials, the sabbaticals, the cultural snobbery and the neo-feudalism of much of further and higher education – and they give it the thumbs-down. In 1983, manual worker union representatives at one famous British university even went so far as to ask for discussions (no more than that!) on an educational leave agreement; the employer's arrogant refusal on the grounds that there could not possibly be any relevant course that could benefit them rather confirmed their views on academics. Is it any wonder that they exhibit few ambitions for themselves, let alone for their children, in further education?

## Why Paid Educational Leave in Working Hours?

We need a well coordinated plan to reverse this situation, and a key element in this plan is, I believe, Paid Education Leave (P.E.L.) – that is to say, time off during working hours on full pay, the time spent studying. However, a distinction needs to be drawn between two routes to paid, post-school education: the first involves full-time and/or long-term study and would attract statutory grants under the proposals outlined elsewhere in this book; the second would involve part-time and short-term study *in working time and on full pay*. The remainder of this chapter is predominantly concerned with the latter.

What is the purpose of Paid Educational Leave? It would be wrong to argue for it as an end in itself. Quite the reverse: P.E.L. should be seen as a means to a number of specific ends. Here are a few:

* the acquisition of the information and/or skills that the course purports to offer (e.g. spoken or written language skills, safety legislation);
* political education;
* cultural education;
* the acquisition of the self-confidence necessary for one to function positively in standing up for one's rights in private and social life, at job interviews and promotion boards, in dealings with management and in trade union debates;
* to act as a *trigger* for people hitherto alienated by the education system to taste it again at no cost and with the minimum inconvenience – and hopefully go on to other further or adult education under their own steam (it is a way of destroying the myth that education ends at 16).

(It would be quite wrong to imagine that *all* of these aims should be found in *each* P.E.L. course. Each P.E.L. course has a combination of some of the aims referred to above, as can be seen from the courses illustrated on pp. 124–5.)

Present provision comes nowhere near offering the kind of opportunities envisaged here. And in addition to the negative perceptions mentioned above, there are two more aspects of post-school education that are critical: the first question is what kind of training needs to be available. The current offerings of degree and diploma courses cut very little ice (they appear remote and inaccessible) and vocational courses often seem blissfully irrelevant when viewed against the background of high unemployment.

Another reason for people being put off these courses is the very stringent entry qualifications: these are a reminder that the tertiary sector is expecting people to be enthusiastic when they have been miserably *failed* for the most part by previous experiences of education. Their memory is of being told to jump through hoops and over hurdles, and then being put down and made to feel foolish or failures. The examination system has a lot to answer for – which is not to say that P.E.L. should concentrate exclusively on people without 'suitable' qualifications: this is simply an area which needs special treatment.

To expect literally millions of educationally alienated people to approach the status quo in a positive frame of mind is little short of sadistic. If our education system wishes to hold out a genuine welcome to everyone, it must (at least in part) turn itself upside down: instead of thinking of new ways of keeping people out, it must devise ways of facilitating people in. Middle-class people have long known the rules of the game and been able to mould the system to suit their own purposes – and white-collar trade union agreements often contain a P.E.L. scheme, something that is almost invariably excluded from manual worker agreements even in the same firm. Research for a trade union negotiating guide, published in 1981, was able to unearth virtually no manual worker agreements whatsoever.[1]

If one of the besetting problems is a widespread lack of confidence in taking on the alien and alienating business of learning something new, it follows that we need courses that aim to sow the seeds of confidence. Assertiveness training and other types of confidence-giving courses (see pp. 124–5) give a hint of what can be done if the will and imagination are there.

It is also absurd to expect people to sign on for F.E. courses if they have significant problems with reading and writing. Language and literacy courses of the type outlined on p. 124 have already been wonderfully successful in directing people towards a wide variety of further educational courses. These courses (sometimes called 'basic skills courses') frequently include an English as a Foreign or Second Language component for migrant workers, and have managed to nurture considerable increases of self-confidence among a good proportion of the students: a measure of this is the significant number of (successful) applications for promotion.

The second critical question concerning paid, post-school education is *when* the courses are supposed to take place – we can put on the most appropriate, tailor-made courses in the world, and all to no avail if the people that the courses are targeted at can't get along. The instinctive response to this question from many seems to be that P.E.L. should normally take place in the evening. Here are a few drawbacks:

* some people actually work in the evening (and some of this work enables evening classes to be lit, heated, etc.);
* some people work shifts (in other words, they will not have (say) every Wednesday evening off);
* some people have unavoidable domestic duties;
* all people have social lives (there is something masochistic about the expectation that enjoyment has to be sacrificed for the improvement of the mind – and we *are* trying to lure people who feel alienated!).

The remaining possibility is that the courses take place during the day, but it is obvious that a very large number of people are at work then too, and few can consider giving up paid employment even for a short period of time.

The solution is not to hunt round for scraps of time at the beginning or end of the working day (this can be logistically inconvenient and can put domestic life under unacceptable pressure): the solution is to opt for *courses during working hours on full pay* – the necessity for full pay is a reminder that the vast majority of the people in particular need of introduction to further education are in low-paid (often part-time) jobs.

## Negotiating P.E.L.

At the very mention of paid release from work, it is customary for a lot of people to throw up their hands in horror with claims that employers will never agree, particularly during a period of severe economic recession. Workers and their trade union representatives can be quite easily dissuaded from this viewpoint, however, by stories of the mouth-watering arrangements abroad and even in this country recounted on pp. 122–3. Experience shows that employers, too, can have their heads turned by such accounts. They too, it appears, need to keep up with the Joneses.

This is an appropriate point at which to say a few words about the role of the employer in the setting-up of a P.E.L. course. It is definitely ideal for the employer to have a formal policy commitment to the ideals of further education for all, and there are good examples of this in the University of London and the Greater London Council (see pp. 124–5). Apart from making it easier for the trade union(s) to negotiate the paid release in the first place, it enables the trainers (working in *close* collaboration with the union(s)) to identify the *real* needs of the potential students in the course of their outreach work. All the parties to P.E.L. projects can easily fall into the trap of notching up flattering statistics.

It is also worth commenting here on the crucial, decisive role to be played by the trade unions. Unions occupy a contradictory position with regard to P.E.L. in so far as they spend sometimes quite considerable sums of money on training their full-time and lay representatives, but fail to take the next logical step and make it a negotiating item with employers – we still need to devise ways of persuading most unions to do this. The key function for a trade union throughout a P.E.L. project is to retain control: far from confining itself to negotiating the time off, the union must also concern itself with the content and aims of the course by means of meeting regularly with the tutors and employer representatives.

Close cooperation with the employer also makes it easier to avoid the whole impetus of the training being destroyed by some elements of line management. To avoid this happening, it is certainly helpful to be able to hold the employer to policy commitments; this is the sort of thing that can happen even when the employer at top management level takes a favourable stance:

* supervisors dividing workers who are not on the course against those who are;
* no cover arranged – that is to say that the work not done during the hours while the lesson is taking place has to be squeezed in by the student on his/her return or by colleagues who receive no extra pay – and who not unnaturally may feel somewhat embittered;

* students being taken off a course *in mid-lesson* to finish some work;
* workers unaccountably not being paid for the hours they are away from work on the course.

Mention of this kind of harassment and intimidation should not be construed as grounds for not pursuing the objective. It needs to be borne in mind as yet another struggle for people who want (or who have been persuaded) to try out some post-school education. I often feel that people who battle their way through quite so many obstacles on the way to further education are nothing short of heroic. Those who fit it all in by their early twenties have it so easy by comparison.

The 'you'll never do it here' school of thought has many, many adherents – they can even point to Britain's position in the West European league table for further education provision: third from bottom, just above Portugal and Ireland. However, a way of countering that rather defeatist approach is to point to what *is* going on elsewhere: if others can have it, why can't we? In this more optimistic spirit, I shall first look at the huge advances made abroad, and then at more recent (and very exciting) developments in this country.

## Examples in Other Countries

One of the most audacious experiments, admittedly in the sphere of higher education, is to be found in the U.S.A.: in 1974, Wayne State University, Detroit, set up its University Studies and Weekend College (U.S./W.C.) to provide an interdisciplinary course of study leading to a bachelor's degree within four calendar, or five academic, years *while the student remains in full-time employment*. Many thousands of workers have been able to take advantage of this scheme, including an increasing proportion of shop-floor manual workers. Much effort is expended by the U.S./W.C. to gear the courses to suit the workers/students – for example, the car worker students who are members of the trade union U.A.W. (United Automobile Workers) attend classes in their union halls. Furthermore, television courses can be watched *at home* via local channels, workshop courses are usually held just before or just after shifts, and there are conference courses held over full weekends.[2]

Developments nearer home have been broader-based, if less dramatic. One of the better-known schemes is the union-negotiated '150 hours' agreement in Italy: this statutory minimum entitlement – it can be spread over three years – has been particularly effective both in enabling young Italians to get basic educational qualifications and in initiating long-overdue occupational health and safety training for union representatives.

Means have been increasingly devised in other West European countries for placing Paid Educational Leave on a secure financial footing: the West German and French governments, for instance, have raised a training levy by imposing a payroll tax on employers. A significant feature, particularly in France, has been a massive boom in provision in the private sector (some of it of a very variable standard), and a characteristic of the German scheme too has been the relatively low take-up by manual workers.

Educational leave in Sweden, on the other hand, has been characterized by a strictly enforceable legal entitlement and by widely available state provision. Students in upper secondary school can temporarily leave their studies to take up gainful employment or to look after their own children, as long as the period of absence lasts between fifteen months and three years (up to four years if the student is over the age of 25). Also, a feature of the Swedish 'gymnasium' (the British equivalent of a tertiary college) is that there are dual facilities for both gymnasium school students and for returning adults. An informative account of these, and other, advances made in Sweden can be found in Arthur Gould's recent discussion paper.[3]

## Developments in Britain

Things may also be beginning to look up at home, too. In London alone, there are now a number of highly encouraging examples of paid release during working time for employees to do courses which they actually need and want. In the University of London, for instance, nearly 500 manual workers have been on language and literacy courses during the five years up to September 1984. Employees and management alike have pronounced the courses excellent and thoroughly helpful from personal and work points of view. Organized originally under the aegis of the N.U.P.E. Basic Skills Project, the courses were transferred in 1984 to a broader-based body called Workbase, but representatives of the trade union concerned (N.U.P.E.) are intimately concerned with the philosophy and day-to-day running of the training. They have also produced a highly readable account of this exciting project.[4]

Workbase has also started similar training in the Greater London Council (G.L.C.), but of equal note are the assertiveness-training courses put on by the G.L.C.'s own Equal Opportunities Unit. These courses, lasting 2–3 days, are specifically aimed at those groups of employees that traditionally do not take up opportunities for further study, such as women and members of ethnic minorities, and they have been outstandingly successful in giving them the confidence to apply for promotion and to take a more active role in their unions.

These classes have also seen the development of mutually supportive relationships among the students, and the employer has facilitated the formation of support groups that meet at other times during the week in rooms specially booked for them. A feature of the teaching is that there is always one white tutor and one black one (only women tutors for women's courses), and a permanent objective of the training is the demystification of the teacher – anyone can be one! In brief the students are made to feel special, and the courses have been very successful and popular from the outset.

Other courses put on by the G.L.C. include a 20 × ½-day course for typists: this course is deliberately held outside County Hall in a nearby technical college, and introduces the typists to the other educational possibilities at the college – and thence to other career choices. Interview skills are also taught. A feature of the organization of the course is that it takes place on *half-days* as a specific encouragement for part-timers to attend. Of comparable interest in the G.L.C. are the foundation courses for manual workers: these act as access courses to further education, and concentrate on the problems of the inner city and on the ability of the G.L.C. to supply a high quality of service to the community of Greater London.

The success rate of these courses has been most heartening. By the autumn of 1984, twenty-five manual workers had undergone 'Basic Skills Course' training, and this is what only some of them have already achieved:

* 4 have obtained clerical officer posts in the G.L.C.;
* 7 have enrolled in adult literacy courses in adult education centres;
* 1 has been promoted to leading hand in the cleaning department;
* 1 has become a N.U.P.E. shop steward.

It is of some significance that the Greater London Council has felt it necessary to put on such courses when it has the Inner London Education Authority (I.L.E.A.) on its doorstep: the I.L.E.A. is rightly noted for its excellent provision in further and higher education (by comparison with education authorities elsewhere in the country), and for being flexible and responsive; it regrettably proves the case that even relatively unconventional approaches to this area of education make little or no impact on very large numbers of the population.

We had looked forward with particular interest to the G.L.C.'s undertaking to give sixty working days' study leave (spread over two years and on full pay) to *all* employees with over five years' service. The study has to be relevant to the person's employment with the Council, but may include 'taster courses' for quite different careers (e.g. women in manual craft trades).

## Conclusion

In this chapter, we have looked at the perceptions and experiences of education of a massive proportion of the population who are disenfranchised and alienated from the system. The proposals for remedy do not pretend to be all-embracing and definitive. To take only a few examples: there is an underlying assumption that the education/training should be at all times supplied by the state – whereas there are certain areas of study which are extremely well covered by outside agencies (e.g. photographic clubs); there would be practical problems about release from very small undertakings; and there is no mention of provision for groups of people who are (wrongly) ignored by trade unions – the unemployed and the not-employed (e.g. people looking after their children).

Something else not referred to is exactly how the right to study can be *enforced*. The decisive role in this respect will be played by unions, but the campaign for P.E.L. will always have to be strongly supported by a *statutory* right.

There have been a number of interesting proposals in recent years. The Merseyside Paid Educational Leave Group has conceived of a two-tier statutory entitlement: thirty days' study leave per annum on full pay (the employer recovering the money from a fund set up by the state), and the right to unpaid leave for higher education based on government grants. A given course of study would be run by an approving body consisting of shop stewards, members of community organizations or unemployed centres, and past and present students. It would be serviced by local authorities and other 'responsible bodies' (e.g. extra-mural departments, the W.E.A., the T.U.C.), which would provide professional information, expertise and practical resources.[5]

Another idea is the Minimum Educational Grant for Adults (M.E.G.A.). This argues for a one-year mandatory grant for those aged 19 and over, this time to be taken as and when the student wishes – and also in periods of weeks or months or a whole year without a break. M.E.G.A. specifically excludes people who have received two- or three-year government grants for study.[6] The above proposal is very similar to ideas put up in the Labour Party manifesto in 1983, except that the latter gave the right to 18-year-olds.

At all events, any viable statutory entitlement to time off work for study purposes will need to give clear assurances about such things as job-back and the protection of promotion and pension rights. And there would need to be a statutory obligation on employers to give the time off! The outstanding successes to date of P.E.L. in this country show quite definitively how popular such a move would be – particularly with those very people who have never tasted it before!

*Notes*

1 Michael Cunningham, *Non-Wage Benefits*, Pluto Press, 1981.

2 P. Bertelsen, P. Fordham and J. London, *Evaluation of the Wayne State University's University Studies and Week-end College Programme*, UNESCO, 1977.

3 Arthur Gould, *Swedish educational leave in practice; the Gothenburg experiment*, Association for Recurrent Education, 1983.

4 *'S' is for Statutory Sick Pay*, N.U.P.E. Basic Skills Project, 1983.

5 *Why should we have to pay for it twice?*, Merseyside Paid Educational Leave Group, 1983.

6 *Minimum Educational Grant for Adults*, Association for Recurrent Education, 1983.

# 6
## Claiming Our Space: *Women in a 'Socialist Alternative' Post-18 Education*

ROSEMARY DEEM AND JANET FINCH

You do not necessarily have to be a socialist to see the need for improving and maintaining women's position and opportunities in our present system of higher education. But with the return in June 1983 of a Conservative government whose official view of women emphasizes their role in the home[1] (while at the same time encouraging schoolgirls to take science and technology), it is more important than ever to consider what steps can be taken to secure a space for adult women in post-school education.

In this paper, we want to move away from the terms in which such debates are commonly constituted (e.g. how to improve women's access to the full range of existing courses; whether to adopt a strategy of positive discrimination for women studying and working in H.E. and F.E.) while recognizing that these issues are important. Our argument assumes an expanded form of post-18 education of the kind envisaged by other contributors to this volume: some form of universal entitlement, and a blurring of the institutional boundaries between higher, further and adult education. We see our task here as an exercise in mapping out the kind of spaces, opportunities and finances which women should be claiming in this alternative structure.

Argument for Post-School Alternatives:
How Do They Apply to Women?

We began by looking at some of the main arguments put forward by contributors to this volume and asking: how do they apply to women? Broadly, our answer is that taking women seriously as potentially equal participants with men in post-school education does entail re-examining some of the strategies being proposed in this volume. If this is not done, there is a real danger that a 'socialist alternative' post-school education would perpetuate educational structures which are geared to male needs, and tolerate women only on those terms.

Education and Life Patterns

The model of H.E. which sees it as a straight-through route following straight on from compulsory schooling fits very badly with the life patterns of many women and goes some way to explaining why women have been 'left behind' in the present system and its structure of opportunities. The present structure could be modified by adding much-improved systems of child care, which would help adult women students, but since many women (indeed many men as well) may not *wish* to go straight from school or college into higher education, what is needed is a rethink of conventional H.E. routes. An essential component of an alternative system is to break the dominance of the straight-through route, and create a number of equally viable but different routes so that mature and women students are no longer seen as following deviant variations of the major avenue through higher education.

Seen within this context, therefore, the present strong commitment of the main political parties to developing education and training policies primarily for the 14–19 age-group is understandable, but also worrying because it misses so many other deserving groups. Although there are many good reasons for developments in the 14–19 area (not least high unemployment rates), concentration implies such a continuing commitment to straight-through educational routes, and does not break through the restrictions which this school-to-F.E./H.E./M.S.C. notion involves.

To take one example, the Labour Party's policy document on 16–19 education[2] is committed to women's education in this age-group as a matter of 'equal opportunities'; but it fails to acknowledge that some 16-to-19-year-olds are mothers and therefore neglects to envisage a form of educational provision which would accommodate them. Clearly the needs of the 14–19 age-group require integration into a much broader policy and strategy for opening out all post-school educational opportunities. Part of this must entail a much clearer separation between 'education' and 'training' (a distinction commonly blurred in much current discussion of provision for this age-group), and a commitment to providing for women as well as men in both of these areas. If this does not happen we could perpetuate an educational system modelled essentially on the life-patterns of young white male school-leavers and their employment prospects or job training. An education system which took seriously the pattern of adult women's (and parents') lives would look very different. It would offer a variety of routes which would enable students to select between a range of alternatives with no single route more privileged and prestigious than the rest. So far as qualification- or exam-oriented routes are concerned, it is important for women and for flexibility generally that educational packages are designed so that students can collect bits and pieces at different times and in different places. The argument that a 'bits and pieces' approach undermines the intellectual integrity of educational experiences is not totally convincing, in our view. It does, however, require the exercise of creative imagination to design packages very different from those currently on offer in most institutions; and there would need to be safeguards built in, to ensure that those who did still acquire their 'post-school' education full-time and immediately after finishing school were not treated as an élite.

In this respect, we regard the kind of proposals put forward by the Leverhulme study[3] as potentially helpful to women; its exhortation that universities, polytechnics and colleges should 'adapt to new tasks and to the needs of new types of students' points in the right direction. One 'new task' might well be to offer more educational possibilities to larger numbers of adult women. The Leverhulme Report's well-publicized proposal (in line with suggestions put forward at about the same time by C.N.A.A.[4]) for the introduction of two-year, less specialized initial courses of higher education with part-time study packages at other times, might also be helpful to women students who look for post-school education well after leaving compulsory schooling, or who do not want to undertake it all in a single, full-time block. On the other hand, at the time of writing it is rumoured that the forthcoming Green Paper will include such proposals, which are most likely to commend themselves to the present government on cost-cutting grounds (that is, two-year courses are cheaper than three-year courses). If this happens there might be further reductions in women's opportunities. Much depends on the arrangements for financial support, an issue also to be included in the Green Paper, following the re-emergence of student loans on the political agenda in 1984 (see Fulton, in this volume).

## Financial Support

A model of higher education which takes seriously the needs of women would require an appropriate system of financial support for all students. Full-time and part-time courses would have to be treated as equally worthy of mandatory awards, with a very flexible approach to entitlements covering shorter or longer periods (but with a maximum period of support). There would also be implied financial support for a range of courses which do not count as advanced further or as 'higher' education, as presently defined. For example, currently, many women are faced with the hurdle of A-level courses for which they receive no support, in order to be able to qualify for the courses for which they can get awards. This would make no sense in an educational system genuinely committed to creating a variety of routes.

It is in this matter of mandatory financial support that we find the Leverhulme proposals worrying from the perspective of women. Since they envisage that mandatory grants would be available only for the initial two-year degree courses, they are offering proposals which any government wishing to control levels of public expenditure might gratefully accept. The arrangements which the Leverhulme Report envisages for the financial support of students beyond the first two years most definitely do not favour women. These arrangements include scholarships for the 'exceptionally talented', industrial sponsorship, grants for subjects where there is a national need, grants for the long-term unemployed, and student loans. In the first three of these, the 'straight-through' route followed by unbroken employment – that is the 'male' model – fits most neatly. Even the proposal for special grant-aid for the long-term unemployed is unlikely to benefit adult women who, although unwaged, are often technically non-employed rather than unemployed and therefore presumably would not be eligible. So far as loans are concerned, their disadvantages from the point of view of younger women have long been recognized (the so-called 'negative dowry' effect), although this could perhaps be reduced by a scheme similar to those operating in some Scandinavian countries, where a loan only has to be repaid if the recipient is in full-time waged work.[5] Even so, the whole notion of loans is based on the assumption that a student can make a financial investment in his or her own future. This can be questioned on grounds of lessened employment opportunity, but also assumes once more that the straight-through route is the basis model of participation in post-school education. Yet this latter, as we have already argued, needs to be questioned from the perspective of women.

A number of alternative proposals are suggested in this volume and by the Labour Party's working party[6] which would open up higher education to a much wider range of people, especially more working-class students. Among these are existing proposals about paid educational leave, and educational 'sabbaticals' as an entitlement, financed by employers. While we have considerable sympathy with these proposals on other grounds, we are concerned about their implications for women. Any policy which relies on entitlements to education based upon (usually full-time) paid work is likely to advantage more men than women, since women's employment patterns (including part-time work and interrupted periods of paid work) would make it more difficult to build up such entitlements.

A strategy for financial support based on sabbaticals and the like would have to be complemented by proposals which apply especially to women and those not in paid work. A more fruitful line to pursue, however, is the notion of universal entitlement, which applies equally to men and women. The Labour Party's 1983 proposals are clearly a step in the right direction, if a limited one, since they envisage a one-year entitlement only. A universal entitlement which entails no additional rules of qualification is the mode of financial support least likely to disadvantage women, provided that two types of criteria apply to its operation. First, it must be a benefit which could be 'cashed' at any time during the individual's life, in whole or in part. Second, it must be available for any type of course(s) suited to the individual's needs, interests and capacities. If those two conditions are met, then it could well be the means of opening up the kind of space which we are envisaging for women in an 'alternative' post-school education.

## Paid Work, Domestic Work, and Educational Provision

It has become commonplace to note that women's participation in higher education is hampered by lack of child-care facilities. While the extension of such facilities is an important immediate struggle in particular institutions, in terms of developing an alternative strategy, we think that the debate needs to be broadened, since to keep it at this level fails to challenge the ideological assumption that child-care is a women's problem.

It could perhaps be argued that our discussion so far falls into that very trap by emphasizing, for example, the need to create more flexible routes through post-school education to accommodate women's child-care commitments. While we would share a strong preference for a society where women were not obliged to be the full-time carers for their own children, we do not believe that we have to wait for that particular social change to happen before we can contemplate improving women's position with respect to education. Our concern here is to offer a vision of the kind of post-school education which does not ignore the reality of many women's lives, but which seeks to offer them maximum access to educational experience despite the limitations which other social arrangements impose.

We believe that the starting-point for this is to create a pattern of educational provision which genuinely makes participation possible for people in employment, those not in paid work and parents of both sexes. Of course this entails the provision of good child-care at *all* times when educational activity is taking place. But it also entails looking carefully at the hours at which educational activities *do* take place, in relation to the hours of paid work, school hours, and at the implications of all those hours for the pattern of people's domestic commitments. An educational system which seriously seeks to be a resource for the users would have to be available at times, and in ways, which everyone actually can use. The implications of this may be uncomfortable for some of those who teach in H.E., and who are used to ten-week terms and day-time weekday teaching. There will be a need to talk constructively to teaching unions about proposals that teaching should take place routinely and extensively in the evenings, at weekends and at holiday times, where this does not happen at the moment. Obviously, however, the hours (and time off in lieu of unsocial hours) and conditions of work for employees within the educational system need to be carefully considered if one group (providers) is not to be exploited at the expense of another (students).

Issues of Curriculum

## What Constitutes Post-18 Education?

Claiming women's space in post-school education entails re-thinking basic issues about what constitutes legitimate educational activities and aims, and the development of much broader conceptions of education. An important aspect of this is to challenge the distinction between 'vocational' courses on the one hand (which are commonly treated as requiring no justification and are inherently worthy of financial support), and 'non-vocational' courses on the other hand, which are treated as 'private' activities which must either be self-supporting or, if given public support, require extra justifications and depend on 'what we can afford'. Needless to say, in many cases more women are found in non-vocational courses than in vocational ones.

Current Conservative Party policy favours scientific and technological courses above others, with emphasis on job relevance, the need for education to be 'efficient', and providing value for money. These strands of policy imply that there is a close link between higher education and jobs, assume that education is not a right or an important part of personal development but rather see it as a product whose provision must be organized as cheaply as possible and along strictly utility lines. However, as other contributors to this volume have argued, one of the most important tasks of a socialist 'alternative' higher education is to reformulate the relationships between higher education and the labour market, and to demonstrate by the distribution of resources that substantial importance is also placed on the personal gains which individuals derive from good educational experiences, and upon the social and political benefits to an open and democratic society in which all citizens are equipped to participate actively regardless of gender, class or race.

An alternative strategy needs to reject the notion that we want an education system which mainly serves the needs of the economy and to put aside the tenuous vocational/non-vocational distinction. Most people do not spend all of their lives in paid work, and that applies especially to women. Concentration on the economy only diverts our attention from and prevents us from recognizing the educational needs of those who are not currently participating in the labour market – for example, the disabled and elderly dependants plus those who care for them, most of whom of course are women. Any socialist, alternative strategy needs to unpack carefully the education–economy link and its implications. A first step might be to recognize that there are interlocking sets of interests which education could potentially serve. One example might be promoting child-care courses for men, to facilitate women parents' more active participation in the labour market.

Like other contributors to this volume, we recognize that the principle of universal entitlement to post-school education raises the question of what kinds of courses should be on 'open' access and what kinds should be restricted to those with formal qualifications. The same issue can be raised in the form: should all courses (even where there is open access) in this sector of higher education lead to some diploma or qualification? We do not claim to have neat answers to these very difficult questions of the proper balance between excellence and egalitarianism in a socialist post-school education. But we do see it as important that women whose experience of compulsory schooling has left them with a very limited view of their own capacities beyond the domestic arena should not thereby be automatically excluded from many courses on offer at the post-18 level. The development of access courses (see below) is clearly an important strategy here. It may also be that profiles rather than credentials acquired through assessment might be appropriate in certain sectors of post-school education. However, that could lead to first- and second-class 'higher' education: a development likely to leave higher proportions of women in the 'second' class, not the 'first' (qualification-oriented) class, thus reinforcing their disadvantaged position in labour market competition. Perhaps the best hope is that credentials themselves would, in the long term, become less important in a labour market which was less segmented and less wage-differentiated.

*The Content of Education*

First and most obviously, the curriculum of an alternative system would need to eliminate the many sexist biases currently found in the content of many higher education courses, and in the routes which women take through different courses.

We do, however, have some doubts about some of the 'positive discrimination' strategies currently being pursued; for example, the encouragement of more women to take courses in science and technology (cf. Rose, in this volume). Do we, for example, really want to see more women participating in the arms race? Issues about encouraging women to participate in areas of the curriculum from which they have hitherto been absent raises broader questions about what counts as science and who is it for. We do not wish to encourage women into nuclear physics without considerable assurances about what they will be doing; although, as part of an alternative strategy for science itself, we might well want to facilitate women's full participation. Indeed, women have a great deal to contribute to the development of such alternatives. In medical sciences, for example, the experience of the women's health movement has great potential for altering the direction of research and developing quite different bases for resource allocation.

More broadly, we see the need for an alternative strategy to seek to create an educational system in which education – among other things, but as a high priority – acts as a *resource* which individuals and groups can use, including women's groups. On a practical level, this means creating resource centres – say, on the model of teachers' centres – in which physical resources and human facilitators are available on open access. On another level, it involves recognizing and welcoming the oppositional potential of education. The task of those who work in higher education can and should be to share their intellectual skills with those who can make use of them, for a variety of purposes, not merely to use those skills to further their own careers or to help maintain the status quo. In this context, education could be much greater use to women, both individually and collectively, in helping them to equip themselves better to challenge their subordinate position in society.

## Issues of Organization

### Breaking the Institutional Boundaries

Like other contributors to this volume, we envisage an alternative educational system in which there is a considerable blurring of the distinctions between the various institutions of higher and further education, including those between the élite and less élite sectors.

From the perspective of women, one of the most important aspects of this is a blurring of the distinction between 'adult' and 'higher' education. In particular, provisions which enable women to re-enter education when they have had a number of years in full-time domestic work and child-care, and provisions which offer a 'second chance' to those people (whether or not they are in paid work) who left compulsory schooling with few credentials, should be brought into a far more central position within post-18 education and resourced accordingly. Models of successful practice of both types of provision are already available. Schemes like the Open College system in Lancashire already offer a 'second chance' route which seems to be of increasing importance for women. Early evidence of the operation of this scheme indicates that more women than men use this route, especially women in the 25–36 age-group, that is, as a way 'back in' after their initial child-bearing phase is completed.[7] Elsewhere 'second chance' facilities are well established, including a number of residential colleges, for which bursaries and grants are available for long full-time courses. Unfortunately only one of these, Hillcroft College, provides solely for women. The percentage of women students relative to men students on full-time long courses at the mixed adult colleges is mostly quite low, although where colleges also run shorter courses the proportion of women is higher. This suggests that being away from home on a full-time basis for a year or more may be difficult for many women. The Open University has also provided many women without formal qualifications with the opportunity to study for a degree part-time, although the rising cost of so doing may deter some working-class women. An expansion of all types of 'access' provision would be an important step forward for women.

We also think that it is important to challenge the assumption that educational activities have to take place within educational institutions. How, for example, are we to meet the educational needs of the many elderly people who cannot easily get out of their home, or travel very far? Again, this group contains considerably more women than men because of women's greater life expectancy rates. Various strategies are possible: tutors who could visit the homes of the elderly and disabled people unable to get to local centres; an expansion of the use of television for educational purposes, linked in a coherent way to visits from tutors, for example; or the greater use of schools (the educational institutions most easily accessible to the majority of the population) as bases for other educational activities, either separate from or combined with schools' existing work with young people. There are obviously many possibilities here, and considerable space for creative experimentation.

## Control of H.E.

The kind of educational system which we envisage, and which would take women seriously, would have to be considerably more accountable to its users than is our present higher education structure, especially universities.

Proposals for developing a structure of regional government for this purpose do have some attractions, because of their potential responsiveness to local needs while not being too parochial. However, the example of regional organization in the National Health Service is not encouraging, having merely removed consumers still further from the focus of power, decision-making and accountability. To repeat this in education might be disastrous. Local control of education ought to mean responsiveness and local influence, not simply bureaucratic petty-mindedness.

On the whole, we think that women's interests would best be served if this accountability were tied in with elected local government. While women of course are in the minority there, they are still considerably more conspicuous than in politics at national level. Greater accountability to local government could be linked to a strategy which facilitates the participation of more women in local politics, especially by changing the financial basis of being an elected council member. (So that those without full-time employment or private incomes are not disadvantaged or discouraged from becoming elected members of local authorities.)

*Single Sex Provision: A Proposal for Post-18 Education*
So far, our discussion has been fairly closely in line with proposals discussed by other contributors to this volume: essentially we have been suggesting modifications which we believe to be necessary if women's interests are to be central, not peripheral, to an 'alternative' post-18 education. But in so far as these are modifications to proposals already broadly acceptable within a socialist strategy, they may be regarded as relatively uncontentious. In this final section we put forward a quite separate and additional proposal which (as we have learned from discussion in various settings) is by no means uncontentious, nor is it acceptable to all socialists. We wish to propose that an 'alternative' post-18 educational system should provide opportunities for women who wish to participate in single-sex settings.

A significant feature of changes in the higher educational scene over the past decade is the loss of virtually all our women-only institutions. This has happened partly because of the decision of most of the former women's colleges in the universities of London, Oxford and Cambridge to admit men, and partly because of the closure or amalgamation of a number of women's teacher training colleges. We believe that an alternative strategy for post-18 education should reverse this trend, although not necessarily by recreating single-sex institutions in their previous form. Many educational activities which currently fall outside the state-funded post-18 educational system already are *de facto* or intentionally single-sex; for example, many day and evening classes and the activities provided by Women's Institutes, Inner Wheel and the Townswomen's Guild. Hence to offer single-sex education in the state system of post-school education would be to extend a practice which already constitutes an important (if often unacknowledged) way of organizing education for women.

We believe that single-sex provision within post-school education is important for a number of reasons. First, a convincing case has been made by many people that girls' and women's educational performances and experience are improved when they are educated without men.[8] There is therefore a clear case for offering them these opportunities on grounds of positive discrimination – or indeed simply of equity. Such facilities could be provided in separate women's colleges, but equally, existing institutions could be encouraged to consider single-sex provision within their existing pattern of educational packages. Of course the tutors on single-sex courses must be women, who would be providing positive role models for women students. This consideration about improving the academic performance of women of course applies principally to credential-oriented courses.

Second, we think it is especially important that women re-entering the educational system after a considerable gap, or just getting started in post-school education, should be offered a supportive environment which is non-threatening (both sexually and otherwise). Thus offering women single-sex educational opportunities may be especially important in preparatory and first-stage courses. It also forms part of a strategy for broadening educational opportunities, especially to working-class women who in the present system are doubly disadvantaged by their class and by their gender. Where they have the choice, women often choose to participate in single-sex groups (in women's organizations or in evening classes, not just in the women's movement), and many working-class women especially are simply not used to the company of men, outside of closely circumscribed domestic and sexual encounters.

Third, the women's movement has long recognized the importance of women-only groups in developing strategies for combating sexism. There are lessons here for the post-school educational system. Any alternative, socialist strategy which is seriously concerned with using the educational system to foster a more equal, democratic society will have to acknowledge the special needs of those groups who have lost out in existing structures of inequality. So far as women are concerned, this means using the educational system as one means available for combating sexism within social and political structures, and enabling women to take a full place in democratic processes at every level. If this is seen as one of the legitimate tasks of a post-18 educational system, then the lesson from the women's movement is that the task can be accomplished most effectively in women-only groups. The same argument would apply to racism and provision for black groups.

We have spelled out in some detail the arguments for expanding single-sex provision because we recognize that they are contentious and because we believe that it is important to put this issue on to the agenda of any discussion of 'alternative' education provision. It is a proposal which highlights more clearly than others which we advocate that any 'socialist' strategy designed to reduce or eliminate existing social inequalities will eventually have to face up to points at which the interests of various groups do not readily coincide. In so far as single-sex provision for women appears to be one such point, we hope that by highlighting it and making it explicit we will advance the debate about the real character of socialist, alternative strategies.

*Notes*

1 For further discussion of this see, for example, J. Gardiner, 'Women, Recession and the Tories', in S. Hall and eds., *The Politics of Thatcherism*, M. Jacques, 1983; M. David, 'Thatcherism *is* anti-feminism', *Trouble and Strife*, No. 1, Winter 1983.

2 *16–19: Learning for Life*, Labour Party, 1982.

3 Leverhulme Report, *Excellence in Diversity*, Society for Research into Higher Education, 1983.

4 *Future Development of C.N.A.A.'s Academic Policies at Undergraduate Level*, Council for National Academic Awards, 1983.

5 A system of this sort is envisaged by one of the contributions to the Leverhulme study: O. Fulton, 'Principles and Policies', in O. Fulton (ed.), *Access to Higher Education*, Society for Research into Higher Education, 1981.

6 *Education After 18: Expansion with Change*, Labour Party, 1982.

7 K. Percy, J. Powell, C. Flude and M. Langham, *The Open College in the North West: a Research Report*, Further Education Staff College, Coombe Lodge, 1980.

8 See R. Deem (ed.), *Co-education Reconsidered*, Open University Press, 1984.

# 7
# Autonomy to Accountability

PETER SCOTT

By the standards of the rest of Europe and even of the United States, higher education in Britain enjoys remarkable freedom – still. Universities are self-governing institutions, and polytechnics and colleges virtually so. Each university, and often each department within it, teaches what it likes in its own way; there is no attempt at national coordination, let alone control. Polytechnics and colleges have to have the structure of their courses approved by the Council for National Academic Awards (C.N.A.A.) and other external validators, and their teaching is assessed, occasionally, by H.M. inspectors. But even in the non-university sector institutions, faculties, departments, course teams and individual teachers have wide discretion. Britain still operates one of the freest higher education systems in the world.

But in the last few years that freedom has suffered serious setbacks. The present government plans to strip university teachers of the tenure which they have traditionally enjoyed and which protects them against arbitrary dismissal. The inspectors are being sent back into polytechnics and colleges to check on suspicions of sloppy teaching. A wide-ranging inquiry into validation in the non-university sector has been established, apparently because the government believes it has been too slack. The social sciences have come under particularly severe scrutiny, and the Social Science Research Council (now the Economic and Social Research Council) barely managed to survive an inquisition in 1981.[1] The University Grants Committee (U.G.C.), established in 1919 to negotiate a block grant with government and then distribute it among the universities, is no longer regarded by many since the 1981 cuts as the ally of the universities but as an arm of government. Both the U.G.C. and the National Advisory Body for Local Authority Higher Education (N.A.B.), its counterpart for the polytechnics and colleges, have been sent increasingly detailed and even peremptory 'advice' by the Department of Education and Science. For the first time the intellectual preferences of the Secretary of State for Education and Science and his cabinet colleagues are seen as a legitimate consideration in deciding priorities in higher education. There seems today to be an accelerating takeover of higher education by the state. The freedom of universities and colleges is in full decline, while the pressure to make them more accountable to the government, and in the market-place, grows stronger day by day.

Why has this happened? The argument in this chapter is that the traditional view that British higher education has been exceptionally free was always something of a myth. The ties of dependence to the state may have been more gossamer-like and more tortuous, but they were just as strong. The post-war expansion, although it temporarily strengthened the position of university and college teachers, was bound to increase the pressure to make higher education accountable for the vastly increased sums of public money which it now received. In this sense the rising tide of accountability, however uncomfortable, has been a sign of success. Yet even within a much larger and more democratic system of higher education the claims of autonomy can never be ignored. After all, academic freedom is underpinned by professional autonomy which in turn is guaranteed by strong and independent institutions. So the task for higher education in the rest of the 1980s and the 1990s will be to try to establish a new concordat between autonomy and freedom on the one hand and accountability and democracy on the other. To take a practical example, we will have to learn to distinguish that part of the traditional practice of academic tenure which still effectively guarantees proper intellectual freedom from that part which has degenerated into an anachronistic dons' freehold.

This chapter is divided into four sections: first, the rise of the academic profession; second, the decline and fall of what has been called 'the donnish dominion'; third, the slide from autonomy to accountability; and fourth, prospects for the 1980s and beyond.

## 1 The Rise of the Academic Profession

Compared with other systems of higher education, British universities, polytechnics, and colleges have two remarkable characteristics. The first, their exceptional autonomy, has already been described. However *dirigiste* the University Grants Committee has become, however much it has collaborated with the government over recent cuts in public expenditure on higher education, and however much universities have deferred to its advice, Britain's universities enjoy a freedom from detailed administrative control that is unknown in the rest of Europe and uncommon in the United States. Similarly the polytechnics and other non-university colleges, for all their lack of formal autonomy, are allowed a discretion in setting their own teaching and research priorities that is also considerable by international standards.

The second characteristic seems a puzzle. For, despite their great formal independence, British institutions of higher education have not become the home of an oppositional intelligentsia. Indeed, what is remarkable is the exceptional solidarity with political society and even the 'establishment' displayed by British higher education. A superficial assessment might suggest that this is a paradox. After all, one might expect a highly autonomous system of higher education also to be highly critical of society because it had the freedom to criticize with relative impunity. Yet a deeper analysis, one rooted in the historical experience of British higher education, suggests that the opposite is true; that the state allows higher education unusual autonomy because it knows that this autonomy will not be used to develop a sustained critique of its activity. It is a deal: freedom for silence.

A century ago British higher education, with the exception of Oxford and Cambridge, was not at all autonomous. Most of the civic universities established in the North and Midlands in the second half of the nineteenth century were created by local civic or commercial élites. Cadburys, Palmers, Rowntrees, these great industrial dynasties were often the driving force behind the new foundations. The academic profession, which in any case was just ceasing to be regarded as a peculiar form of clerical employment, played no part. Nor did the grand Victorian intellectuals who saw themselves as part of an élite political society in the tradition of Macaulay or people with predominantly aesthetic responsibilities like Ruskin. So, although they were later to come under the commanding influence of the dons, universities were established by lay people usually with severely practical intentions. Until well into the present century universities suffered from a chronic financial insecurity which inhibited any early or easy consolidation of the academic profession. Only a few senior professors secured safe jobs and properly rewarded careers, and universities remained dependent on a mixture of philanthropy, industrial sponsorship, and student fees.

Only Oxford and Cambridge had the social eminence and secure resources, and so the independence, to pursue the more elevated roles of scholarship and élite pedagogy. For the rest it had to be 'useful' science and technical training. As with the rest of the industrializing world, the theoretical sciences grew out of the practical sciences rather than the other way round. Artillerymen became mathematicians and later physicists (and so back to artillerymen, some would sigh, in the nuclear age). However, in Britain two special factors intensified the practical bias of the early modern university. The first was the pragmatism of the British intellectual tradition. The second the fact that universities, although sponsored by the state, were not part of the state machine. Their teachers were not, as in so many countries, civil servants. This left them chronically dependent on private subsidy and so without the dignity or influence to insist that the practical sciences should be subordinated to the theoretical.[2]

But while these two factors discouraged the consolidation of the academic profession in the nineteenth century, in the twentieth they had the opposite effect. The pragmatism of the British intellectual tradition inhibited the development of an oppositional intelligentsia which might have made its natural home in higher education (and so provoked the hostility of the established order). As a result the state had no reason to discourage the growing autonomy of higher education. The second factor had a similar force. The state's lack of a strong financial interest in the early universities allowed them to develop autonomous forms of government, which have been maintained even though public expenditure has become the only serious source of income for universities. This could not have happened if university teachers had been civil servants and vice-chancellors appointed by the government.

The outcome was that the state and the academic profession gradually became allies. The keys to the successful consolidation of higher education's autonomy can be found in these same two factors. Higher education's commitment to practical sciences, reinforced by the pragmatism of the British intellectual tradition, meant first that the knowledge being produced by the universities was not seen as subversive, and second that universities came to be seen as an essential element in an industrializing society. The First World War was a decisive period and it is no coincidence that it was in the 1920s and 1930s that the autonomy of higher education was finally consolidated. In 1919 H. A. L. Fisher, president of the Board of Education, wrote that at the start of the war 'there was a most inadequate apprehension of the results that might be derived from the laboratories and brains of the universities'.[3] Significantly, during the war the Department of Scientific and Industrial Research, the forerunner of today's research councils, was also established. The Ph.D., that grand apprenticeship for the academic profession, was first introduced in Britain at the end of the war.[4]

This new appreciation of the material benefits of higher education led naturally to greatly increased state subsidy. Already before the war R. B. Haldane's *ad hoc* University Colleges Committee had recommended that there should be a permanent Advisory Committee on University Grants, which in 1919 became the University Grants Committee. The two latter were made up almost entirely of members of the academic profession, and the last was made responsible not to the Board of Education but to the Treasury in official acknowledgement of the universities' advancing status. By the eve of the next war over a third of the income of universities came from the state and after 1945 this rose rapidly to two-thirds. But the effect of this growing subsidy was not to reduce the autonomy of the universities but to increase it. For state grants not only offered an alternative source of income to the old mixture of philanthropy, subsidy, and fees, but also encouraged industry to redouble its own support for higher education for reasons very similar to those which the state had found so persuasive. The universities found both that their services were now regarded as much more valuable because of the progress of science and technology, and that these services were being bid for by both state and industry. So the strategic position of the universities and of the academic profession was greatly improved. On the brink of the 1960s British higher education seemed to be poised for the final, even triumphal, affirmation of its autonomy. The early years of the expansion so powerfully endorsed by the Robbins Report in 1963 did nothing to destroy these hopes.[5] But the seeds of decay had already been sown.

## 2 The Decline and Fall of the 'Donnish Dominion'

For this post-war 'donnish dominion', to borrow a phrase from A. H. Halsey, had never been unconditional. It was subject to two main restraints, both of which have become very clear in the last few years. The first was that, paradoxically perhaps, one of the unintended consequences of the state's enthusiastic subsidy for the practical sciences in universities was to increase greatly the negotiating position of university teachers and so give them a new freedom to pursue their natural academic inclination to place more emphasis on theoretical sciences. If this led to the splitting of the atom or the invention of penicillin who could complain? But higher education had to use its new bargaining strength with care. In the 1960s it may have pushed its luck too far.

The great expansion of higher education triggered off by the 1956 White Paper on Technical Education[6] and by the 1963 Robbins Report was clearly seen by government as an investment in scientific invention and technological excellence. Yet, because of the pattern of school-leaver demand and the random distribution of promising lines of academic inquiry, much of this investment was diverted into the expansion first of the humanities and then the social sciences and their dependent para-professions. The first hint of government irritation with this unexpected development was Anthony Crosland's binary policy, which modified the Robbins formula for expansion and tried to ensure that the practical sciences got a fair share of the extra resources by building up the new polytechnics. Later hints have been less oblique and constructive, culminating in the crude emphasis on immediate industrial utility that has now been established as the orthodox attitude of government, of whatever party, to higher education.

What was perhaps forgotten, until the crisis of the last four years, is that the 'donnish dominion' and the autonomy of higher education in which it was institutionalized were always conditional. They were one side of a bargain. They had been tolerated, even encouraged, by the state because of the universities' utilitarian potential rather than because of the state's liberal endorsement of higher education's broader intellectual or cultural roles. The result has been a backlash, at first discreet but most recently forceful, a demand for a new accountability to rein in the independence of higher education. Its roots can be traced as far back as 1946, when the U.G.C.'s terms of reference were revised to include a special commitment to meeting 'national needs', a stipulation included of course by a Labour government. But its full force was only registered during the 1960s – the creation of the polytechnics, the interest in manpower planning, the development of national policies for higher education that were not simply glosses on the priorities of the academic profession itself, the present cuts, the attack on tenure, all are evidence of this growing backlash.

The second restraint on the 'donnish dominion', the guarantee of political neutrality, has always been treated with greater circumspection by higher education perhaps because it chimed in with the political timidity of many university leaders. The state allowed the universities exceptional autonomy because they could be trusted not to exploit this independence to promote ideological causes hostile to the predominant interests of the state. On the whole higher education has accepted this hidden but powerful restraint on its freedom. Teachers in British universities and colleges have kept to the narrow role of the 'academic' and avoided the more contentious role of the 'intellectual' – which may be a way of saying that they have been wary of following theoretical preoccupations through into social or political action. This may account in part for the strain of philistinism that runs through the academic profession in Britain. It may even explain the strong establishment prejudice against the social sciences.

The conflicts that do occur between the state or industry on the one hand and higher education on the other can be much more easily explained by higher education's desire to establish the conditions of professional autonomy than by any strong enthusiasm to develop a radical critique of the established order. The failure of British higher education to establish enduring examples of general education rooted in contemporary experience rather than historical tradition can perhaps be explained in similar terms. For this could only be successful if higher education was prepared to ask fundamental questions. When higher education was confined to a political and administrative élite, a general education based on the classics and the traditional humanities or on the dignified professions like law could be constructed. The values of the don (especially in Oxbridge), the senior civil servant, and the barrister were sufficiently similar to come together in a common view of the purpose of higher education. By the 1960s all this had changed. The values of the new students of a much expanded university and college system were so heterogeneous that an attempt to impose a new pattern of general education would have to be an explicit operation which asked fundamental questions that might challenge the existing social order. Better to play safe and do nothing. The advance of the social sciences in the 1960s seemed to be just beginning to compromise the apolitical character of higher education. The phenomenon of student revolt, mild as it was in Britain, touched a raw nerve because it could be interpreted as an attempt by higher education to break this concordat of apolitical autonomy.[7]

This analysis of the character of higher education's autonomy, if it is correct, casts doubt on some important assumptions that are made about its value in maintaining a free and critical intellectual tradition. No institution better illustrates the ambiguous quality of this autonomy than the University Grants Committee, a Janus-like institution that enshrines professional autonomy while acting as a channel through which the commands of the state can pass to the universities. For it is difficult to argue that the U.G.C. does not to some degree embody the collective views of the universities, at any rate of their leaders. What was depressing about the hierarchies of relative excellence that emerged in the U.G.C.'s selective distribution of the much reduced university grant in July 1981 – some universities were not cut at all and some by up to 40 per cent – was not their arbitrary quality but rather their dull familiarity. Yet it is equally difficult to deny that the U.G.C., almost as part of higher education's folk memory, does not embody an exact understanding of the terms of the unwritten agreement between state and the universities (and polytechnics), in faculties and departments, and even in the assumptions and values of individual teachers.

So far from stimulating a tradition of a free and critical inquiry, our present forms of autonomy may actually inhibit such a tradition. The concordat between the state and higher education, after all, is freedom for silence. Systems of higher education in other countries, which in formal terms have been less free, seem nevertheless to have provided environments in which it has been possible for individual teachers and researchers to be less silent. Perhaps this is because in such systems the rules of conduct are written down and so open to scrutiny and to change, while in Britain the very ambiguity of what is allowed and not allowed leads to excessive timidity. It is much easier for a government to make use of all the hints and signals it can command to indicate its displeasure with, say, the social sciences, confident that they will be transmitted as if by osmosis throughout the system, than to take direct action for which it can be made immediately accountable. Sir Keith Joseph's failed attempt to abolish the Social Science Research Council in 1982 seems to be an example of this paradoxical phenomenon; the state can exercise more effective power in those areas where it has no formal standing, than in those where it is acknowledged to have the legitimate power to decide.

There is little evidence that the exceptional autonomy of British higher education has led to exceptional intellectual or critical freedom. Indeed it may not be a coincidence that in the very years, just after the First World War, when university autonomy and the 'donnish dominion' were being consolidated there seemed to be a parallel decline in the radical and populist ambitions of higher education. Summing up this period, Brian Simon writes in *Education and the Labour Movement 1870–1920*:

> The aim of opening a way into the universities for mature students from the working class receded into the background while attention concentrated on developing an extra-mural form of further and higher education regarded as complete in itself. The idea that education is valuable for its own sake, an idea born of the very real desire for knowledge on the part of the working class and the idealism of those who set out to realize it, paradoxically enough contributed powerfully to limiting horizons. It was not to get on in life, to escape from their class, that these workers sought knowledge, but rather to enhance their own cultivation without wish of entering either a university or politics. The universities themselves were well content to support this solution rather than opening their doors to the working-class students . . . Working-class education, as many of the rank and file in the Labour and socialist movement conceived of it, could only be furthered outside this orbit in close connection with industrial and political activity directed to winning rights for labour in a wider field.[8]

Certainly the history of British higher education shows that there has been no automatic congruence between the autonomy of universities, and to a lesser extent of other institutions of higher education, and a free and critical intellectual tradition or the reform of higher education to meet the new needs of a more modern and more democratic society.

This conclusion, however, has become easier even for those in higher education who place the highest possible value on intellectual freedom to accept because cracks have begun to appear in the once-impressive façade of higher education's autonomy that can no longer be disguised. The University Grants Committee has ceased to be clubbable, a private and informal committee that shares out the grant made available by the government to universities according to the well-worn principle of 'informed prejudice'. Instead it has become a bureaucratic agency that, however unpalatable the idea may be to many of its members, has a predominant control over the shape and direction of the university system. The universities themselves have ceased to be a loose association of autonomous institutions and have become the semi-independent sub-sectors of a national system.

Research has come under equally dominant national discretion. Lord Rothschild's customer-contractor principle, a new version of the old principle 'he who pays the piper calls the tune',[9] has led to a much closer relationship between research councils, the state (often government departments other than the Department of Education and Science), and high-technology industry. This has led to new devices like teaching companies and joint research directorates. In the case of the polytechnics and non-university colleges, recent events have made it clear that 'social control' is to be maintained in the important sense that these institutions are not to be allowed to come under the exclusive influence of the academic profession. It is this desire to keep the dons down, rather than any strong commitment to local democracy, that has allowed the local authorities to maintain their proprietorial stake in higher education.

At a more detailed level the erosion of formal autonomy is even more obvious. Universities which have exceeded the total number of students allocated to them by the U.G.C. in the 1981 run-down of university numbers have been 'fined'. The distribution of the so-called 'new blood' lectureships, 200 new academic posts a year which have been established to try to bring new talent into the universities, was decided centrally by the U.G.C. in consultation with the research councils. This was the first occasion in Britain when universities had to be given permission by a national authority to make an academic appointment. There are many other examples of this rising tide of detailed interference which have undermined the formal autonomy of higher education. Although there has been little formal change in the status of universities, and ostensibly a move towards greater autonomy for the polytechnics and colleges, the last ten years have seen a remarkable shift towards greater accountability in higher education. The decay of the donnish dominion is there for anyone to see.

## 3  Autonomy to Accountability

In the late 1960s a group of left-wing teachers in higher education, concerned by what seemed a rising tide of panicky authoritarianism among university and college leaders in response to the emergence of the New Left in general and student revolt in particular, came together to establish the Campaign for Academic Freedom and Democracy. Their programme, as the title they chose suggests, was first to defend individual teachers who were discriminated against because of their views or reputation or because they offered moral or practical support to radical student movements, and second to campaign for greater democracy within institutions of higher education so that junior teaching staff, non-teaching staff, and students could have more influence in their government.

During the 1970s the efforts of the C.A.F.D. met with moderate success. The victimization of individual teachers has remained a rare phenomenon in British higher education. The sacking of Robin Blackburn from the London School of Economics in 1968 did not lead to a more general campaign against left-wing staff. The long-drawn-out dispute at the University of Lancaster involving the English lecturer, David Craig, in the early 1970s was eventually resolved by a compromise that was probably unhelpful to the university authorities. Nor have personal rule by vice-chancellors or the oligarchy of senior professors, which had been the common patterns of university government up to the 1960s (with the exception of the élite and wholly exceptional academic communes of Oxbridge), escaped modification by the reformers. By the end of the 1970s university government had become a much more participatory business, and the authority of university leaders had become much more conditional, although the chief credit for this change should probably go to the rise of trade unionism among university teachers – the Association of University Teachers moved rapidly away from its past professional commitment and joined the Trades Union Congress in 1972 – rather than to the more fundamentalist campaign for reform conducted by the C.A.F.D. and its allies. In the polytechnics and colleges, although the 1970s saw the modification of the previously almost absolute power of the principal or director, powerful oligarchies of senior academic staff persisted. Too often the new academic boards were dominated by *ex officio* placemen.

Yet this moderate success in holding the line against the erosion of academic freedom and stimulating the spread of academic democracy within higher education was overshadowed by a growing failure to persuade those beyond the campus to continue to respect the values of intellectual freedom, and an increasing pressure to make higher education accountable, not to those who are themselves engaged in the processes of teaching and research, but to the state as paymaster, industry as an over-mighty customer, and students as clients. So as the cause of reform made progress within higher education it lost ground outside. University leaders may have been persuaded that purges of left-wing teachers are not compatible with the preservation of a proper academic community. But government felt less and less inhibition about interfering in higher education. Under the 1974–9 Labour government, higher education had already had to begin to dance to a new and naïvely utilitarian tune. Under the present Conservative government this subordination of 'academic' to 'industrial' values has broadened into a full-scale attack on 'useless' subjects, the more vulnerable humanities and the more political social sciences. So individual teachers may have largely escaped discrimination because of their personal views, but whole categories of teacher have come under attack because their discipline has fallen into political disfavour.

During the same period, and indeed as part of the same process, the pressure to make higher education more accountable also intensified. In many cases, the spread of academic democracy within institutions led to a closer identification between institutional priorities and the values of the academic profession. This identification was seen as an obstacle to broader democratic accountability, to elected politicians, to community representatives, or to free-market customers. The domination of senates and academic boards by a donnish interest, in the eyes of some, became a barrier to the modernization and democratization of higher education.

Such views are fairly evenly distributed across the whole political spectrum. On the right they take the form of a nostalgia for tough-minded management by strong vice-chancellors or principals and a resentment at the failure of their successors to 'carry' their institutions with them in plans for wholesale rationalization. In the eyes of the present government nothing has been more damaging to the reputation of the universities than the spectacle of vice-chancellors' rationalization proposals being overturned or watered down by senates. So academic tenure has become a key issue because it is seen as the basis of this donnish interest. In fact the protection it gives university teachers and so the obstacle that it presents to institutional flexibility have almost certainly been over-estimated. University teachers have shown themselves more than willing to sell the jobs of their future colleagues for generous pay-offs, or to abolish the jobs of their non-tenured colleagues on short-term contracts to protect their own. Yet in the eyes of the government tenure remains a key symbolic issue, a symbol of a donnish dominion that is now discredited. For this reason it plans to send in commissioners to remove tenure clauses from university statutes.

On the left there is a similarly strong belief that the donnish interest is a conservative interest. So minor shifts of influence between professors and more junior staff within that interest are of little significance. Higher education is an élitist business and the academic profession has élitist values. So the only way to nudge higher education towards a more populist role is to abridge the donnish interest's power in universities (and increasingly in non-university institutions also) and to introduce countervailing influences into the government of higher education. For the left, therefore, the binary policy, and the continuing role for local authorities within higher education, are key issues. To abolish the last vestiges of popular democratic control over higher education, however inadequate its processes have become, seems to many on the left to abandon the hope that higher education can play a more positive role in the building of a more equal and more modern society.

The principles of autonomy and accountability, which when the C.A.F.D. was founded fifteen years ago were regarded perhaps too optimistically as complementary, have come into sharp conflict. So long as autonomy was defined in terms of the intellectual freedom of the individual teacher, and accountability in terms of equal rights to participate in the government of higher education for all those who were actively engaged in teaching and research, it was fair to regard these two principles as complementary. Democratic self-government was probably a sufficient guarantee that the individual teacher with unpopular views would not be penalized; it was in the collective interest of teachers to show mutual solidarity and toleration, and the values of the academic profession were and are, at any rate superficially, liberal. More recent budgetary pressure and external political interference have shown that this solidarity could not be absolute, and this liberality was sometimes only skin-deep as engineers ganged up on sociologists after the 1981 cuts. But nevertheless, academic self-government seemed a better guarantee of intellectual freedom than the arbitrary discretion of a managerial hierarchy.

Today the definitions of autonomy and accountability would be rather different. Autonomy is no longer seen so exclusively in terms of the intellectual freedom of the individual teacher, but more in terms of the collective autonomies on which such freedom has to be built, whether of the discipline or of the institution. There may be other ways in which academic freedom could be entrenched, but in Britain it is largely dependent on the autonomy of the institutions in which academics teach and research – which, of course, is why it is so important that their internal government is collegial rather than managerial. Accountability, on the other hand, is now seen in terms of the relationship between higher education on the one hand and the state, society, and the market on the other, rather than in terms of internal government. Yet such accountability can only be made effective by abridging to some extent the autonomy of higher education which in turn threatens to undermine the conditions for academic freedom.

## 4 Future Prospects

This slide from autonomy to accountability raises fundamental issues about the relationship between higher education and society. It also suggests an immediate paradox. Reformers have traditionally placed great trust in the benign potential of the state, while the defenders of tradition have placed the highest value on the preservation of autonomy. Yet in the practical world of the 1980s these roles seem to have been reversed. The left looks with great suspicion on the slide to greater accountability, while the movement towards a higher education system under the direct tutelage of the state has been most rapid during the present period of Conservative government. A further paradox arises from the clear historical fact that the power of the academic profession and the expansion of higher education owe everything to the sponsorship of the state. The great bursts of university development, between 1550 and 1650, after 1850, and during the 1960s, were all the result of direct state (or at any rate lay) intervention.[10] Having built up and sustained the donnish interest for so long, the politicians now seem to have turned against it.

Some reformers will seek to reverse the tide by claiming that they fully accept the ultimate claims of a just state to make higher education accountable to it, but that because our present state cannot claim to be just, higher education is entitled to maintain the highest degree possible of institutional freedom. Autonomy, according to this argument, is a necessary protection against the encroachment of the predatory and philistine state because it provides an ideology, even a morality, that justifies the survival of 'safe house' institutions in which intellectual opposition to the existing order can be generated. The difficulty with this argument, apart from its impractical utopianism – when exactly will the state become sufficiently just so that its claim to make higher education accountable is legitimate? – is that it fails to come to terms with the very active possibility that institutional autonomy may be preserved by sacrificing intellectual freedom.

Other reformers will argue that autonomy is a barrier to the modernization of higher education to meet society's needs, and that in some cases it has become a conservative ideology that justifies intellectual irrelevance and even irresponsibility and, in extreme cases, a fig-leaf for privileged semi-property rights (like tenure?). This argument perhaps undervalues the danger to intellectual freedom posed by making higher education more directly accountable – particularly when the question of accountable to whom has not been satisfactorily resolved.

The safest conclusion, therefore, is that a balance must be kept between the claims of autonomy and accountability and that this balance must be constantly reviewed. But such a bland conclusion must be unpicked in some detail. We cannot remain deaf to the exceptional claims of intellectual freedom, partly because of our centuries-old tradition of liberty, partly because democratic society can only be built on the freest possible exchange of knowledge. Equally we cannot accept that higher education should stand apart from society as an almost anti-democratic institution. This has never been the role of higher education in Britain and is even less appropriate for the semi-élite, semi-mass system of higher education that has been built up in Britain as a result of the Robbins and Crosland expansion. Keeping the balance has two aspects, the first of which is practical. It is important to be realistic about the degree of autonomy which British higher education presently enjoys. Some university leaders may imagine that it is worth hanging on to the theory of autonomy long after its practice has been eroded, perhaps on the grounds that it acts as a barrier or brake to future encroachment. This view can be contested for two reasons. First, it is historically naïve.

The record of actual events suggests that the constitutional autonomies of higher education have done nothing to make the interference of the state more difficult; they may indeed have made it easier because the state has been able to exercise its influence in a more informal and therefore more flexible manner. This may be relevant to the present experience and future aspirations of the polytechnics and other non-university colleges. They feel they are discriminated against because they are held more directly accountable to local authorities and bodies such as the Council for National Academic Awards which validate their degree courses. But these formal relationships may make it easier to establish patterns of procedural justice that can be defended. The absolute lack of these formal relationships has made it impossible for the universities to define such procedural justice. In the years of expansion and advance this may have been to their advantage but today it leaves them vulnerable to unregulated pressure. The average polytechnic at least knows where it stands with its local authority or the C.N.A.A., and can define when they step over the approved mark. The average university has no similar certainty about its relationship with the U.G.C., or for that matter the U.G.C. with the government.

The second reason is that institutional and professional autonomies are means to an end, the protection and increase of intellectual freedom, not ends in themselves. It may be better to accept that the U.G.C. has in effect become a national universities board. The next step is to reform the U.G.C. in ways that reflect this real role and also hold it accountable for its real powers. It may also be better to accept that the state plays a dominant role in the making of higher education policy. Then the next move is to formalize these formidable powers so that their limits can be defined and their exercise checked.

The second aspect of keeping the balance between autonomy and accountability is the ideological. Here there are two sets of questions. The first concerns the hierarchies of knowledge with which we are confronted. Some forms of knowledge enjoy a social prestige that entitles them to privileged autonomous practice; others do not have the same privileges and are closely subject to political or market controls. Why? Or, to put it another way, what are the criteria of demarcation that distinguish between those forms of knowledge that deserve to be institutionalized in higher education and so enjoy all the protection of autonomy and those that do not? Any claim for autonomy to be granted to practitioners in any form of knowledge has to include some explanation or justification of why others should be excluded. This is an issue that has been rarely addressed.

The second set of questions concerns the rival claims of accountability. Just as we must ask *who* and *why* some should be allowed exceptional intellectual freedom, in the positive sense that they are given the resources to maintain this freedom rather than just in a passive or permissive sense, so we must ask *to whom* and *on what criteria* is higher education ultimately accountable. Should higher education be as accountable to labour as to employers, to citizens as to the state, to local democracies as to Whitehall bureaucracies? Trade unions rarely have the resources and the capacity to influence the shape of higher education as effectively as boardrooms. More crucially perhaps, they often do not have the interest or feel they have the right to exercise such influence. The same can be said of informal communities and local government in opposition to the central state and its bureaucracies. So the first task is to assert the rights, and provoke the interest, of such groups in higher education. Only when that has been achieved can the difficult practical questions of how these countervailing interests be expressed be tackled.

The absolute autonomy of higher education has never been on anyone's active agenda. On this the record of history is clear. The autonomy of higher education has always been modified by the circumstances of history and the demands of society. In any case intellectual freedom can have no validity, or perhaps even existence, in a social vacuum. All these factors, the cultural context, the historical tradition, and the immediate demands of society, are forms of accountability.

But in a deeper sense they are also sources of significance and forms of meaning without which free intellectual inquiry cannot proceed.

## Notes

1 *An Enquiry into the Social Science Research Council*, H.M.S.O., 1982.

2 Margaret Archer, *Social Origins of Educational Systems*, Sage, 1979.

3 H. A. L. Fisher, *The Place of the University in National Life*, 1919.

4 R. Simpson, *How the Ph.D. came to Britain*, Society for Research in Higher Education, 1983.

5 Robbins Report, *Committee on Higher Education*, H.M.S.O., 1963.

6 *Technical Education*, H.M.S.O., 1956.

7 Peter Scott, *The Crisis of the University*, Croom Helm, 1984.

8 Brian Simon, *Education and the Labour Movement 1870–1920*, Lawrence & Wishart, 1965.

9 *A Framework for Government Research and Development*, H.M.S.O., 1972.

10 Lawrence Stone, 'Social Control and Intellectual Excellence: Oxbridge and Edinburgh 1560–1983', in Nicholas Phillipson (ed.), *Universities, Society and the Future*, Edinburgh University Press, 1983.

# 8
# Cultural Studies: *The Case for the Humanities*

BILL SCHWARZ*

For all who work and study in higher education, and especially for those who teach humanities, the past few years have brought with them moments of dispiriting gloom. The buoyancy of an earlier time all of a sudden seemed to give way to an endless round of actual or threatened cutbacks, a dreary institutional drama which has come at times to dominate the routines of the working day. In such situations it has been difficult to concentrate the mind on anything but the immediate defensive task of resisting the next blow. To have the will and the energy in the midst of these set-piece syndicalist engagements to argue creatively about the intellectual content of the courses we teach is, to say the least, demanding, and might easily appear to be no more than the aspirations of a deranged optimist. Yet if we are ever to reverse this current situation, to break through the contracting encirclement which presses in on us, then this shift from the defensive must be accomplished and the terms of the debate made our own.

The case for the humanities is not easily achieved contending with governments of the stamp of the Conservative administrations which have been in power since 1979. Delegations of academics can troop through the corridors of the

* I would like to thank Michael Rustin for comments on an earlier draft, and also other friends and colleagues on the Cultural Studies course at North East London Polytechnic, especially Alan O'Shea.

Department of Education and Science pleading the merits of their own particular discipline to no great effect. Despondency can quickly set in. But too often the case is conceded before it has even been properly formulated. It is symptomatic of this general situation that at the prestigious Leverhulme seminar convened to discuss the place of the arts in higher education the conference was reported to have made its initial response with a 'rather nervous liberalism' which sank during the course of the proceedings to a 'hard-headed and even conservative pragmatism'.[1] What seems to lie behind such retreats is a lack of confidence in our own work, a sneaking, half-acknowledged belief that perhaps after all there really is little point in teaching year in and year out the arts or the humanities, an activity which does precious little to halt the increasing barbarism and ruin which is all too evident in 'the world outside'. Yet it is against this perspective and this lack of faith that I want to take issue. The central difficulty is this. If we begin to defend the humanities from the position of a 'rather nervous liberalism' then we can only end up with a rather nervous, pragmatic solution which can easily be countered by the managers of the education system without too many people even noticing, and probably fewer caring. But how to shift from this perspective is by no means obvious, for the paradox and great difficulty is that the very conception of the humanities is one which was founded within a liberal idiom, and it is the liberal tradition which has bequeathed the set of questions which confront us today. The resolution to this problem depends on extending and transforming the liberal premises on which the idea of the humanities is based, advancing gains which have already been accomplished, such that a more assertive, democratic and intellectually coherent and forceful position can be elaborated.

However, it may be as well to begin by emphasizing the fact that the contemporary political right has developed its own intellectual programme. This is true in two ways. On the one hand it has fashioned its own philosophy and ethics which provide a more or less coherent idea of the cultural project which its adherents seek to fulfil; it can be argued, even, that this has formed one of the great strengths of Thatcherism and the radical right since the 1970s, and contrasts significantly with the sloppy and ultimately disastrous pragmatism of Labour and Labour administrations in the period leading up to the 1979 election. This is not to suggest that the Conservatives have not at various points been forced into adopting more cautious and pragmatic tactics, especially perhaps in the field of higher education whose institutions still harbour the spectre of forces sufficiently dedicated to democracy and intellectual pluralism as to make the imposition of the full programme of the right a formidable task. But nonetheless Thatcherism can boast a vision – indeed a utopianism – of the future with its attendant philosophical and moral objectives. On the other hand this has the most direct consequences for education, for it is through the schools and colleges that this programme for the future can best be realized.[2] Contemporary Conservative policy, therefore, is concerned not only with the reorganization of the institutions of education; it is as concerned with the curriculum and the forms of knowledge appropriate for each social sector. The education system is central to the job of 'regaining the commanding heights of the moral and intellectual economy'.[3]

To those with some commitment to the humanities, the Conservative ideal of the educational curriculum can often appear grossly philistine. This does not need to be elaborated here. But simply to castigate the philistinism of Conservative apparatchiks misses the extent to which a specific set of ideals have been formulated as Conservative policy, explicitly conceived as an antidote to a democratic intellectual culture. It is clear, for example, that the interminable threat of cuts not only refers to attempts to dismantle public education from the inside but – and more important in the context of this chapter – also carries with it the deliberate intention of reconstructing the forms of knowledge produced inside the educational system and the content of courses *across* institutions. This latter aspect is obviously more difficult to grasp than the rate of establishment cutbacks. Here especially there is no single political or utilitarian determinant at work, as the fierce attacks on the technological universities demonstrated. At most, it is possible to point to a general strategy whereby the implicit process of streaming within tertiary education would became accentuated and more forcefully institutionalized, and in which the objective is to segregate and police more rigorously the place and content of courses such that they come to exist in their appropriate streams and institutions. This overall pressure appears to favour a remodelling of the traditional binary-based hierarchy of education in which the élite minority pursue the time-honoured liberal and arts courses while the vast majority are trained specifically to occupy the middle or lower ranks of the technical and commercial intelligentsia. It is this stress on traditionalism, however drastically revamped, which provides the ground for the convergence between the academic managers of the University Grants Committee variety (mouthing the outmoded platitudes of a specific stratum of traditional intellectuals) and the more narrowly utilitarian calculations of Tory backbench opinion. The streamlining of institutions to fit this hierarchical conception has been the source of multiple conflicts, already demonstrated by various territorial disputes, and it is unlikely that any smooth and pure settlement will be achieved, matching exactly the blueprints. But it remains more than likely that, if ever successful, at one end there would be Oxford and Cambridge with their subaltern, parasitic universities close in tow, and at the other an amalgamation of the present infrastructure of anonymous colleges and polys, generating a much greater degree of demarcation within tertiary education than exists at present. In effect, it would ultimately mark a full reversal of the social programme which led to the creation of the polytechnics.

The effect of this is not to abolish the humanities from the curriculum. Rather, it is to regulate much more severely than at present who is to be allowed access to arts courses. Even more than now these would become the preserve of a relatively tiny élite of the population – the 'cultured' accredited by a lopsided educational system in previous generations – and, moreover, there is every likelihood that all the most intellectually backward and conservative elements of such courses would once again dominate.

This has a nightmarish quality to it, commensurate with the tradition of twentieth-century dystopias which evoke the mores of societies founded on extreme divisions between mental and manual labour. It is, of course, only a projection. But in the light of these Conservative objectives it becomes all the more clear that what is needed to counter these moves is a real and credible educational and cultural alternative, one which is democratic where the Conservatives are élitist, pluralist where they are sectarian, and intellectually imaginative where they are traditionalist. It is in this spirit that this chapter is written, not in the belief that an alternative will suddenly take shape in these pages, be formulated as some future blueprint and a new policy be born, but rather to shift away the rubble so that issues can be clarified.

Whatever one thinks of it, notwithstanding its intellectual poverty and philistinism, Thatcherism has provided the right with a coherent educational programme which has gained a measure of popular support; on the other hand there exists as yet no easily available socialist alternative, in the sense of a set of cultural objectives sufficiently persuasive to convince even the bulk of our colleagues at work. This point can be elaborated by reviewing, very briefly, the main traditions of dissent which provide the critical syntax in which to engage with current Conservative ideas on the educative role of the humanities.

In the past the dominant source of critique has derived from what might be called the labourist reflex. Traditionally the greatest concern here has been with the vital questions of access to post-18 education, the opening up of the tertiary system on the principles of universalism, the right, in other words, to receive further education. This is dealt with extensively in other chapters and calls for little further comment here. All that needs to be said is that in the past the Labour Party has shown very little interest or curiosity in the content of the courses which the new entrants are to 'receive'; at best, after the Robbins Report and in the climate of the new technocratic utilitarianism of the early sixties, there was a wish that 'more science' should be taught; but on the question of the humanities, historically Labour has been all but silent.

The second source of critique can be identified as the student radicalism of the late sixties and early seventies, elements of which are still active, although in attenuated forms. It is difficult, now, not to caricature this and fall for the slick platitudes of retrospective representations which fail to see the highly contradictory nature of the intellectual manifestations of the period. These were heady times. The starting-point for the student response was the recognition that there was something dreadfully wrong with the content and peda-gogic assumptions of many of the courses, in the humanities above all. The deep intellectual conservatism of the universities was no mirage. As a student of English literature at a new university in the early 1970s I remember I had no idea of what was required of me intellectually; I enjoyed the reading, but beyond that was lost, mystified in the end by the lack of any critical seriousness. Beyond personal pleasure there seemed to be no further justification, and in the political climate of the period this appeared pretty thin, as it still does. In addition, it became startlingly clear to students of our generation that the curriculum represented 'a particular set of emphases and omissions' – as Raymond Williams had put it much earlier in *The Long Revolution*. This drove many of us, not just from the humanities, into a mind-bending whirlwind of alternative study-groups, desperately and unsuccessfully trying to make sense of Lukács or Lacan, Fromm or Foucault in successive sessions, knocked sideways by our own naïve eclecticism and intellectual immaturity. To some degree, however, the impulse behind such endeavours deserves respect. We were trying to make sense of our world, and given our belief that our teachers had abdicated their collective responsibility we had few guidelines. The positive legacy was the range of critical journals and magazines produced in each discipline which attempted, albeit often in rudimentary form, to develop critiques of the dominant traditions. Many of these journals still exist, following the same concerns, and they have published some important work. But in other respects this radicalism was outrageously misguided, short-circuiting crucial complexities. Thus while rightly identifying higher education as a source, ultimately, of the reproduction of relations of inequality and power and also, again correctly, suggesting that the intellectual content of the courses must at least partially be determined by these institutional settings, this radical critique could at times become stretched into the belief that universities and colleges were *only* machines for the reproduction of the dominant ideology and thus all disciplines taught in universities were irretrievably contaminated. The only conclusion to be drawn from such an analysis was that everything to do with the humanities, as constituted, was to be written off and the utopian search for brand new forms of knowledge to begin forthwith. Paradoxically, given the awful theoreticism of this quest, but not illogically, this combined with a shallow libertarianism in which an uncritical notion of experience became elevated as the touchstone to anything which was perceived as academicism.

In such a context the whole idea of the *critique* of dominant intellectual forms – as opposed to their obliteration – disappears. But, shorn of the appalling excesses, there was a body of work begun in the academic institutions in this period which continues to be of great importance. Just as the Labour emphasis on democratizing access is indispensable, so too is the attempt to break the élitism of traditional humanities courses and to open them to new areas of investigation. It will be necessary to return to this point. But precisely because of the significance of the work which grew out of student radicalism, it is as well to specify carefully two major points of departure from it, both of which are peculiarly relevant to the role of the humanities.

The first concerns the characterization of educational institutions as sub-systems locked into the larger capitalist system, directly reproducing capitalist relations. This needs to be qualified to the extent that what is produced in higher education, especially in the humanities, is not a product *directly* transferable to the market, in which exchange values are dominant, but rather a use-value – skills, knowledges, learning in the broadest sense. These clearly are shaped and organized by the bureaucratic form of the institution, and at various moments are assessed and gauged according to competitive and market criteria, especially in the moment of final examinations. To put this in a more technical way, in having a *similar* structure to a commodity in capitalism, the learning which is produced in higher education (discounting for the moment those margins which are privately controlled) is made up of both use-value and exchange-value, but in the humanities it is the former which is most often in dominance.[4] This is a categorically different way of conceptualizing the situation to that which supposes that all forms of knowledge in colleges and polys can be reduced to their market-value, irrespective of their intrinsic use to the particular student. As teachers and students know well enough, this contradiction lies at the core of our work and is often the cause of much bitterness and conflict. However, as teachers it would be irresponsible to pretend that the exchange-value dimension does not exist and thus to deny others the possibility of gaining the certification which we ourselves hold and which for us has been the key to remunerative and relatively pleasurable employment. But what we can also do, given the constraints of the institutional setting, is to struggle to ensure that in our courses the elements of use-value come systematically to dominate the imperatives imposed by the market and the exchange of commodities.

Second, and this is a related point, it simply is not possible to rely any longer on ill-thought-out conceptions of experience to which intellectual coherence must become subordinate. It is necessary for students who embark upon further education, who choose to do so voluntarily, to take seriously their decision, to come to terms with the disciplines required to carry through intellectual inquiry and produce work of a high standard. This is not simply a pedagogic point (although it clearly is that) but one which is political in the most immediate sense. A naïve libertarianism in which student experience alone determines the form of education has proved not only to be a fatal breach through which the right could press, but more importantly it has drastically limited the potential of education to little more than the reproduction of a subordinate and corporate culture circumscribed by the idea of experience. To put this more fully, alongside the positive connotations associated with the idea of popular experience.

> . . . what, under our present socio-economic system, 'experience' teaches is also how to be subordinate, how to be second- or third-rate, how to have second- or third-class expectations, how to be run by someone else's agenda of life, how to lose. It also 'teaches' ways of resisting that, and of surviving. We have to work with, but also *work on* experience. We need to bring something to bear on experience. We need to be able to deal with it critically. Above all, we need to be able to see round; that is, to understand the principles and invisible structures on which 'experience' rests and which determines its shape, beyond the naked eye. No curriculum 'tells itself'. It has to be *told and learned*. To evade that hard issue – an issue, yes, of local control and discipline for the sake of a wider freedom – is to short-change the people we teach.[5]

This may seem a hard argument to swallow, but so far as it is necessary to take up and extend the intellectual radicalism of the sixties and seventies, necessary to *use* these insights, it is a crucial antidote to the misbegotten extravagance of that moment. The impact this has on the appropriate forms of pedagogy is a complicated question which will be touched on later.

The third intellectual formation in which dissent coheres is the tradition of the humanities itself. Because this is the most complicated of all to unravel, the greater part of the remainder of this chapter will highlight the most contentious issues and problems. This first requires an abbreviated historical contextualization.

The liberal disciplines which form that amorphous group of intellectual positions we know today as the humanities – the study of English literature pre-eminent among them – were, against all contemporary appearances, formed only in the mid-nineteenth century. Even today the assumptions on which these studies are based seem to suggest that there is nothing more natural, obvious and eternal than the close reading of literary texts, nor anything which can compare in its ethical and humanizing potency. Yet it is a function of these beliefs and practices, as ideologies, that they conceal the historical conditions of their own emergence. In the last century the right and proper education for gentlemen consisted of the classics, so far as education was ever thought to be necessary for the upper classes. That English literature should become a serious component in education appeared to many a scandalous idea, for after all, wasn't discussion of English literature merely one aspect of polite, cultured conversation, without the heavy-handed resort to formal teaching? Just as one discussed the qualities of certain cuisine or the merits of favoured horses alongside such weightier business as prospective marriages or the state of the stock market, so there existed a recognized discourse in which taste and preference for literary works could be aired, not as a great issue but primarily as a mark of cultivation.

Yet the first decisive moment in the institutionalization and academicization of the 'humanities' touched neither the upper classes nor the universities but rather those educational establishments – mechanics' institutes, working men's colleges and so forth – which were designed for the enlightenment of the working class.[6] It was in this way, as the appropriate means for the development of a *moral* education, that the study of literature virtually came to overlap with the great ethical concerns championed by the foremost liberal humanists of the period, of whom Matthew Arnold must stand as by far and away the most astute. At this point 'English' came to equal the human and moral disciplines. This implantation of English as an appropriate discipline for working-class education was frequently believed by its advocates to be *the* great means for the creation of social cohesion and for the dissemination of an outlook which favoured the unity of classes in matters of ethics and human progress. There is no need to unearth a conspiracy in order to demonstrate this point. It is clearly there in every page written by Arnold and his epigones. But at the same time the force of this moral education derived precisely from its critique of utilitarianism and the values associated with *laissez-faire* capitalism. Thus from their foundation the humanities both represented the form of educational knowledge preferred by the dominant liberal ideologues for the working class, a dominant ideology to put it at its most reductive, and were a means by which a critical and even at times a popular counter-ideology could be organized against the dominant economic and political order. It is worth remembering in this context the extent to which socialists of the late nineteenth century often understood their socialism in terms directly appropriated from Ruskin and the cultural critics, including of course Morris. The practical consequences of the adoption by working-class radicals of this cultural critique of capitalism has been the matter of debate. For some it marked a shift which was wholly positive, broadening the discourse of socialism to incorporate humanist and utopian dimensions absent from many of the usual definitions or theories of the socialist project. For others this appropriation is evidence of a political immaturity and accounts in part for the continuing subordination of the English socialist tradition, still mortgaged to its liberal philosophical precursors. This is an important debate but cannot be followed or resolved here. That there is this contention, though, may suggest that those forms of knowledge, organized in the mid-nineteenth century as the humanities, began their institutional life as a profoundly contradictory and even dislocated intellectual formation, with no easily determined political effects and never settling in their ordained space in the educational institutions as their advocates had wished.

The second great moment in the development of literary studies *as* the humanities was their eventual incorporation in the universities, especially in Cambridge and Oxford, evolving into the supreme humanist discipline sufficiently universal in its moral scope that no social class or group concerned with the cultural conflicts and complexities of the modern world could afford to be excluded. The names associated with this decisive intellectual transformation – which, given the quirky peculiarities of English intellectual culture, was analogous in many ways to the great intellectual revolutions in continental

Europe in which classical sociology or 'western' Marxism were fashioned – are those of F. R. and Q. D. Leavis. According to one recent commentator, the Leavises and their evangelical co-workers 'blasted apart the assumptions of the pre-war upper-class generation. No subsequent movement within English studies has come near to recapturing the courage and radicalism of their stand. In the early 1920s it was desperately unclear why English was worth studying at all; by the early 1930s it had become a question of why it was worth wasting your time on anything else.'[7] The vehemence and conviction of their lower-middle-class nonconformism was the detonator adroitly placed beneath the assumptions of the upper-class connoisseurs of literature, a conviction driven by a passionate concern about the world and by the fear that all was about to tumble into an unspeakable chaos in which culture – the great ethical and aesthetic testaments to human civilization, to be located first and foremost in the literary tradition – would be no more. So far as these ideas were developed conceptually a gentlemanly reliance on taste could have no place. The study of English literature became perceived as the exclusive field of serious philosophical and moral inquiry in which all the fundamental questions were to be pursued, its practitioners comprising a vanguard in the civilizing mission. Literature became the great defence against a turbulent world powered increasingly and remorselessly by the machine and the market, the historic negations of 'life'. Only a close *relationship* to literature, based on careful and systematic study, could recreate a sensibility sufficiently powerful to resist the encroachment of this ever-expanding utilitarianism.

It should be clear that however breathtaking and audacious the extremism of the Leavis position, it carried forward some constitutive features of the humanist philosophies of nineteenth-century liberalism. Negatively, in concentrating so determinedly its vision, the effect of the Leavises' intervention was to bind more tightly the humanities to the academy (as evidenced in their writings by the mystical role attributed to the university in general and the magical qualities of an imaginary Cambridge in particular), and to elevate to an astonishing degree the redemptive powers of critical encounters with literature at the cost of understanding even the relative merits of other approaches to cultural and subjective matters. On the impact of this intellectual explosion, the humanities and literary studies became encased in a mould which was fundamentally élitist, a description which has become a cliché in describing, but also impossible to dissociate from, the work of the Leavises. The contemporary effects of this liberal tradition, as reformulated through English studies in the 1920s and 1930s, are active today across a range of institutions and cannot be thought to be confined to particular departments in particular universities.

The creation of a voluntary association of élite intellectuals, devoted to the reproduction of a hierarchical national culture and aspiring to civilize the popular masses at the moment of their political enfranchisement, was a cultural transformation of deep and long-lasting significance, redrawing the cultural field of force in civil society. The ideological sedimentations of this transformation exist today, carried forward by the work of the Leavises in the 1920s, not only as the staple of intellectual provision in the ancient and not so ancient universities, but as the received conception of teaching the humanities. It codifies as much the official discourse of the Council for National Academic Awards or schools examinations boards as it does the tutorial in Oxford or Cambridge. To be trained for the élite and to encourage social emulation on the part of the uncivilized masses depended on a belief in the centrality and potential force of the individual sensibility and on the contention that personal development, in an autonomous mode, would contribute to the forces battling for the preservation and enrichment of the national culture. The irony is that such conceptions were clearly redundant even by the 1880s (the moment when the term 'intellectual' first gained currency), a decade which witnessed the beginnings of an unprecedented expansion of professional intellectual workers and the complex reorganization and internal differentiation of the various sectors of the amorphous British intelligentsia.[8]

It is easy to see how an intellectual programme so carefully devoted to the ideals of the academy, and one which spurned so vigorously any manifestations of popular culture, could do little but run aground from the time of the sixties so far as it maintained its pure profile. It was exactly the numbing élitism and outrageousness of this conception of the humanities which compelled so many at the end of the sixties to swing round to a naïve radicalism which complemented and mirrored in their excessive brio and self-importance the underlying assumptions of the intellectual order with which it was engaged. But if this was all that the Leavisite conception represented, then why all the fuss?

The problem is that their version of the humanities has *also* led directly to the contemporary field of cultural studies and the current attempts to reorganize and extend the humanities in a more popular and democratic spirit. Driven by a profound cultural pessimism, the Leavis entourage turned their attention to the study of popular culture, pioneering such inquiry in England, in order to convince others of the deleterious effects of the culture of modern capitalism. The importance of this work lies in the empirical investigations which attempted to show how popular culture was connected to, but also relatively autonomous from, the economic and political relations of advanced capitalism. This stress on the specificity of cultural forms opened a more fruitful means for the analysis of popular cultures than the overbearingly economistic Marxism which predominated in Britain in the 1920s and 1930s and which existed as the primary intellectual resource for socialists. As Raymond Williams commented retrospectively, in matters of cultural analysis in the 1930s Leavis was right and the Marxists wrong. Loosened from their literary and élitist moorings, it seemed to socialists as if the Leavisite approach might provide the starting-point for richer cultural analysis in which the humanities themselves might be advanced beyond their initial liberal premises. And so it has proved.

More needs to be said on this point. But first it should be emphasized that *all* the contemporary political readings of the humanities have been informed by Leavisite positions. Thus the current perspectives of traditional academics, existing not only at the apex of the educational system, but still all too frequently heard in the daily chit-chat of senior common rooms, converge with traditionalist Leavisism in expressing the idea that the humanities must continue to service a minority to create a cultured and disinterested ruling group.

Equally, a version of Leavisism influences those who accord an absolute importance to autonomous personal development, and for whom the contemporary right is best understood by its philistinism. It is this perspective, drawing strongly from the militant humanism of the Leavises themselves – in which to summarize crudely but not inaccurately the purpose of studying literature and the humanities was no more and no less than to make the student a better person – which still forms today the common-sense of teachers in the arts and humanities. This is of polemical value in countering the gross philistinism and utilitarianism of the Thatcherite philosophers. But its polemical strength is not matched strategically. It is exactly this sort of response which, when it comes to putting a political position, can receive a polite but irreversible 'no', and then disappear. This is partly due to the untransformed conception of politics it carries within it. In the 1980s nothing seems more absurd than to suppose that the development of the individual personality, inside the academy, could possibly do anything to reverse the barbarism of the social world. It must be said that this is the redundant illusion of the political liberalism which underpinned the philosophical structures of the humanities in their founding moment.

And so too those attempts to extend and transform the humanities, which anticipate the disintegration and displacement of the humanities as an essentially unified pedagogic enterprise, were also formed in the first instance by the Leavis heritage. The key here was the move away from a narrow conception of culture, premised almost exclusively on literature and high culture, to a much broader understanding of cultures as the lived relations in which men and women make sense of their material world. This shift had its roots in the urgent need felt by the first-generation Leavisites in the 1930s to get to grips with popular culture, not out of reverence or respect but from a feeling of anxiety about future social development. But in their derision for popular culture they unwittingly provided the explanatory and analytic means for its recuperation. Nor did it require, in different hands, a great methodological upheaval for the political tables to be turned so that the exploration of popular culture came to be imbued with a strong democratic purpose. This move away from the pre-eminence of literary culture has been under way for a long period and no longer demands the constant justification which its pioneers had to endure. However, it is interesting that this has now taken a new twist. Terry Eagleton, an Oxford don as well as a sprightly Marxist theorist, has in his most recent works playfully insisted that this move from a narrow to a broad definition of culture does no more than inherit the authentic and traditional perspectives of English critical thought which were dominant before they came to be so exclusively appropriated by the literary critics.[9]

Historically this shift to a more critical and usable intellectual practice in the humanities originated mainly on the peripheries of the educational system, and crept only slowly towards those institutional bastions at the hub which constitute the central intellectual edifices, and it may be this which explains the publicity given to the recent academic 'scandals' which reverberated through the English faculty at Cambridge. It has been a process of the weakest links breaking first. An insurmountable contradiction has arisen in the past couple of decades, a period in which these broader concerns in the study of culture shifted from voluntary organizations existing outside the reach of the state to inside the state sector itself. The greater the expansion of higher education, the greater the likelihood that the élitist forms of the central paradigms in the humanities would crack. At one extreme, ten minutes of teaching literary criticism to day-release students should be enough to convince anyone of that. Transplanted into the polytechnics and colleges, traditional arts degrees brought with them, in terms of their own conceptual structures, very little which could actually hold them together under the force of these pressures.

In a difficult but highly perceptive essay Raymond Williams attempts to locate the forces which lie at the root of this process, looking not only to institutional developments but also to the formative intellectual moment in which these issues took their contemporary form, the heroic moment of modernism at the turn of the century.[10]

Williams writes in the belief that the decay of Cambridge, or Leavisite, English has set in. He fears that in its wake there could arise a resurgence of the most backward traditionalism in which even the premises of Leavisism would appear, once more, as dangerously advanced: '. . . there is now so strong a push to re-establish forms of order and discipline based on projections of past greatness and specifically of great Englishness that it would be astonishing if certain inherent tendencies in the constitution of English literature as an enclosed subject were not congruent with, even actively recruited and contributing to, this assertion of order through a version of tradition.' To counter this Williams is careful to distinguish the decay of Cambridge English as currently codified – 'failing – deeply failing – to meet the full active interests of students' – from the formal definitions and aspirations on which the subject was founded. He identifies the disjunction between English literature, the long history of the cultured and the powerful, and English literacy, the relatively much shorter history describing a crucial aspect in the cultural development of the dispossessed, in order to signal the relations of power and cultural unevenness which lie at the heart of the contemporary organization of English literature and the humanities. Implicit in this analysis is the idea that the project or objective of a new programme for the humanities is to reconcile this disparity, not – as the student radicals of the sixties supposed – by some modern millenarianism but by a protracted process of critique and self-reflection. This is based on the paradox that the aspirations of Leavisism can only be realized once the primary illusion of Leavisism itself, namely the reliance on a 'central base in literary criticism', has been dislodged.

In a powerful reconstruction Williams re-examines the critical moment of modernism, that great series of intellectual and aesthetic breakthroughs which dominated the avant-garde from the 1890s to the 1920s, suggesting that it represented not only a series of innovative achievements but that it has now come to represent *for us* 'the major intellectual formulations through which the unevenness of literacy and of learning has been lived with and either mediated or rationalized'. He argues that modernism, for all its avant-gardism, was a response to the underlying uneven development of literacy and learning characteristic of the metropolitan nations in advanced capitalism, and that Cambridge English, although formed by this moment, 'at a certain stage ... refused its further development and tried to reconstruct a common-sense tradition from its limited materials'. The specificity of the intellectual trajectory of modernism, which has constituted our current perceptions of the humanities and of which Leavisism was a distinct though unfinished strand, lies at the source of the separation of the intellectual and the critic, the difficulties and abstraction of language, in part the *academicization* of aesthetic and cultural practitioners and commentators.[11] More emphatically he proposes that 'What happened in modernism was at root defensive: an intransigent response to a general failure, in which the unevenness ... of literacy and learning was decisive.' Williams suggests that it is precisely by engaging strategically with and on this central cultural unevenness that new and emancipatory developments in the humanities will occur, activating 'a dislocation that is beginning to reach, harshly but instructively, into the old privileged places'.

Thus if a strategically democratic transformation of the humanities is to be accomplished it demands not only advancing those insights already developed within the framework of the humanities, but also the extension of the terrain of the debate itself, drawing in the traditional socialist emphasis on access as well as the sixties critiques of institutional power. It is this which holds the promise of overcoming the crippling unevenness of cultural development of which Williams writes. It is the combination of perspectives assessing the historical formation and current institutional location of the humanities as a totality of social relations which provides the basis from which a strategically flawed liberalism can be transformed into a democratic and plausible case for 'the humanities' – under whatever name might be adopted in the future.

We can now pull together some of the implications of this argument in summary form. At present, within the human and social sciences there is a range of distinct strands which at various points carry forward and transform the idea of the traditional humanities. These can appear institutionalized in university or college departments as courses or options in cultural or communications studies or more or less centrally in a variety of literature, history or sociology degrees, and have formed crucial inputs into new work such as women's studies. It is precisely the diversity of the various positions, the scope of approaches encompassed within the broad rubric of 'cultural studies', which is testament to the vitality of the new possibilities fashioned in the wake of a traditionalist idea of the humanities that is still moulded by a conception of culture more appropriate to the late nineteenth than the late twentieth century. This is not to conceal the fact that this brings with it many pedagogic difficulties, and can invite an uncritical eclecticism which simply inverts the excessive traditionalism of the mainstream disciplines. There is an important sense in which the intellectual rigour required in defining and getting to grips with a specific field of inquiry is absent from much current cultural analysis, to its loss. However, the general lines of development are clear enough that a polemical schema can serve to conclude this chapter.

First, we must emphasize the shift from a literary discipline, with a highly specialized sense of aesthetics, to one which investigates much more broadly the whole range of signifying practices which make up any society. This, in itself, can be said to underpin the shift from what we have called here Leavisism to the new strands of Cultural Studies. At present this extremely broad and loose formulation is possibly the only common denominator in the various experiments aiming to extend the range of the humanities. Eagleton, at the end of his survey of two centuries of criticism, comes to the following conclusion: 'These pursuits have no obvious unity beyond a concern with the symbolic processes of social life, and the social production of forms of subjectivity.'[12] Potentially this approach can do much to democratize conceptions of culture – dismantling common-sense or received ideas of high culture and the attendant notions of a culture to be enshrined and guarded in order to preserve the aura of treasured artefacts. Conversely, it invites study of lived cultures, and particularly of those subordinate forms of cultural practice previously neglected as suitable objects for serious investigation. Thus questions of aesthetic judgement and ranking lose their hold on the humanities as a defining, organizing principle, although this is not to suggest either that a complete relativism can take their place or that aesthetic problems disappear.

Second, with such loose formulations at its foundations, work in the humanities can only thrive so long as it remains committed to the principles of intellectual pluralism. This is not the same problem, touched on above, of eclecticism. It is more an argument against the establishment of orthodoxies and the settling of accounts such that they become transmuted into sectarianism. This becomes a vital principle in engaging with traditionalism and contemporary 'philosophical' versions of conservatism which are all too keen to discover heretics (with insufficient regard for constitution, family, nation – or even culture) and to pronounce forthwith the illegality of further pursuance within the academy. This is a villainous practice, dangerous politically and disastrous intellectually. It is impossible to imagine either current cultural studies courses existing without a historic input from a wide plurality of intellectual sources, nor them advancing in the future without this process being deepened. Furthermore it is crucial to have faith in our ideas – in the belief that we can explain the world better than the ideologies of the right and not be frightened to engage in debate. This, after all, is one means by which our own positions can be strengthened and the enemy's weakened.[13]

Third, it is necessary to define in a preliminary way the purpose of such academic ventures. Perhaps it still needs to be repeated that the objective is not and cannot be one which is 'political' in the sense of recruiting people to a particular party, or intellectual or philosophical position. A basic knowledge of pedagogy should deter even the most ardent proselytizer from embarking upon such an enterprise, for there is a known tendency for students to resist vehemently attempts to impose upon them particular views, and with good reason. On the other hand this does not imply that teachers of the humanities must concede all and fall in with those who piously wish that education has 'politics taken out of it'. Education is inevitably political; specific definitions of culture carry with them determinate political effects, however neutral they may at first appear. And the humanities, for a good part of their history, have been vigorously critical, a discipline encouraging the questioning of the dominant ideas of the day. In this spirit a working definition, drawn from Gramsci, might be to suggest that the broad aim of such courses today should be the 'critical analysis of the philosophy of common sense'. This implies that the purpose of an extended idea of the humanities is to reveal to students their position as social and historical individuals, to uncover the historical make-up of their own identity such that they can understand better the world they inhabit. In the process a new sort of intellectual is created. What conclusions, political or otherwise, they then choose to draw from that point are, so far as we are concerned as teachers, their own business. This again is not to suggest that for socialists the relationship between our work and politics is non-existent or contingent. The political importance lies – not in the 'humanization' of either ourselves or our students – but in developing a mode of analysis which can adequately explain symbolic processes and forms of subjectivity and in this limited way create the conditions for a critical and political engagement able to counter the barbarism of the contemporary world.

Fourth, this directly relates to the question of pedagogy.[14] I argued earlier against the idea of an easy libertarianism. This cannot mean, however, that student contributions to the construction and teaching of the course are prohibited, nor that we revert to old-style classroom teaching. That too carries its own dreadful politics. On the other hand when we attempt to reveal to students their own historical subjectivity, neither can we be in the business of confrontationalism as if in some grizzly re-education programme in which student ideas – be they racist, sexist or whatever – are hammered out of them as if we as teachers are the holders of absolute truth and reason. It is precisely in this context that a sense of the subjective formation of ideologies (taking into account philosophies and emotions) is crucial for students and teachers alike in attempting to *reveal* rather than confront head on; and in demonstrating *how* ideologies work one shows at the same time the determinate social conditions in which an ideology is formed, transformed and reproduced, and in so doing breaks from a relativism – to which at times students of cultural studies not surprisingly become particularly attached – in which all ideas have an equal validity. Deep problems remain, however, which never fit easily with the ideas gleaned from traditionalist courses; most particularly, how students respond personally and emotionally to courses which may turn them upside down must also be our concern and responsibility.

Fifth, in thinking how courses can be developed it is mistaken to concentrate exclusively on the internal conceptual workings of the humanities and the confines of the institution. The only hope of the humanities or cultural studies thriving in an academic environment is to make a virtue of their connections to the non-academic world and expand these where possible. This openness to influences produced from outside the given protocols of the discipline is essential if the disjunction between literature and society is to be narrowed, and to ensure that the programme of cultural studies does not in turn become fossilized, boasting a daring and risqué radical vision but in practice succumbing to the manifold day-to-day pressures and compromises imposed by the dull compulsion of institutional life. The outline provided in this chapter has been deliberately conventional in its scope, focusing on the relationship between formal intellectual disciplines and educational institutions. A very different account of the humanities and cultural studies could be written from other perspectives. The most obvious, for example, would be to investigate how in the past decade the feminist movement, as a political intervention, has effected an extraordinary upheaval in the *conceptual* categories which constitute the humanities and which until this moment had been taken on trust by the great majority of its practitioners. Or again, it would be possible to trace the connections between the recomposition of popular cultural forms in the past twenty or thirty years, looking at the transformation of the labour process, patterns of consumption, family life, new technologies and the revolution in mass communications and so on, and see how these too, up to a point, have impacted back on the shifting concerns of cultural studies, although, given the startling innovations in the systems of mass communications since the Second World War, the wonder is not why there are so many books on the media but so few.

Yet these are exactly the ambitions which the right are determined should be halted on the grounds that such concessions to ephemeral and contingent 'fashions' badly jeopardize the standards of academic work, pandering to the lowest common denominator. This belief needs to be dispelled once and for all. For on the contrary our job is to undermine the isolation of the old (and new) 'privileged places' even if the experience does indeed prove to be as harsh as it is instructive. In attempting to extend the very conception of the academic we begin to force the pace of educational innovation and determine its direction.

The key to this shift in perspective lies in the necessary recognition of the extent to which education already takes place outside the sphere circumscribed by the accredited institutions, in forms which may sometimes appear alien to us, as an *active* process and sometimes even defined in conscious opposition to the academy. The voluntary and autodidact culture is still a very strong element within civil society, and is, whether we be conscious of it or not, reordering the assumptions of academic ideologies. We can take a relevant example. In order to understand fully the transformation of

Leavisism one would have to assess not only the competing academic ideologies but also look at, say, Mass Observation, the educational practices of the labour movement (including the Communist Party in the 1940s and 1950s), C.N.D., the British Film Institute, a variety of women's groups, the W.E.A. and probably many other groupings. The critique of Leavisism would never have been achieved had it not been for the alternative positions elaborated in these non-academic, voluntary and private movements, all of which are or have been the sites of a popular pedagogic practice, often combined with a forceful notion of citizenship or public and political duty. It is significant that many of the founding theorists of cultural studies, holding now their professorships and fully accredited academically, escaped the traditional academic routes and were intellectually formed in one or more of these alternative associations. Raymond Williams, who has been referred to earlier in this chapter, is but one example.

In the more recent social history of England and Wales this situation has changed in so far as there now exists in theory a much greater possibility for large numbers of people, who in previous generations would have been exclusively involved in their alternative associations, to enter the state sector, perhaps as mature students, and with some finance. That this promise has never been adequately fulfilled is one of the great missed opportunities. Nonetheless the state sector now has to respond as never before to a much broader range of intellectual demands in post-18 education. As it is argued throughout this book, this offers a great chance for higher education to be re-fashioned. To be successful it is necessary to provide courses which can meet this challenge. This is not an imperious ambition, out to compete with and undermine the great plurality of educational ventures, an impossible objective in any case. The distinct voices must remain, but a bridgehead established between state and non-state.

It is here that worries about standards are most often expressed. There is, however, no reason for this. On the one hand not all courses need to follow the conventional profile of the current honours undergraduate course. But even where they might, all the evidence suggests that the contributions and links to organizations outside the academic institutions enrich rather than impoverish the intellectual work, and that standards as conventionally understood are raised, which is hardly surprising if the enthusiasm of the students can be generated and their real needs met.

There are many different models for this. One which has been particularly successful is that of the history workshop movement, drawing together to an unusual degree socialist and feminist intellectuals from the established educational institutions and from a variety of private and alternative associations – women's groups, local societies, trade unions and so on. In the past ten years it has perhaps become the major intellectual organizer in the field of history, extending the terrain of our understanding of history to include areas previously spurned by academic historians and producing a body of work of exceptional merit. It has done this by providing a public space for a wide range of different types of historical practice, and in the end by producing intellectual work which in its imaginative grasp can equal anything produced in the normal run of history departments.

The sixth point needs only to be noted here. I have argued throughout this chapter for the need to understand the links between the educational institutions and academic disciplines. In this context it is essential that the institutional space is defended both intellectually and from other threats financial or whatever. This is part of the job of defending, through trade unionism, the institution as a whole. There can be no special pleading for innovative courses: in one language this smacks of sectionalism, in another of an untransformed Leavisism. Little has been written on the sometimes tricky relationship between our intellectual practice as teachers and our role as trade unionists, but it is a crucial issue.[15]

Last, it is essential to argue the case for the humanities in terms of universalism, to press home an idea of the rights of students to develop the full range of their capacities and not be condemned to the bottom streams of some utilitarian programme in which 'training' for non-existent jobs is all that is on offer. Thus it is important to conceptualize the humanities as constructing and extending a new range of social rights, comprehensive and universal in their scope. In this way it may be possible to democratize further the means of intellectual production and to give new meaning to the idea that all men and women are already their own philosophers.

## Notes

1 *The Times Higher Education Supplement*, 23 April 1982.

2 It is necessary to recall at this point the role played by the notorious *Black Papers* on education in the ascendancy of Thatcherism.

3 Martin Walker, *Guardian*, 1 March 1983.

4 For an elaboration of these points, Claus Offe, *Contradictions of the Welfare State*, Hutchinson, 1984.

5 Stuart Hall, 'Education in crisis', in Ann Marie Wolpe and James Donald (eds.), *Is There Anyone Here from Education?*, Pluto, 1983, p. 8. This collection is exemplary in its critique of some of the fallacies of educational progressivism.

6 See the elegant account by Terry Eagleton, *Literary Theory. An Introduction*, Blackwell, 1983, Ch. 1; and Christopher Baldick, *The Social Mission of English Studies*, Clarendon Press, 1983.

7 Eagleton, *Literary Theory*, p. 31.

8 T. W. Heyck, *The Transformation of Intellectual Life in Victorian England*, Croom Helm, 1982.

9 Eagleton, *Literary Theory*, p. 206, and *The Function of Criticism. From 'The Spectator' to Post-Structuralism*, Verso, 1984, pp. 123–4.

10 Raymond Williams, 'Beyond Cambridge English', in his *Writing in Society*, Verso, 1983.

11 For a parallel interpretation see the fine essay by Fredric Jameson in Ernst Bloch *et al.*, *Aesthetics and Politics*, Verso, 1980.

12 Eagleton, *The Function of Criticism*, p. 124, and *Literary Theory*, p. 205. Important in this respect is Richard Johnson, *What is Cultural Studies Anyway?*, Centre for Contemporary Cultural Studies Occasional Paper, University of Birmingham, 1983. For one of the earliest theorizations of this shift from literature to signifying practice, via a discussion of modernism, see Peter Wollen, *Signs and Meaning in the Cinema*, Secker & Warburg, 1969, a text clearly marked now by its historical moment.

13 I have found useful here Michael Rustin's *What is Cultural Studies? The Virtues of Pluralism*, unpublished paper, 1983, which discusses Basil Bernstein's work on the curriculum.

14 On general questions of pedagogy there were many useful articles to be found in the now sadly defunct *Screen Education*; here I have drawn from Ian Connell, ' "Progressive" Pedagogy?', *Screen*, 24:3, 1983.

15 For an exception see Jenny Taylor, 'The University Cuts', *Screen Education*, 41, 1982.

There now exists an Association for Cultural Studies which functions as a network and liaison for those concerned with developing cultural studies in colleges and institutions of higher education. It can be contacted through Mike Dawney, Middlesex Polytechnic, Cat Hill, Barnet, Hertfordshire, EN4 8HU.

# 9
# Art and Design:
## *Time to Think Again*

GORDON LAWRENCE and DAVID PAGE

> A sort of top-hat view of life had been reached, and a theory of
> education had been developed which seemed to pride itself on its
> ignorance of work, and was based on books and abstractions. It
> was an education in words, in the knowledge of what can be said
> about things rather than knowledge of the things themselves.
> Indeed, modern education, directed from the old Universities,
> seems naturally to fall into the disease of putting 'subjects' in the
> place of substances . . .
>    Now mere word-knowledge about things is often paralysing
> and sterilizing, and we must aim at doing and making, at high
> purpose in production and quality in labour, at a clear, strong,
> national spirit, at economy in consumption, at creation rather
> than possession.
> (William Richard Lethaby, from 'Education for Industry', in
> *Handicrafts and Reconstruction*: notes by members of the Arts and
> Crafts Exhibition Society, London, 1919)

Art and design developed separately for most of its history.
The long, muddled process of evolution consequently hatched
out a different set of strategies for further education in this
area, strategies which ought to be carefully examined precisely
for their difference: many of the disciplines which have been
snotty about art and design could learn from it, with a little
humility. Naturally the same applies in reverse: art and design
has its own arrogance as well. But it is worth saying, at the
start, what is unequivocally good about art and design education.

First of all, it is about knowing how to make and do things, and proving it (and in this it has more affinity with the best primary school practice than with other levels of education). Respect is earned by the concrete realization of ideas rather than by the abstract manipulation of ideas (so that in *bad* academic courses, thinking is a process which never touches the ground at all). It seems particularly absurd, for instance, that we have a whole range of English degree courses in which the ability to make anything with words is irrelevant. This situation continues to be defended, in spite of the strictures (for instance) of F. W. Bateson decades ago, while fine art courses, in which visual making constitutes at least 80 per cent of the work, continue to make a mockery of the defence.

The sector has evolved a range of teaching methods and corresponding ways of assessing creative intelligence displayed in making, as well as the craft ability involved in realization, and the sensitivity not to confuse the one with the other. It is sceptical about immediate end-products, preferring to stress process and the development of skills for the next forty years of working life. It does not go in for firsts by acclamation; indeed, most people in the sector regard the classification of degrees as a retrograde ritual imposed by barbarians from elsewhere. What counts is what you can do, not the pieces of paper you have picked up along the way. This is the sector in its ideal form, of course: it often falls below this level, but the ideal remains there, and shared.

For students this way of working entails a high level of self-motivation and satisfaction leading to the emergence of a confident, flexible, creative person, who finds, or creates, employment at least as well as anyone else.

Structurally the sector has thrown up a way of organizing the school/higher education transition effectively, without pressuring schools into premature specialization. We cannot expect schools perpetually to develop new areas of skill to a high level to match the profile of emerging courses: this distorts the secondary school purpose, namely to provide an education which is basic, and adapted to children of all ability levels. Most students move to art and design courses via a one-year foundation course, which (also in its ideal form) offers a generalist introduction to art and design studies before any specialist bias is developed. In spite of the visible success of this two-stage structure and its necessary development elsewhere (access courses, though intended as remedial, may be expected to grow in this direction), there has been a concerted attempt to whittle it away. Regrettably some of art and design's own commentators have turned on its main structural innovation, perhaps wishing to demonstrate that they cannot be out-Heroded by Herod.

So far as staffing is concerned, the characteristic form in art and design, of a full-time core plus a cluster of part-timers who are simultaneously practitioners, presents a better model than the tenured monastic community of Academe. It is both educationally and organizationally more dynamic and reflexive: many areas – science and engineering, for instance – would work better with such a structure. It is, further, much more adaptable to likely future patterns of part-time working, job-sharing and career flexibility than the present case-hardened norm. L.E.A.s and administrators, instead of regarding it as an anomaly, and cutting away at the part-time area every time there is a crisis, should consider it carefully as a much better model.

Finally the sector is and has been, at least at student level, sexually balanced and traditionally open to women: one area, textile fashion, is overwhelmingly female. This is not true at staffing level, nor, unfortunately, is the sector free of imposed class distinction which has nothing to do with merit. But it can be said that there *has* been an egalitarian tradition, and that resistance to the sheep and goats act springs up continually and naturally from the ground.

There is no reason (apart from all the usual reasons) why we should not develop the art and design model into a more apt and powerful vehicle for preparing students to grapple creatively with the slippery possibilities of the post-industrial society, for generating ideas and projects on its own initiative, and for self-renewal through a fruitful critique of its own knowledge.

A Short Critical Survey of the Sector's History

Art and design education was established in 1837 for broadly commercial reasons;[1] as time went on the sector acquired three aims which have competed ever since, to train:

1. design artisans;
2. artists and dilettantes;
3 art and design teachers for schools.

It was controlled, in isolation, by the state (Board of Trade, Department of Science and Art, and successors), with central examinations, until 1963, when it acquired its own controlling Council (the National Council for Diplomas in Art and Design), and notional local autonomy. Only in 1973 did art and design (against majority sentiment) come into the national educational mainstream with the merger of N.C.D.A.D. and C.N.A.A. Once again the 'reform' was administrative; C.N.A.A. swallowed the existing structures whole. Spiritually and organizationally, art and design stayed *out there*.

The system was briefly captured, towards the end of the nineteenth century, by teachers with an agreed socio-political framework in which to place educational objectives. The Arts and Crafts movement (1888 seq.) was built on William Morris's analysis of society, politics, and art. Some did not follow him all the way, but there was a solid area of agreement. Morris believed that art was 'the pleasure of life'; hence any decent work, however rough, done by human beings could in principle produce 'art', a name which should not be reserved to certain 'higher' or intellectual categories. The medieval period, during which not only were irreplaceable and astonishing masterpieces (the cathedrals) made by the cooperation of craftsmen, using a crude technology and a very small population, but during which also virtually nothing was made which was ugly, was followed by the rise of industrialization and divided labour, which, given the lack of control by the workmen ('drudges') over purpose and process, and the dominance of the profit motive, inevitably led to the production of shoddy, and ugly, goods, alongside the isolation and increasingly the incomprehensibility of individual artists – the only people left who could control the whole process of making from beginning to end. To this situation Morris opposed the dictum 'Have nothing in your house that you do not know to be useful, or believe to be beautiful' (there was no real opposition here since he believed that the sparely functional would not, at any rate, be ugly). He did not, however, believe that beauty could be brought back to life under the social conditions and mode of production of capitalism, and saw socialism as the precondition for the re-flowering of a human art: 'I do not want art for a few, any more than education for a few, or freedom for a few.'

The Arts and Crafts movement sought to re-establish respect for the whole range of design and production, mainly on a craft basis. Radical teachers from the movement began to dominate the sector in the nineties and finally captured it altogether. Walter Crane, designer and socialist, a leading apostle of Morris, became head of the Manchester School in 1893, art director of Reading College in 1896, and principal of the National Art Training School at South Kensington (which had recently been ennobled as the Royal College of Art, and was in need of reorganization) in 1898.[2]

William Lethaby, an architect and critical thinker, became principal of the L.C.C. Central School of Arts and Crafts in 1894, subsequently described by Muthesius as 'probably the best organized contemporary art school'.[3] The Arts and Crafts movement had thus captured the commanding heights. Muthesius had been sent to investigate by the Prussian Board of Trade and subsequently set up the *Deutsche Werkbund*, an association seeking to improve German design. Through this and his support for standardization he was the forefather of the *Bauhaus*. The importance of Arts and Crafts, therefore, was that it provided a unifying field-theory relating art design and society, and channelling the energy usually absorbed in internal conflict into a productive explosion on a European, not only a British, scale.

In line with Morris's view of a social continuum of creativity, with art growing out of craft rather than constituting a separate category, the prima donna tendencies of fine art were restrained. But the clear vision faded in England (breaking out later in Germany); by the First World War the art schools were still expressing themselves, like a bad habit, in Arts and Crafts forms, but the content had leaked out.[4]

The most significant movement between then and now was the child art movement, stemming from Cizek and Marion Richardson, and later promoted by Herbert Read's substantial *Education Through Art*.[5] Although this was a liberating movement, in the thin atmosphere of the time it had the enfeebling effect of stressing the expressive at the expense of the constructive, and encouraging an irrationalist approach.

By the early sixties the schools seemed dominated by nineteenth-century drawing and painting, and 'craft' subjects haunted by the ghosts of Morris and Crane.[6] The new Diploma in Art and Design was meant to lead out into the real world of the twentieth century; what actually happened was, in content, a reduction of craft (hand production) in favour of design for industrial production, within apparently broad but effectively restrictive categories favouring the new professionalism of designer groups (e.g. textile and fashion designers, and graphic designers. These latter had since the war acquired respectability by way of the uneasy labels 'commercial design' and, earlier, 'commercial art'). General studies was tacked on to provide academic rigour. In function, the system, previously unified, was split into an élite 'degree-equivalent' level, with the residue designated 'vocational': the sector's early categories had been rearranged, with artists, artist/designers and art and design teachers at higher level, and design artisans below. Concern for 'standards' then chased out the part-time day and evening courses for local people (which had made the art colleges community institutions even at their least vital), and the lucky élite became isolated centres of a dubious excellence.

Historically, then, art and design has regressed under D.E.S. pressure from a system which, with all its serious faults, had substantial virtues: it was open, unified, egalitarian, and based in the community. At the same time no attempt was made to remedy the system's serious failings: to reconsider, in view of the twentieth century's massive change in technology, media and cultural concepts, the nature of its subject-matter; to reconsider the place in society of its product and mode of production, and out of these considerations to develop a theory of its knowledge, and a pedagogy.

## How We Got Here

> 'Of all things British muddle is the worst'
> (Warrington Taylor to Philip Webb)

The present state of art and design has long roots: the examinations introduced in 1913 were reorganized and renamed the National Diploma in Design with only minor alterations. All those who had any claim to understand the problems of art education in the twentieth century were united in their belief in, and desire for, fundamental changes to its structure even though they consistently failed to agree about how these might be achieved. As far as the Board, and later the Ministry of Education, was concerned, all that was missing was a set of appropriate instruments for its reformation.

In 1932 Circular 1432 set in motion a process of reclassification of the existing schools which, by that time, numbered in excess of 200, catering for more full-time students than the whole of the technical sector. On the basis of the available evidence it would seem that all subsequent decisions about the provision for art education had their beginnings with this circular. Nonetheless it was not until fifteen years later that the first of the instruments for control were developed out of the deliberations of the Bray Committee in 1947.[7] Many of its members were drawn from the Association of Art Institutions (A.A.I.), the most influential institution in the world of the art colleges, which, at that time, was claiming that the history of art education had consisted of a 'century of haphazard development and the absence of any coordinated policy', providing, with isolated exceptions, 'sanctuaries for the determined and refuges for the idle'.[8] In the wake of the *Report on Higher*

*Technological Education* in 1945 – the Percy Report – and the setting up of the Regional Advisory Councils in 1946, the recommendations of the Bray Committee led to the establishment of a standing National Advisory Committee on Art Examinations, the Freeman Committee.

Bray himself repeatedly recommended the unification of art and technical education under the umbrella of a national certificate system[9] (virtually what happened twenty-seven years later with the merger of N.C.D.A.D. and C.N.A.A.). In 1946 Bray wrote that the objective was 'to give our major art colleges the same academic freedom, or as much as possible, as obtains at universities, and to do this we must trust the teachers'.[10] But the art school heads trusted neither themselves nor their teachers to meet the requirements of a national certificate. A senior H.M.I. replied to Bray: '. . . an approved course implies a syllabus to be followed. Ninety per cent of the work in Art Schools is done under individual tuition and not through class teaching. An approved course, plus an approved syllabus, will impose a far greater rigidity on Schools than we have ever done and will be opposed by every Principal worth his salt.'[11] And it was.

The history of the period is the history of resistance to both unification and the development of specific curricula related to learning in the field of art education. The failure of both Bray and Freeman lay in the fact that no effective controls were established over the institutions which were to run the courses leading to the award of either the Intermediate Certificate or the National Diploma in Design between 1947 and 1958.

It was not until the establishment of the successor to the Freeman Committee, the National Advisory Council for Art Education (the Coldstream Committee), in 1958, that it was possible to provide a means of legitimizing such an undertaking. This new Council recommended that the N.D.D. be replaced by the creation of the National Diploma in Art and Design (the Dip. A.D.) along similar lines to that of the National Council for Technological Awards' Dip. Tech., and that a similar body be set up to administer it. Accordingly the

National Council for Diplomas in Art and Design (the N.C.D.A.D) was set up under the chairmanship of Sir John Summerson in 1962.

This Council only granted approval to twenty-nine colleges to run a total of sixty-one courses from September 1963. The fact that it had received 201 course applications from eighty-seven colleges left many feeling that the Council had acted in a draconian fashion. This response had been totally unexpected and left colleges, which in anticipation of expansion had established large pre-diploma courses, with insufficient Dip. A.D. places for students who had gone through them. It was clear that this new executive arm of the Coldstream Council had one overwhelming priority in the eyes of those who created it, as Sir William Coldstream's statement bears witness: 'We inherited an enormous number of art schools. We were appointed to get rid of art schools since it was regarded as uneconomic even if the small schools pooled resources.'[12] And although Summerson did not acknowledge Coldstream's view, he accepted that there was continuity in the decision-making and demonstrated it through his Council by granting recognition initially to twenty-nine colleges and, under severe pressure, to a further ten in the same year. This number was to be increased only by two in the next ten years. Throughout, this Council provided the focus of resistance to amalgamation with technical education in the form of the Council for National Academic Awards, set up in the following year.

Provision was reduced progressively over the period from 211 establishments, which by 1950 catered for over 100,000 students, to 111 establishments in 1970, catering for 42,000, of which only forty were to become B.A. centres in 1974. In this increasingly confined area it was a struggle for power in which the Councils, the weaker combatants (although the official bodies for art and design), stood no chance of success, for the process was one in which formal consultation, their only weapon, played no effective part.

Although significant improvements were effected in facilities for those colleges fortunate enough to have been designated as Dip. A.D. centres, there was no evidence that the same improvements had been effected in the educational process. It was a case of *plus ça change*. Areas of study were in four meaningless divisions, with art history and complementary studies tacked on to preserve the illusion that the courses were somehow other than thinly disguised technical courses concerned primarily with the unsystematic development of psycho-motor skills at the expense of any form of understanding.

Throughout, it was clear that there would be no attempt to develop a democratic educational structure, which would involve a debate about the educational issues. One can read the minutes of the N.A.C.A.E. and the N.C.D.A.D. committee meetings and encounter, in the ten and twelve years of their respective lives, no significant concern with any form of educational issue and certainly no debate about their collective purpose in terms other than the politically expedient. What emerges is a sterile debate covertly legitimizing fundamental changes in the organization of the provision, reducing its scope and potential for development. The argument about education never took place.

The real battle was between those concerned with providing a rational employment-linked provision and those seeking high academic status for a small part of it. Their views coincided in the practical matter of trimming the provision to fit their different concepts of its function, but in no other respect.

Both sides shared the same assumptions and fought only over how they could exercise their little bit of control over a torpid system. And, notwithstanding the development of D.A.T.E.C. (the system of courses run under the Technician Education Council's Committee for Art and Design), the outcome of this struggle is already evident in the relatively small growth of the degree courses at the expense of all the rest.

The influence of the teachers in the institutions generally has not been effectively challenged by the D.E.S. For while it may coerce them in the interests of reducing the overall provision, it cannot seem to wrest the control of the curriculum from them. And why should it, since their willingness to accept the 'rationalization' of the provision is only matched by their tenacity in maintaining an iron grip on course content? A grip maintained for the most part by the old guard, aided and abetted by those who wish to take their place.

The fears of those in art and design education who opposed national validation on the grounds that it would entail dictation of methods and content were ill-founded. Content remains unravished. L.E.A.s have the responsibility for the major part of art and design provision, excepting the B.A. degree, and, in the absence of positive guidelines in the form of a nationally validated sub-structure of courses, are progressively cutting it back. It is widely believed that the non-B.A. sector has little value in training people for jobs, and it is generally thought to be over-subscribed, despite the clear evidence to the contrary established in the Ritchie Report (1972),[13] research which has never been updated. Consequently these courses are regarded as politically unimportant and, in the absence of powerful advocacy for their existence, every chill economic wind that blows only serves to visit further misfortunes upon them. Course closures, fund reductions, and refusal to pay discretionary awards to students, together with a general lack of encouragement, form the background to their struggle for survival.

In sum, while recent provision has been slightly better than stagnant, prestigious middle-class courses have grown at the expense of working-class courses, while marginal changes have been made in the name of social utility not merely unsupported by, but in face of, the (inadequate) evidence available. The establishment account of this period is of course quite different.[14]

Meanwhile the failure to provide evidence of a coherent educational philosophy, or practice – in a context where there is a lack of clarity in objectives, unevenness in levels of staffing, resources and facilities – casts doubt on the educational or vocational utility of art and design generally. The key to this state of affairs lies in the control which throughout its history has been exercised by examinations and subsequently assessment procedures, which were based largely on practical activities, and led to, or ensured from the beginning, the lack of a curriculum structure which took a holistic view of the learning process in the arts throughout the educational cycle from the earliest age. This led to courses with characteristics based on heuristic, implicit learning at a purely practical level.

The deliberate policy of using as part-time staff people engaged in the world outside education had (as we have said) some clear advantages. They were required to bring to bear a heightened sense of reality by spelling out what professionalism meant in the 'real' world – as they might do with value in a dialogue. But the other half of the argument was not there in art and design, and their style and values have tended to dominate, correctly seized by students as more vital than whatever else they were being offered, but reinforcing hostility to structured, systematic and explicit learning strategies.

## The Structure of Knowledge in Art and Design

> 'My mind does not work, but my work does not mind'
> (Fine art department lavatory wall)

The move in the early sixties to an élite specialist ('degree equivalent') qualification created intellectual tensions as well as social ones. Two problems immediately arose: first, what was now the subject-matter of art and design, and how could it be categorized? Second, where was the theoretical study ('academic content') in these activity-based courses which could make them degree-worthy?

Four areas of study were announced: fine art, textile/fashion, graphic design, and three-dimensional design, labels which broke a prime rule of taxonomy, that terms should be of the same order. This jumble of dimension, technology, quality and description led, from the start, to absurdity. In what sense is it useful to segregate two- from three-dimensional design, for instance, and where, in terms of this system, did we place film, video and tape-slide, new media of communication which immediately began to penetrate courses? How was it possible to justify communication courses being designated a subset of graphic design, rather than vice versa?

The point is not so much the inadequate categories as the lack of importance attached to rethinking the area's current and likely scope and purposes. This blank failure to respond continued, and the *Joint Report* of 1970[15] merely remarked that the categories were serviceable but should be more flexibly interpreted. There was no discussion of Norman Potter's far more rational scheme: product design (things); environmental design (places); and communications design (messages),[16] which would, however, immediately have raised the question why architectural and art and design education were conducted separately.

The second issue, that of 'academic content', was to prove more embarrassing. The problem with art and design's theory was that apparently there was none. The same sort of problem occurred when English degrees were being set up: sitting around reading novels and poems was obviously jolly fun, whereas in classics, translation had ensured that, whether or not enjoyable, it *was* hard work. The solution was to bolt on Anglo-Saxon, if not also Old High German, Old Norse and Gothic, which, if irrelevant, were definitely difficult.

Bolting on a general studies element – art history plus the undefined complementary studies – was not a sufficient exorcism. The move to actual (C.N.A.A.) degrees led to an ever-increasing demand for more evidence of theory everywhere. There was by this time a deep neurosis among art and design staff, leading to two characteristic stances: the rejection of poncing about with theories as a substitute for *getting on with it*; and cringing inferiority leading to the acceptance of all and every theory and theoretician encountered, including the bogus. And yet all the time a basis for real theory was there, but masked, because implicit rather than explicit. A colleague has described the situation like this:

> Students have learnt by working alongside other students in the workshop or studio. Learning to paint or draw by this method

may be compared with the way in which children learn a verbal language: the child learns to speak by acquiring the rules of language at an unconscious level within the speech-community. Similarly, in art schools, the typical learning situation was the life class: staff and students implicitly accepted a rather narrowly specialized 'visual language' whose rules were acquired, for the most part, at an unconscious level. Learning to paint or draw in this way is easy and natural and can be highly effective; but the process only works if the 'language' which the community shares is widely accepted and not subject to rapid change. This does not seem to be the case with the visual arts today, and teaching by workshop or studio practice alone is, unfortunately, no longer effective.[17]

Whether as a cause or a result, the sector has no structures which might promote theory. Postgraduate work is in continuation courses (i.e. more of the same), not scrutinizing the subject-matter of the sector: its leading (and only entirely postgraduate) institution, the Royal College of Art, is dominated by such courses. The sector's former Councils never carried out any research, and teacher education is a Cinderella currently near to death from starvation.[18]

We have to lay heavy stress on the degree of backwardness found in this sector with regard to theory. Compare, for instance, the state of reading teaching with that of visual language. Unlike reading, which is thought to be of paramount importance and the centre of a continuous debate about how it might be more effectively and systematically taught, the skills associated with visual learning are regarded as inessential and are, consequently, relegated to the fringes of the educational debate. Furthermore, the child in the art lesson is believed to be involved in a mysterious activity which loses its potency when attempt is made to direct it. This view persists throughout the education system right up to, and including, graduate level. Hubbard's statement, written ten years ago, still seems to represent the present situation accurately:

> ... art educators possess no great ideas in common except those which sound important but which no one can define with the

approval of the profession: ... we in art education have not merely to intensify our goals; we need to define them ... Is the task of developing vision handled at all systematically in schools – or anywhere else for that matter? No it is not ... Do we find explicit, detailed statements coming from the art education profession as a whole to the effect that art teachers are dedicated to the goal of systematically developing visual mastery (maturity) and visual efficiency? No we do not ... art curriculums themselves are not even commonplace occurrences.[19]

Adequate learning really cannot take place, in visual communication (including fine art), without the formal teaching of a body of explicit theory which provides students with a common critical language and the conceptual means to transfer the implications of particular practical learning.

This can only be provided for by ensuring that the critical/analytical aspect of their education is continuous with practice. More time is needed for reflection, and this reflection, to be effective, must be structured through a deeper understanding of the historical and critical aspects of their study. Less time needs to be spent on the practical aspect of learning by doing, and more direct attempts made to structure the means.

A serious problem here is that art and design staff are generally chosen for, and judge themselves in terms of, their ability to develop specific executant skills. A diversion of part of learning time into theoretical study, in pursuit of a (hypothetical) greater conceptual grasp for the student, will be resisted – the more so because, unlike art history and complementary studies, it impinges directly on what is taught in the studio.

The object, nonetheless, must be to equip students to think effectively in terms of the knowledge they possess, and at the same time to allow of learning which challenges all abilities and interests in a diverse group. The scope of content would be determined by the range of important ideas and concepts within the field of knowledge, together with a methodology of interpretation. These two factors have simply been ignored in visual education despite the fact that they are vital to any effective teaching enterprise.

The intention is not to turn courses into that chimera of the Coldstream Report, 'a liberal education in art', but to develop a powerful field within which learning by doing could operate more fruitfully, enabling art and design courses to meet the spirit of C.N.A.A.'s criteria for 'the balance and aims of a programme of courses' (particularly 3.2 and 3.3) – which at the moment most of them do not.

Where is one to look for the constituents of appropriate theory? Related post-war work on (for instance) communication, the mass media and linguistics is often of direct application. Even more importantly, this in turn has stimulated work central to the sector's concerns, on the nature of representational systems, and the acquisition of drawing ability in children.[20] Such work may enable a coherent blueprint for visual education to emerge, replacing the crazy school merry-go-round on which uncritical enthusiasm for 'child art' of one moment is totally eclipsed by simple-minded 'problem-solving' the next, as if the constructive and the expressive, like matter and anti-matter, would cancel out if they inhabited the same space.

Finally, particular areas have developed 'workshop rules', usually tagged in a local jargon and thought of as highly specific, but often relating to principles which apply across the field (so that, to take a simple example, communication's 'noise in the channel' turns up as 'fussy' drawing, or 'busy' typography). This implicit knowledge of the sector can be made explicit.

Work which contributes to the development of appropriate theory is being done, and will continue to be done. If it does not co-opt this appropriate theory, acquiring in the process a degree of self-respect, the sector will be vulnerable to continuous whittling away. And it is not too fanciful to say that, if the pressures increase, built as it is round a vacuum, it will implode.

The Prospect

We have concentrated on the structure of knowledge in art and design because this yawning gap seems of central importance. It is also linked with the problems of subject-matter, social consciousness and purpose, structure of courses and so on. But consideration of these seems to be entailed in the debate we propose. For example, any general account of the nature of visual representation and how it is learnt presupposes consideration of the full spectrum of ability. Hence we would commit ourselves to a definition of purpose along the following lines:

> The function of art and design education is to equip children and students to understand and model visual reality, to design and create places, things and communications appropriate to the needs and desires of themselves and their fellows, account taken of all necessary constraints; these skills being specialized applications, recognized as such, of general and transferable abilities, produced by, and feeding back into, an education system which addresses itself to all levels of human ability, and which seeks to develop and connect all areas of human ability.

This switch of emphasis away from specialized élite education to that of the whole population would require greater integration between all levels (primary, secondary and tertiary) and the recreation of a coherent unified structure of courses, full- and part-time, with one validating body. This body, however, would have to be far more democratic and responsive than the C.N.A.A. as at present constituted if we are to break free from the sequence of oligarchies which have determined the sector's nature since the fifties.

At the same time the scope of the sector needs to be redefined, linking with architecture at the constructive end, along with the audio-visual media; given the interlacing of language, sound, image and movement which the latter employ it should probably link with performing arts and music at the expressive end. The need here is not for the creation of a new orthodoxy of categories but for a breaking of the unreal exclusive dominance of the visual *per se*; indeed, since so many educational categories need rethinking (for instance, the category 'English' is really about verbal communication, just as 'drama' represents the expressive development of self-presentational communication skills), the greatest generality and fluidity should be sought in the definition of areas of knowledge.

Of course the above programme is ideal. Looking at immediate reality we can see two contrary pressures. One now acting is the drive to 'rationalize' and reduce educational spending. In this process the individual parts of the sector most at risk are foundation and fine art courses, which can be represented as *unnecessary* provision. More generally there will be pressure on the whole sector based on alleged *over-provision*.

Hard on the tail of this assault will come a demand for an expansion at lower levels to absorb an increasing number of the young unemployed completing schemes which suggest some progression.

The lack of a coherent ideology in the sector makes it difficult to mobilize resistance; hence there is likely to be at least a decimation of provision. On the other hand, energetic surviving centres may be enabled by the second pressure to pursue some developments not too wide of our ideal programme. The most likely outcome is a pragmatic muddling-through of part of the sector. And that is where we came in.

*Notes*

1 Early history is described in Quentin Bell, *The Schools of Design*, Routledge, 1963; later history more cursorily in Stuart Macdonald, *The History and Philosophy of Art Education*, London University Press, 1970.

2 For Crane's reforms, see 'The Manchester School of Art' by A. Lys Baldry, in *The Studio*, Vol. 5, 1895, pp. 104–10.

3 N. Pevsner, *Academies of Art Past and Present*, Da Capo Press, 1973, p. 265.

4 See Charles Holme (ed.), *Arts & Crafts*, a special number of *The Studio*, 1916, which reviews work at 'the leading Art Schools' (thirty-one are reviewed).

5 Herbert Read, *Education Through Art*, Faber, 1943. For an assessment of pioneering work with child art, see 'Art and Craft: Marion Richardson and Robin Tanner', in *Adventures in Education* by Willem van der Eyken and Barrie Turner, Allen Lane, 1969, pp. 97–124.

6 See for instance Quentin Bell, 'The Fine Arts' in J. H. Plumb (ed.), *Crisis in the Humanities*, Penguin, 1964.

7 *Report of the Committee on Art Examinations*, H.M.S.O., 1948.

8 Association of Art Institutes, *Annual Report 1947–1948*, p. 43.

9 A.A.I., *Annual Report*, 1949, pp. 15–17.

10 Public Records Office, ED 46/384. Correspondence between Bray, Dickey and Dalby from 10 to 18 December 1946.

11 ibid. Letter from Dalby to Bray, 16 December 1946.

12 Sir William Coldstream in conversation with G. R. Lawrence, in G. R. Lawrence, *The Role of Consultation in the Formulation of Policy for Art Education in the Higher Education Sector between 1946 and 1974*, unpublished Ph.D. thesis, 1979, p. 125.

13 J. Ritchie, C. Frost, and S. Dight, *The Employment of Art School Leavers*, H.M.S.O., 1972. Showed *inter alia* that 72 per cent of 1968 leavers took three months or less to find their first art or design activity.

14 See Robert Strand, 'The Art Schools' Progress', in Kate Baynes (ed.), *Young Blood: Britain's Design Schools Today and Tomorrow*, Design into Industry Ltd/Lund Humphries, 1983. Strand was a senior officer within N.C.D.A.D. and then C.N.A.A.

15 *The Structure of Art and Design Education in the Further Education Sector*, H.M.S.O., 1970.

16 N. Potter, *What is a Designer: Education and Practice*, Studio Vista, 1969, pp. 9–10.

17 John Willatts, 'The Role of Theory', unpublished paper, Communication Design Course, North East London Polytechnic, 1980.

18 The number of students entering Art Teacher Diploma/Certificate courses has fallen dramatically – from a peak of 765 in 1970 to 277 in 1979.

19 G. Hubbard, 'A Revision of Purpose for Art Education', in G. Pappas, *Concepts in Art Education*, Macmillan, 1970, pp. 247–8.

20 See for instance F. Duberry, and J. Willatts, *Perspective and Other Drawing Systems*, Herbert Press, 1983. Willatts has also published numerous research papers, e.g. 'What do the marks in the picture stand for? The child's acquisition of transformation and denotation', in *Review of Research in Visual Arts Education*, Winter 1981.

# 10
## What Should Be Done About Social Science in Higher Education?

JENNY SHAW

### Social Science: Now and Then

The 1960s were a heyday for the social sciences in which they expanded even faster than higher education generally. The new universities and polytechnics found that the social science courses they offered were highly attractive to students and, in those days, to employers and governments too. The 'Robbins principle' of higher education for all who were qualified was accepted in a climate that barely recognized how radical a proposal it was. Compared with the natural sciences the social sciences were cheap and, as such, they offered a quick and easy solution to the 'problem' of the post-war demographic bulge reaching university age.

Today the wheel of fortune has turned, expansion has halted and, by some at least, the social sciences are treated as irrelevant and costly, remnants of a 1960s intellectual fashion. Yet despite contemporary attacks they deserve their place within British higher education. From being cheap and cheerful subjects suitable for the rapid expansion of higher education they are now essential to the maintenance of a free and democratic society.

The opportunism involved in the early support that they 'enjoyed' is apparent in the speed with which it is being withdrawn. Colleges of Education have been warned not to treat graduates with degrees in child psychology, politics or sociology as suitable for admission to teacher training. The research council responsible for overseeing and administering social research has been denied the honour of calling itself a 'Science' council. Ironically, for this, as Harold Silver points out, is a replay of the hostility meted out to the natural sciences in the nineteenth century.[1] The Open University periodically suffers smears and attacks on its (always) social science courses, most recently economics but in previous rounds education and sociology. In the name of economy essential and accessible government publications of social data have been abandoned or curtailed, making planning more difficult and inaccurate. It has become harder for those other than 'experts' to find their way around official statistics and, most important of all, the basis on which verifiable claims that living standards and welfare are deteriorating can be made has been obscured by attenuating series of data and by changing the bases on which a number are calculated, e.g. unemployment data and the Retail Price Index.

In a sense the social sciences have become academic scapegoats, partly because of the somewhat self-indulgent directions they took during their expansionary phase, but more particularly because of the role that they must play in relation to governments and policy-makers. It is the collective responsibility of the social sciences to maintain a forum for the discussion of moral, political and social issues and to use what financial and intellectual independence they have to tell governments what they do not want to hear or know rather than simply what they do. Because the subject matter of the social sciences is of universal significance they are bound to be more or less controversial. As such they ought also to be highly accessible, and it is in this respect that social science education clearly needs an overhaul.

The fragmentation of the social sciences as a whole and the absence of specific career-related objectives have together produced a situation where the aims and objectives of most social science courses are either rarely discussed or simply subsumed under the general objectives of promoting 'power of the mind', 'critical ability', 'insight', 'judgement' or 'thinking for oneself'.[2] This will not do. The objectives of higher education have to be firmer and less vague, and it has to be clearer what the social sciences can contribute to them. Which, in brief, are methods of social investigation and interpretation coupled with an awareness of the broad historical processes of change which provide the context in which current developments have to be viewed.

## Reskilling and Investigation in the Social Sciences

Compared to some other subjects the social sciences have a greater responsibility to establish themselves by making their skills commonplace, rather than by straining primarily for theoretical recognition and respectability. One aim of the social sciences should be to 'deprofessionalize' themselves in order to create a population familiar and at ease with the use, and abuse, of social science methods. Had this been the case the Cyril Burt hoax, in which phoney research played a key role in the debate about the nature and determinants of intelligence, might not have lasted so long and had such serious consequences for generations of children, teachers and educational psychologists. Although they are not supported by industry in the same way, this objective should be similar to the drive now under way to make us all computer-literate.

This means that teaching must be a high priority and that it must include the transmission of research skills as well as the production within the students of whatever degree of theoretical self-consciousness is currently thought desirable. However important it is for students to be able to see themselves as social products, this is not the only goal of social science education, although it is to this that much 'critical' social science teaching has been narrowed. For too long radical social scientists have interpreted their duty as being to criticize positivism and then, at a loss for what to do next, have retreated into the history of ideas, albeit Marxist ones. Much of the valuable work of the last twenty years of legitimizing Marxism, getting Marxist ideas firmly established in the curricula of nearly all the social sciences and creating theoretical journals of outstanding quality, is undermined by its links with a contempt, mistrust and often ignorance of empirical social science. At the student level the attack on positivism often results in nothing but an empty relativism, with the result that the production of evidence is more likely to be abandoned to the right. In a sense it is a vicious circle: the more unsympathetic the 'facts' seem to be, the less likely are people on the left to do empirical research. Other potential sympathizers may even regard the alienation of the evidence as an insurmountable product of consciousness itself.

Thus an unintended, but serious, consequence of the 'ideas' approach to social science has been to distract or even detach social science teaching from problems of evidence and to deny its students a sense of competence. This has not happened evenly over the social sciences, but in some subjects such as sociology, anthropology, politics and education it has been near terminal. Meanwhile certain other social science subjects suffer from the opposite problem. A frequent complaint of economics and social psychology is that they are too empirical, pseudo-scientific in the extreme and far removed from the concerns that led students to want to study them in the first place.

With hindsight we can see that the 'ideas approach', as a reaction to positivism, was a cul-de-sac entered because there appeared to be no other orthodox 'body of knowledge' to teach. With the result that the opportunity offered by the fluid nature of social science material to make learning in these fields less hierarchical and more democratic was missed. Sadly and paradoxically social science, which ought to rely extensively upon discussion and the development of interpretive and analytical skills, thus having, as cause and effect, a narrowing of the distinction between teaching and research, went in the opposite, traditional and élitist direction. In fact the retreat into the history of ideas reinforced the hierarchical aspects of social science education. Practitioners defined themselves more as 'academics' interested in the esoteric than as 'intellectuals' concerned with broad social and political issues.

It is important to make clear that wanting to shift the balance of social science teaching away from the history of ideas and towards a more investigative approach is not simply a plea to return and rehabilitate positivism. There were, and are, many fair criticisms to be made of the way positivism skewed social science research and teaching up until the mid-sixties. Certainly it failed to question the status quo and appeared to teach that there had to be unemployment, educational failure, bad housing. It produced conclusions that were widely disseminated, such as that mothers should not work else they risked their children becoming disturbed or delinquent, while other issues such as the significance of paternal involvement in child-care were simply ignored.

An immediate and fundamental change in how social science education is viewed must be to break with the idea that research is something that postgraduates do while the best way to teach those starting out is to retrace the cognitive paths trodden by the founding fathers. There is in fact a strong case for reserving that sort of intellectual history for postgraduates and giving undergraduates and others a chance to participate in the investigation of contemporary issues. It is shameful that many social science students graduate ignorant of the methods necessary to produce and use empirical evidence in the most unambiguous forms possible. Even where they have an introduction to epistemology or the philosophy of science it remains unrelated to any understanding of practical research methods and argument. Yet ultimately research methods are about persuasion, about producing evidence in its most persuasive form, capable not simply of persuading others of the researcher's preconceptions but also of changing the researcher's view of the world. Rigorous research methods are simply those which stand up best in critical argument.

Nevertheless, translating this into practical educational proposals is not without its problems. Because the social sciences are skill- rather than knowledge-based they occupy a somewhat anomalous position, within and without education. It is frequently hard for them to respond adequately to the demand that they be 'relevant'. It is all too easy for them to reserve judgement and stand firmly on the side of facts rather than values. Yet this is exactly what they must not do. Relevance has become their weak point and functions mainly as an imprecise but all-round criterion for judging the social sciences. Like the concept of needs, to which it is closely related, relevance is notoriously difficult to define but a version is imperative. In part this is supplied by recognizing the values of the skills themselves.

In short, the argument for research techniques to be more common and to be incorporated more centrally into undergraduate degrees is an argument for greater competence. This is not made simply on the grounds that society would be better off, it is also based on the recognition that in a comprehensive university there will be many older students who are ready to embark on research projects, and indeed to do their degrees by dissertation, much sooner than most 18-year-olds. A more investigative approach to social science would be both more in tune with the needs and experiences of older students and, paradoxically, with shorter courses, as it does not lead to such seemingly certain and disillusioning conclusions.

## Research and Cooperation:
## Alternatives to Hierarchy and Authority in Education

Already older students tend to prefer social science courses, at least initially, often using them as 'gateway' courses into study generally and then into other subjects. Their popularity among these students comes from the clearer sense of purpose and motivation that older students usually have, a strength which not only makes the processes of teaching and learning easier but which must not be wasted. In fact there is a reasonable chance that if universal entitlement to higher education were introduced and older people took up their rights to it then some, at least, of the problems with existing courses would disappear. One of which is how to encourage students to formulate questions about the society they live in.

At present they take as given the questions to be answered, or worse, do not see their work as answering questions at all, rather 'doing topics'. Older students fall into this mode less easily and would probably get most out of more research-oriented courses, but making research a way of learning would benefit all students.

Sometimes it is hard to imagine how a more collective and supportive learning environment could be achieved without a focus distinct from that of individual performance. Integrating research and learning provides a possibility, though, of course, it is not without difficulties. There are still likely to be problems of motivation, of responsibility, trust and conscientiousness, of students feeling that they are being used as cheap labour (shades of the worst aspects of the Youth Opportunities Programme and its successor the Youth Training Scheme). At present many of the research methods courses are the most unpopular and least well taught or understood. Some of this stems from a perceived irrelevance or triviality as well as from the confused equation of empirical work with empiricism. Where higher education is genuinely integrated with practice, as in nursing, there are acute problems stemming from the conflicting needs of the students for a variety of experience as opposed to the needs of the institutions (hospitals) for adequate and competent nursing in all its departments. Furthermore, anyone who has had to arrange and/or supervise placements will know how difficult this can be. Yet without minimizing these difficulties they are not insuperable and if, as I shall argue below, the demand for research is stimulated, solving them will become easier.

There is nothing intrinsically anti-authoritarian or anti-hierarchical about research, but the activity of 'finding out', which is all that research is, involves cooperation and the exchange of ideas in a much less self-conscious way than most conventional teaching and learning situations. If one reconsiders, the nomenclature 'research' is very much like the 'project' work of progressive primary education, and it is hard to believe that it is really much more difficult for practices such as these which stress the capacity to create knowledge to take hold and be incorporated into the freer curriculum of higher education with already accomplished students than it has been in primary schools. Moreover it is a recognized and central tenet of progressive education that it should offer an experience of social relations that are different and better than the prevailing ones, making education a rehearsal for a better world. Of all subjects the social sciences offer some of the best opportunities for cooperative work, although these are stifled at present by the individualism of academic work which prohibits joint work for purposes of assessment. Research offers some relief from this. Those fortunate enough to get part-time or vacation employment on research projects frequently regard them as among their best learning experiences. While this is hard to build in to course structures, it is clear that what makes them good experiences is the fact that they are joint or collective in some way and help to move the idea of intellectual and academic work away from being solely about showing individual ability.

## Research and Democracy:
## Citizenship Rights and Community Resources

The argument so far has rested on the benefits for social science education of increasing the research element, but there are broader issues too, the most important of which is the democratic potential of research and research skills. By making the spread of methodological skills more general, the social sciences can play an important role in achieving greater democratic control, especially as societies become more complex and control is more centralized. At present the momentum for the investigation of social issues is simply too low and too slow. In part this is a matter of funding, and the expenditure on social research is puny, but this might change if the demand for research changed and that might change if there was a greater understanding of its processes and procedures.

I expect that most people will, at some point in their lives, be involved in campaigns, either professionally or non-professionally. These campaigns will, no doubt, be poorly funded. If they are to be successful they need to be well thought out and imaginative, and may well include the collection and presentation of social data which is not generally provided or easily available. A good example of what can be produced by a local community with a sprinkling of skilled people, some community-based experience of publishing, writing and data collection is the book *Brighton on the Rocks*, which records and documents a fight against recurrent cuts in local government expenditure.[3]

It is clear that as an antidote to the present trend of reducing facilities for research and centralizing what is left of them there has to be a revaluation of social research from different quarters. Ideally charities, trade unions, local authorities, community health councils, associations of parents of handicapped children, etc. would all be entitled to command and demand that research from their local institutions of higher education be done into issues that they have defined and which serves their purposes. Centralized agencies such as the Economic and Social Research Committee or the Equal Opportunities Commission simply cannot be expected and should not be allowed a monopoly to define what is researched. Thus it is as a corollary of wanting to see the funding and commissioning of research widened that the patterns of teaching social science in higher education must change too.

This means not only changes in degree courses but the provision of far more in-service training and short courses. It means ceasing to treat the three-year undergraduate degree as a fixed point of reference into which all other courses must fit. Charities, housing associations, play-groups, tenants' associations, schools, self-help groups, parents' associations, etc. should not only be able, as a right, to apply for research to be done, they should also be able to sponsor their members to go on courses to equip them to evaluate their own initiatives.

The costing of this depends, of course, on a commitment to increase resources to higher education and to diversify the categories of student and course eligible for funding. It also touches on the question of sabbaticals of various lengths for educational purposes and the ways in which employers might be encouraged and helped to grant them. The existing arrangements for maternity leave, where state and employer share the costs (not equally, as the state bears the lion's share), are perhaps an example. And the better T.O.P.S. courses indicate the extent of demand for courses of ten to twelve weeks' length. If the proposed increase in research expertise were to be realized and a wide variety of individuals and institutions began to see themselves as involved in its processes it would soon be necessary to find ways of covering research expenses, for they are by no means negligible. The most obvious is to make them tax-deductible, at least in part.

Several problems remain outstanding. Among them is the real but counter-productive confusion over the role of social problems as defining the activities of social science and social scientists. Action research has been called 'gilding the ghetto', and many of those involved in it came away scarred and feeling that ultimately it all amounted to an exercise in managing the poor.[4] Clearly political lessons have been learnt, not least of which is the importance of alternatives to state funding for research.

Another problem concerns the fact that many existing teachers of social science have themselves to acquire research skills. A consequence of the rapid expansion of social science in the sixties and seventies was that many of the first generation of social science graduates became employed in teaching their subjects without ever having had much opportunity to participate in research themselves. But this too is remediable if a more cooperative approach is adopted and indeed if a variety of skill levels is envisaged.

An example of the strategically successful use of fairly basic social science skills comes from a health education unit. There is a David and Goliath quality about most health education. Persuading people not to smoke from a material base of the odd duplicator, one typist and whatever time one health education officer feels they can reasonably spend is not much compared to the thousands of hours spent in thinking and planning sales by the tobacco industry. Nevertheless, though the general imbalance of resources available, including intellectual ones, between capital and labour is enormous, some coups are possible.

Prior to one budget when an increase in taxation on tobacco was widely expected, the tobacco industry organized a petition to protest at any such increase and posted it at every kiosk and newsagent or tobacconist in the land. A counter-petition, though obviously smaller in extent, was mounted locally and showed a majority in favour of raising tobacco tax. A demonstration outside a tobacco industry press-conference provided the occasion for its results getting equal coverage, at least on all the main television news that night.

Similarly, an extremely effective way of finding out how easy it is to flout laws forbidding the sales of cigarettes to children was to use schoolchildren in a survey. The vast majority had no difficulty with their purchases. The design of the survey was simple enough and perfectly adequate. The furore that followed the use of schoolchildren in such an experiment nearly eclipsed the findings, and while efforts were made to highlight the ethics of such an action, the ethics of the chairman of the local health authority who tried to squash the findings, remove the officer involved, etc. could hardly go unnoticed. That chairman was professionally involved with the tobacco industry itself. Conflicts such as these are not uncommon; the point is that research, often of a quite unsophisticated sort, can hold the ring as well as being essential and effective components of the battles.

## What Jobs Should There Be?

Ultimately the case for social science in higher education rests largely on the part it can play in vocational training, even though this cannot be wholly extricated from its role in maintaining a democratic society. Planners, outreach workers, economists, administrators with social science training will be needed in almost any conceivable developed society as much as in the present one, and new jobs will be created making even greater use of those skills. Defending those jobs and that direction of employment is itself a political and democratic process. As politics become professionalized and far from part-time – so does effective opposition.

Its forward thinking accelerated by the threat of abolition, the Greater London Council is a useful guide to a changing occupational structure and to future possibilities of employment. It has recognized the extent of the social information needed for it to function efficiently and democratically and has got it by creating posts which provide current information on transport needs, on ethnic circumstances, on the position of local labour by industry and social characteristics, i.e. age and sex. It has employed people to think constructively on a wide range of issues and not simply report back and gather data, important though that is too. It demonstrates how it is 'people' work in fields such as health and education and research that will be the locus of employment in future.

A society more sensitive to human needs than ours is today will want to invest more in services which meet those human needs. Part of the job of higher education is to anticipate those needs. To take but a small example, the allocation of resources within the health service is both an acknowledged problem and a scandal – it currently depends upon the muscle of individual consultants. A better, more efficient, and rational solution would be to actually employ some epidemiologists with social science skills, but at present they simply do not exist.

These are all manpower considerations and it is perhaps reasonably clear how another administration might view the creation of employment in the service sector and how that would affect the training role of the social sciences. If higher education is to contribute to a more progressive society, the social sciences at least must put their faith more wholeheartedly into empirical research than they have in recent years and face up to the fact that they are and should be 'problem' oriented; which is another way of saying they must make human needs their central purpose. This will be done more easily by increasing the opportunity for those outside the academy to commission research as well as by making research skills more central.

Although not uniquely socialist, there are distinctly socialist reasons for reintegrating teaching and research and for the inter-disciplinary approach necessitated by starting with social problems. The socialist view that natural laws of society do not exist means that the social sciences should not be looking forward to a maturity when they have an established body of unchanging 'knowledge' of society to hand down. Instead, the view that society is in a continuous process of historical creation implies a continuous need to examine the changing reality.

A view of the social sciences as somehow joining the arts and humanities in civilizing and correcting the philistine tendencies of the natural sciences is as false and out of date as it is patronizing. They certainly do have a critical and moral role, but it is by concrete results that they should be known. When Mrs Thatcher celebrated her 1983 victory with a bid to reintroduce capital punishment, an emotive issue likely to serve her purposes well, there can be little doubt that it was research evidence from the social sciences about the deterrent or non-deterrent effect of capital punishment that swayed Members of Parliament and their constituents and produced the vote against hanging. Furthermore, while the social sciences may not seem spectacular in their results, research that shows the effect that low incomes have on life expectancy, if heeded, is just as life saving as a heart transplant, indeed much more so.

In considering what the social sciences have to offer society it is important to remember, as Peter Scott observes in another chapter, that the left asks more of higher education generally than the right; it similarly asks more of its social scientists. The left is helped by a better understanding of social reality while the right depends on denying it. That is not to say that the left has a correct view of the world, only that reality is rather less conservative than even the left believes and in the messy business of trying to understand it social science remains crucial.

Undoubtedly the social sciences squandered a number of opportunities, educational and political, and this, plus the current vogue for accountability in education, has contributed to an odd alliance between radical right-wing critics of social science and higher education and left-wing critics. The first fear that if the social sciences are successful they are also subversive and wasteful, while sections of the left consider that social scientists in higher education have done nothing more than feather their own nests with jobs for life. As with other aspects of the Welfare State, ill-thought-out attacks have coincided with, and indeed overtaken, the processes of re-evaluation and learning from experience that are part of the evolution of higher education.

## Notes

1 H. Silver, *Education as History: Interpreting Nineteenth and Twentieth Century Education*, Methuen, 1983.

2 A. Leftwich, 'Social science, social relevance and the politics of educational development', *International Journal of Educational Development*, January 1982, Vol. 1, part 3.

3 *Brighton on the Rocks*, Queenspark Books, Brighton, 1982.

4 Community Development Project, *Gilding the Ghetto*, Urban Deprivation Unit, Home Office, 1977.

# 11
## Nothing Less than Half the Labs

HILARY ROSE*

It is obvious that the values of women differ from the values
which have been made by the other sex . . . yet it is the masculine
values which prevail.

(Virginia Woolf)

The occupation of scientist or engineer is by and large secure,
technically interesting and reasonably well-paid. It is also
still very much a man's job. Consequently, there are good
equal opportunity reasons for wanting girls and women to
have their share of the scientific and technological pie. Equal
righters have pressed energetically the claims of girls and
women for a fair share of both the educational provisions
and the jobs, and have with considerable ingenuity sought
innovatory mechanisms such as the Manchester *Girls into
Science and Technology* ([1]) (G.I.S.T.) project of the E.O.C.'s 1984
*Women into Science and Engineering* (W.I.S.E.) programme. Yet
for both radical feminists and socialist feminists, who carry
a more transformative conception of the need to change
society to make it serve the needs of women (and of men)
better, the equal rights position is seen as masking the real

* My thanks to the editors for friendly and critical editorial comments. I am
indebted to Steven Rose, who offered not only intellectual encouragement but
also nurturant support during an extended patch of ill-health during which the
final draft was written. My thanks to Pauline Jennings for her typing and to Raja
Pagadala for his.

problem – the oppressive nature of the scientific and technological pie.

Feminists have long been aware that science – and here I use the word 'science' as a shorthand for 'science and technology' – is not simply neutral but actively hostile to the interest of women. And that shorthand, science, for science and technology, is more than just shorthand, for it recognizes, despite the cultural mystification which the separation of terms endeavours to impose, that science and technology are in any practical case indivisible. Back in 1938, before the achievements of nuclear and solid state physics and the advent of the biological revolution had together made possible the bomb, biotechnology, the microchip and the test-tube baby, Virginia Woolf observed 'Science, it seems, is not sexless; she is a man, a father and infected too.'[2] Those with a suspicion that Woolf was right in 1938 have even better reason to be concerned about the state of science and technology today. Do we really want our sisters to enter the juggernaut? Would success be but a Pyrrhic victory in which the sexual composition of the scientific labour force was changed but its character had not?

Here, I want to suggest that equal righters and transformative feminists,[3] with their very different preoccupations about what feminists need to do, don't have to divide and oppose one another, and that in considering the question of women and science education the reformist position of the equal righters opens the possibility of a more radical programme of change. The issue is not 'Are equal righters or transformative feminists right?' To set the question up this way is to enter the dichotomy beloved by masculinist reasoning – all that reform *or* revolution debate. The more useful question is whether the struggle to get women into science and technology is likely to help women and, if so, how? There is no invisible hand of feminism which guarantees a positive outcome, but posing the question this way helps us to look at the structural reasons for the exclusion of women from science which lie within the division of labour in a patriarchal society, and the consequences this exclusion has not merely for women but for the nature and goals of a masculinist science. How could we work for the entry of women into science and technology in such massive numbers that their sheer presence brings in those different experiences, values, needs and demands which will themselves inform and transform the knowledge and applications of science?

## Absent and Invisible Women

It is increasingly commonplace to talk about the absence, or at best limited presence, of women in science and engineering. The new chairman (*sic*) of the E.O.C., the marine engineer, Lady Beryl Platt, launched W.I.S.E. as an initiative to encourage more girls to take science and engineering subjects at school so that the option of them making a career in these subjects is not precluded by choices made as far back as the O-level stage. In similar vein, W.I.S.E. hopes to encourage industry to release its younger scientists and engineers, above all the women, to go to the schools to talk about the contribution women professionals can and do make. The E.O.C. meanwhile provides posters of Hypatia's sisters, as it were, from Hypatia herself to Marie Curie and Dorothy Hodgkin, and glossy pamphlets showing smiling self-confident-looking young women wearing hard hats and standing on construction sites, dextrous and object-oriented in laboratories, or relaxed and totally in control of computing equipment. Positive role models in picture and actuality, together with innovatory teaching strategies, are seen as a way to alter the statistics of the gender distribution of scientists and engineers.

What does W.I.S.E. have to take on in higher education? First, it is true, but only in a particular sense, that there are few women. The academic staff of science and engineering departments is almost entirely male, though the pattern varies from engineering, where there are almost no women staff and only 8 per cent women students, through physics and chemistry, which are a little but not much more mixed, to biology where (depending on the branch of biology concerned) there is the greatest proportion of women as academic staff, although still a small minority. What is special to biology, however, is that many departments have a majority of women undergraduates.

But while there are proportionately few women in evidence in post-18 science and technology education, that is not to say that there are none to be seen at all. Women clean the floors – under the supervision of male supervisors; women act as technicians, under male senior technicians; they work as catering staff under the direction of male catering officers; and they work as secretaries typing letters dictated by male academics and generally smoothing out interpersonal relations. The point is – and it has to be made again and again – that women's paid work, especially in the science or technology laboratory, echoes just what she does at home – except that at least there she is relatively free to get on with it at her own pace.

The very architecture itself reflects the routine expectation that this is a man's world. In engineering blocks built at the height of the 1960s affluence, when the norm was not a stretched and cut budget, it is terribly hard to find a women's loo. Whatever the Robbins principle, it was not about equal opportunities for women. Even now, women are ambivalently wanted as students or colleagues. It's not just the pornographic pictures of women still pinned up in the labs. The new health and safety posters, for example, found in the labs and workshops, are often crudely sexist in their use of women's naked bodies to make sure the men remember the safety points. It was the university that wrongly dismissed Mrs Dicks from her biology research post which was at the same time discussing conversion courses with the E.O.C. for women students who wished to do science or technology but had the wrong A-levels.[4] Even at the most superficial level, higher education is sending out contradictory messages to women about science and technology.

Scientific and technological education in Britain reflects the global, rather than merely national class, race and gender order. Because the body of scientific knowledge is inherently international and the language of communication formal or even mathematical rather than verbal, the practitioners of science and technology need only the common culture of industrialization. It comes as no surprise then that the engineering departments – even more than the science ones – recruit extensively among the rising élites of the newly industrializing societies. These third world students are almost exclusively male; the much smaller numbers of women are to be found in the appropriately 'softer' and more feminine subjects. The indigenous British students are almost entirely male, but also almost entirely white. A handful of British Asians and almost no British Caribbeans thus complete the archetypal membership of the student body of a science or technology department at most British universities or polytechnics. Some institutions and departments have gone some way to contest this stereotype, and it is important to acknowledge their achievement. But they are a minority.

The point is that scientific and engineering education is indissolubly bound up with what science and technology are, and are used for, in our society. This is much more true for science and technology than it would be, say, for arts, history and many of the social sciences. Education under capitalism and patriarchy is fragmented because the division of knowledge, division of labour and division of power are fundamental to both. Capitalist patriarchy is not a monolithic universal category but one which has to be understood in terms of the variations between different societies over time. The deep antagonisms of class, gender and, for that matter, race find their reflection but with differing degrees of intensity within these societies. In certain respects, not least in the continuing resistance to the claims of women to have access to higher education, Britain is a particularly patriarchal society. (Under 40 per cent of higher education students are women as against 50 per cent in most industrial countries.) It is difficult to escape the feeling that it is the relative shortfall of male school-leavers during the 1990s which has moved the male-dominated academy to view the possibility of increasing the numbers of women students in such a favourable light.

For that matter science and engineering are not monolithic either. Although there are some women academic staff in biology and almost none in engineering, the exclusion mechanism works very differently between the disciplines. Biology appears to be the most sympathetic to women; even more girls than boys take biology; but by the time we are looking at the entry requirement into research – the Ph.D. – the ratio of men to women is four to one. In engineering, physics and chemistry the exclusion mechanism seems to operate before higher education rather than during it. Thus any strategies for change in education have to be premised on the very clear understanding that the problems – while they have certain things in common – work out in different ways within the different disciplines.

The question of access into scientific and technological education in Britain is exacerbated because of the early – indeed premature – specialization within the British school system, unlike, for example, the U.S., where the commitment is to a broad general education until the end of the first degree. In Britain you either get a school science education, or you don't. Doing science at school is not about gaining knowledge of the culture of the society of which one is a member, but about taking the first step on the ladder to becoming a scientist or engineer. While the arts and social sciences have worked harder, and found it easier, to provide a second chance at study, universities in particular are remarkably resistant to thinking creatively and practically about a second chance of getting into the sciences. Anyone who has sat through a University Senate debate on the sacred value of three or four A-levels all in the natural sciences will know what I mean. Indeed, even with my hostility to Sir Keith Joseph's educational *dirigisme*, it is difficult not to have a sneaking sense of hope that the A-level strangle-hold might be broken as at least one good thing among all the Joseph losses. Nor has the example of the Open University's success in teaching science and maths to students with no back-ground done much to modify the ideological commitment to premature specialization. Such a commitment is bad news for all disadvantaged potential students; for women, because of the other barriers we now recognize which direct them away from the 'masculine' 'hard' subjects at school, it is extremely negative.

## Science and Technology under Capitalist Patriarchy

However, we cannot consider the question of increasing the participation of women in science and technology education without looking at what science and technology are actually doing in Britain today and asking whether it is the kind of activity which women would want to enter.

The overwhelming majority of spending on science and technology by state and industry, and of the employment of scientists and technologists, can be categorized under two very traditionally male heads – science for military and internal security goals, and science for production and profit. Science for social welfare and for the environment come a very poor third (science for that disinterested goal – knowledge for its own sake – while important within the ideology of science, forms a very tiny part of the whole enterprise). You can see this in the distribution of the science and technology (research and development) budget, now some 2–2.5 per cent of G.N.P. The government's share of this, according to government sources,[5] was £3.38 billion in 1981–2, and about half was spent on military research and development. It is difficult to be very precise about these figures, as a good deal depends on the detailed definitions employed; European Commission statistics,[6] for example, suggest that Britain spends 60 per cent of the state budget on military research and development. However, there is nothing new about this militaristic direction of the British research effort. Since 1945 the figure has oscillated around the 50 per cent level, but has, by any method of calculation, shown an increase since the Thatcher administration took office in 1979. In scientific research, as elsewhere, the restructuring of the pattern of public expenditure has worked so as to promote swords and reduce ploughshares. This high figure for military research is incidentally a much greater proportion than spent by any other industrial nation except the U.S. Germany spends 12 per cent, Japan less than 5 per cent. It is scarcely surprising that the outcomes of research and development reflect the goals of its fund-givers.

However, what is discussed rather less is the fact that these fund-givers, whether industry or the state, are, like the scientists and engineers who carry out the research, overwhelmingly male. Although varied in their class origins and positions, they share certain common assumptions concerning the priority of the needs of the production of wealth and of military defence. It is by no means self-evident that productionism and militarism hold such a priority within the agenda of women. (It may, too, cast a little light on the fact that less than 10 per cent of the research on birth control technology is directed towards men.[7])

Historically, science as knowledge was seen as a liberatory force; scientists were men (and rather infrequently women) critical of the social order, struggling for the greater freedom of the human spirit. An engendered look at that past might well interpret the freedom as being mainly gained for men and offering much less except in a rather abstract and relative way for women. However, even to speak of science as a critical force within culture is to invoke a period long since past. Today science is incorporated into the social order in a way that few other areas of the higher education syllabus are – with the possible exception of management and business studies.[8] And all the evidence is that this incorporation is becoming ever more complete, with the passive support of the present generation of University Grants Committees and Research Council members and administrators.

Throughout most of their history, the development of physics, chemistry and engineering has been geared to the needs of the generation of weapons and profit. But the speed with which even the most arcane of scientific endeavours is pressed into service by state and industry in pursuit of these twin goals, although not fast enough for the technocratic imagination which believes that herein lies the core of the

explanation for Britain's relatively poor economic performance over past decades, is still impressive. There is little space
for autonomy in sciences ranging from astronomy, whose
huge expenses are met with a view to the backhanders which
may accrue to the space race and star war programmes, to
biology, where what twenty years ago was an 'academic'
study of genetics and the molecular components of life has
become a scramble for patents and industrial investment as
the great biotechnology bandwagon with all its promises (and
threats) of genetic engineering[9] begins to roll.

If this is the character of contemporary science and technology, why should we want socialists or feminists (or indeed
anyone) to enter it? But there is more yet. Go back to the
golden age of critical science – or at least the myth thereof. It
is doubtless true that the part science played in the transition
from feudalism to capitalism was a vital one, and that this
transition was part of a liberation of the human spirit and
intellect from the dead weight of the received wisdom of
church, king and custom. Exploring and understanding the
natural world so as to generate the public knowledge which
the methods of scientific inquiry yield were steps on the road
to human freedom. But they were distinctly lopsided steps
taken along a route which was simultaneously capitalist and
male-dominated. Feudal society had, perforce, to endeavour
to achieve some sort of harmonious relationship with a nature
which it had not the means to control.

Critical social theory,[10] less enthusiastic about the role of
science down the mainstream traditions of either reformist or
Marxist socialism, argued that modern science had a fundamentally exploitative relationship to nature, seeking control
and mastery. Domination replaced harmony. Through feminist scholars, notably Carolyn Merchant, we have learnt to
re-read Francis Bacon,[11] acknowledging him as the major
ideologue for both bourgeois and socialist cultural traditions
in modern science, and see the sexual violence of his central
metaphors. Bacon's science is lustfully masculine, his metaphors are unabashedly those of 'uncovering nature's naked-
ness . . . wresting her secrets from her . . . penetrating her

inmost recesses'. They are the metaphors of rape. And this explicitly male goal of domination and exploitation has remained central not merely to capitalist science as it has developed but to the equally masculine traditional socialist view of the purposes, prospects and methods of science and technology.

We have had to wait for Evelyn Keller's[12] study of the geneticist Barbara McClintock, who last year at the age of eighty-two was awarded the Nobel Prize for work done many years earlier (should we ask why so late as well as why so few?), in order to read a detailed account of a radically different relationship of a scientist to nature. McClintock speaks (and it is rightly reflected in the book's title) of *A Feeling for the Organism*. While McClintock made a salutary contrast to the macho imperializing account of the arch-reductionist Jim Watson,[13] Keller is not making an essentialist point concerning the differences between the perspectives. I could cite for example the geneticist J. B. S. Haldane, who practised what he described as a non-violent biology. What feminism is after is a newly engendered perspective and that is not a biological phenomenon.

Nonetheless, Bacon's exploitative view of science and nature has permeated the analysis of both Marxism and labourism through this century. Science and technology through the exploitation of nature were to do nothing less than end want. In Britain (and his influence was international rather than merely national) it is typified above all by the work of J. D. Bernal,[14] who did more than any single person from the 1920s to the 1960s to influence the science policy goals of both the Labour and Communist parties. It characterized Wilson's strategy in 1964 (and Mitterand's in 1980) for the building of socialism through 'the white heat of the scientific and technological revolution'. It was still evident in the Labour Party's election manifesto of 1983, with its emphasis on using new technology to aid a product-based recovery of the economy and on strengthening the links between research in higher education and industry so as to speed innovation. And towards the end of 1984, the scientific and higher education trade unions launched another resolutely backward-looking campaign: 'The Alliance for Science'.

The Labour Party manifesto, to be fair, did call for the increase of girls and women within science and education and made some reference to wider social objectives. But it fell far short of recognizing the new social movements with their very different relationship to science and technology – which see them in no small way as part of the problem.

## Science, Technology and the New Social Movements

This conception of humanity's relationship to nature as one of mastery and exploitation lies at the heart not simply of a particular Labour Party manifesto commitment but of the Labour movement itself. While not sharing the militaristic goals of a capitalist science and technology, the Labour movement is deeply preoccupied with productionism through the exploitation of nature. It is precisely this conception which the new social movements of feminism and ecology challenge. Feminism claims women's rights over their own bodies, above all to choose to have or not to have children. Within feminism women look for a harmonious relationship between their lives and nature, beginning with their own nature. This harmonious relationship with nature intrinsic to feminism finds matching resonances with ecology. From an initial set of anxieties about 'limits to growth', finite natural resources, problems of global pollution and holocaust, an alternative vision of humanity and nature has developed.

To bring this new relationship into existence, both feminism and ecology necessarily reject the split, central to the science of domination, between the living participative 'I' of experience and the external world of nature. Where the old science cut thought and feeling in two, separated subjectivity from objectivity, the new movements seek a reconciliation.[15] The objectivity of science which was claimed as its highest cultural achievement is seen by the new social movements as threatening human survival itself.[16] It is uncomfortably like the old medical joke which similarly split technique from social purpose. 'Yes, the operation was a great success; unfortunately the patient died.'

The difficulty the new movements face in bringing this new conception into the old science and technology and transforming them is nowhere more evident than in the very different trajectories of ecology as a social movement and ecology as a subject within higher education. Born during the optimism of the 1960s and 1970s, the teaching of ecology was seen as a creative response to the problems of pollution and the need to conserve natural resources. As a new strand within biology it found an uneasy place in school, further and higher education syllabuses during the 1970s and attracted students – both men and women – who shared these goals.

Ecology as an academic subject is defined as the study of the relationships between communities of living organisms and the living and non-living world around them. Sustained by the growing public concern with ecological issues, the subject grew steadily. No small part of the credit for this new public concern must be attributed to Rachel Carson's path-breaking book *Silent Spring*. While not a self-identified feminist, her writing was to speak eloquently of the twin risks of human and natural catastrophe resulting from the present technological culture. Today we have Bhophal.

But the sad thing is how far the education courses have become separated from the utopian goals of the movement itself. The social movement stressed holism, the need to live non-violently and harmoniously with nature. The science and the movement look to emphasize the complexity and inter-connectedness of the living world; the belief that it is not possible to understand the present without its past; nor by disarticulating nature into molecular components alone; nor as divorced from human interest and intervention – and hence human values. But ecology as a taught science in the context of a deteriorating economy (to say nothing of the U.G.C. cuts in 1981 which specifically attacked non-profit-oriented biology) became trapped into precisely the fragmented, analytical mode of approach of the classical science disciplines. This captured ecology laid its stress on objectivity, on control, on reductionism, as opposed to the holistic understanding represented by the hopes of the social movement. And where the movement sought to transform the world, ecology courses increasingly turned out a generation of pollution control experts and planners to be snapped up by industry to provide the know-how to manipulate, circumvent and avert planning legislation and pollution control standards.

## Feminism, the Division of Labour and a New Vision of Science

But why does this more harmonious vision of the relationship of humanity and nature flow from feminist theory and understanding? And why is it so conspicuously lacking from actually existing science and technology? Surely it is precisely because of the division of labour between women and men in contemporary industrial society which cuts women out of science.[17] A division of labour which allocates caring and reproductive labour to women and cognitive and productive labour to men is bound to result in the science done by the men reflecting their male priorities and goals. Science can only be transformed from an instrument of oppression and destruction into one of liberation for all humanity by its reorientation towards feminist (which offers genuinely humanist) goals. This is why the project of feminizing science is much more than a simple E.O.C.-type project, however much we need to encourage and struggle for equal opportunities strategies. To be realist as well as visionary requires change on multiple levels. Without such a multi-faceted approach, projects like W.I.S.E., and even G.I.S.T., threaten to become new victims to what has been unforgettably described in policy innovations as 'reinventing the broken wheel'. Other broken wheels have followed the post-Sputnik panic of the late fifties, when the U.S. tried very hard to get more girls and women into science and technology so as to compete more effectively in the superpowers space war. In Britain 1969 was also an earlier year of getting women into engineering. Puns apart, it might be wise to look at these earlier initiatives in the light of the fact that there are proportionately fewer women academics in, for example, mathematics and physics now than there were in the 1920s. It is only medicine as a science-based profession which has made significant space for women. Indeed, in Britain it is particularly critical to examine the relationship between education and training and the labour market. Hakim's work,[18] for example, points to an increasingly segregated labour market, with women taking a diminished share of the skilled jobs, so that despite sixty years of educational reform, women's position in the labour market was relatively worse in 1971 than in 1911.

## What is to be Done?

This critique of actually existing science and technology and technology and its teaching has been root and branch. The need to transform science and technology has never been more urgent, yet at the same time it has never been more possible. The burgeoning social movements of ecology and feminism are challenging the existing order not merely in theory but in a multitude of local practical activities. The socialist cities, London and Sheffield particularly, have fostered a mass of experimentation and innovation, releasing people's creative potential – take the work of the Greater London Enterprise Board (G.L.E.B.) with its programme of local computer and technically-equipped workshops. East Leeds Women's Workshop, which has sought to give women technological skills while simultaneously offering child-care, has been an important pointer to the new directions that we need for a socialist policy in science. It is not surprising that this present government has set cash limits and has refused to support projects designed, like Leeds, to have integral child-care facilities.

Science and the Demands on Women's Time

Women's lives are not organized around paid work like those of men, instead they are threaded between the demands of caring for children, running a home, caring for an elderly parent: each activity must be worked around the next. Extraordinarily few women can leave home in the morning, simply returning at night to eat an evening meal and to sit by the box, read a book, perhaps go out for a drink, or even go to a Labour Party meeting. It is this fundamental difference between most women's and men's lives which creates the problem in getting and *keeping* girls and women in science and technology.

Even studying science and technology in higher education regulates time in a less flexible way than other subjects and, as I have already said, there is a deeper link between studying and doing science than there is in many of the disciplines. An arts or social science student can choose the most convenient place to study – library or home – the science or engineering student, like a factory worker, has virtually to clock in. S/he has to be in the laboratory, to work through experiments, to analyse them on the computer terminal. Much less can be taken home to be fitted around other activities.

What is true at the undergraduate level is even more true at the postgraduate and postdoctoral level. At this stage the young scientist or engineer is expected to spend long hours in the laboratory; extended, even overnight, experiments are part and parcel of the process of becoming a recognized scientist. Even though it is for safety rather than a measure of work, science and engineering students have to sign in when they work unsocial hours. How does this world of exclusive preoccupation with science match up to the multiple demands a woman experiences? When, in an account of the 'surplus graduates', Geoffrey Beattie[19] writes of women biochemists being 'more realistic' and accepting jobs as lab technicians, what the author is really saying is that in order to limit the number of hours demanded of them by science, the subordinate job of a technician is seen as having the merit of defining and controlling the hours of work. Thus, the 'realism' of which Beattie speaks approvingly is that women must in practice submit to the unjust and unequal division of labour inside and outside the laboratory.

A woman's double labour burden means not only that she is likely to find coping with the male pattern of scientific work difficult, but that the paucity of adequate nursery provision pushes her out altogether. There is not a single woman vice-chancellor or principal in the entire British university system (nor for that matter a single woman director of a polytechnic), so it is not too surprising that C.V.C.P. managed to conclude that universities did not have to provide nurseries and crèches. It seems that it is all right to subsidize student accommodation, rugby, football, hockey, swimming pools, sports halls, drinking and catering facilities, but not crèches. We are required to believe that the gender imbalance among the students using these facilities is simply a matter of chance. A much needed piece of simple research is to measure the gender differential usage of student so-called universal facilities.

This lack of good facilities – from birth-to-five crèches, and play provision for five+ children – affects all women students and staff with young children adversely, and those in the laboratory-based subjects doubly so. Without child-care provision – a crucial element in the material conditions of their participation – they are denied access to academic and particularly to scientific life.

Many women simply lack the possibility of carrying on in full-time science and engineering when they become mothers; others want to spend time with their children. Part-time participation in science and engineering is extraordinarily difficult, and the tightening of the academic labour market has by and large eroded such limited opportunities as there were. If she is pushed into or chooses full-time motherhood, getting back into science afterwards is tough. The knowledge base of science is cumulative; 5–7 years out and the re-entry into research is either impossible or at a very junior level.

The much heralded 'new blood' posts (actually paid for

A. D C.

with something which looks remarkably like the monies cut from the social sciences, where women are more in evidence) are a bonus for men. Only one in the first round went to a woman. As Professor Daphne Jackson of the Women in Engineering Society pointed out, the age limit of 35 actively discriminates against women. And while the E.O.C. points with some pride to extending the age limit for women into the executive grade of the Civil Service it has, despite W.I.S.E., done little on the 'new blood' scheme. So even a small equalizing reform requires that the age-bar for women is lifted so as to take account of the average length of time spent in child-care.

There is an acute need for women to have adequate child-care facilities in higher education so as to make the care of children into a public and convivial activity, so that for instance a parent (or any other friendly adult for that matter) can nip across between lectures or experiments to play with children. This itself would help produce a different and more human environment for studying and researching. If we are serious about bringing women into science and engineering we have to bring the children in. But there is no joy in setting up nurseries so that women scientists become like men scientists. It is not simply that women rightly don't want to become men, but that if there is to be a chance of society getting the humane science and technology it so urgently needs, it can only be achieved by bringing into science those whose values are informed by their caring labour.

The provision of nurseries is thus not only to make possible women's entry into science, but also, through encouraging men to share in child-care, to erode the over-commitment to the male scientific work ethic. The changing structure of employment is presently directed by a policy which deliberately requires the unemployment of 4 million people to achieve its economic and political objectives. Egalitarian objectives could seize the opportunities to fashion an entirely new relationship to the worlds of paid and unpaid work. The radical revision of the scientific work ethic which perpetuates the exclusivity of science is desperately overdue.

## Reconceptualizing Science Education

The content and form of science and technology teaching need reconceptualization. Schools used to teach science as a set of received facts about the world, combined with so-called 'experiments' – actually demonstrations designed to 'prove', or rather illustrate, these facts. (Even when the experiments failed, pupils were encouraged to write down what 'should' have happened.) Since the Nuffield science and education schemes, some schools have adopted versions of its explicitly Popperian hypothesis falsification model of science teaching – though there are some indications that it disadvantages working-class children. Many teachers are still uneasy about this divorce of science from lived experience and social context, but are trapped by the rigidities of premature special-ization, A-level and university entry requirements. Socialist and feminist science teachers could and should be encouraged to build new syllabuses based around pupils' 'lived' experience, and to break the barrier between 'science' and 'non-science'. The now clear evidence that girls do better in science subjects and maths if taught in single-sex classes should be recognized.[20]

Higher and further education build on the schools' approach. They receive 18-year-olds accustomed to learning from authority, to separating fact from value, and to the abstract world of taught science. The rigidity of the entry requirements to these subjects makes polys and universities inflexible to the needs of mature students, likely dispropor-tionately to be women. Within the hallowed walls, the author-ity of the research and review paper substitute for that of the teacher. The hierarchies of theory and practice, (hard) and mathematical sciences over (soft) and human-centred ones, are reinforced.[21] Education is pragmatically directed towards, for the brightest, the research career leading linearly to fellowships of the Royal Society and the Nobel Prize; for the rest, into an industry whose unidimensional goals are those of profitability which the student is not encouraged – or given the intellectual tools – to evaluate. Indeed, this cutting adrift of science from social context has now been specifically reinforced by Sir Keith Joseph, who has frowned upon those few 'science and society' courses which were established – mainly in the polys – during the 1970s.

To transform the content of this science and technology, in a way which makes it accessible to women and open to feminist and socialist demands, we must also begin by opening the syllabus towards a more human and social-centred approach. This means more than tacking a few obligatory culture lectures on to the slack parts of the week along with the traditional Wednesday afternoon off for games. We must encourage science to be taught in its context – linking genetics with the implications of genetic engineering and birth-control technology, biochemistry with the drug industry and biotechnology. But we need to be aware of the pressures on students to avoid discussing the perspectives of science and technology in a social context; even where courses are available it is far from unknown for them to vote with their feet.

Getting large numbers of women into science and technology is to bring in that gender perspective stemming from the experience of those whose lives are interwoven between the demands and skills of caring and the demands and skills of scientific research and teaching. It may well be the only practical way of realizing the objective of changing science education from narrow technicism to a socially contextualized approach.

## A Socialist Feminist 'New Blood' Scheme?

Again, we could develop a socialist and feminist version of a 'new blood' scheme by linking formal education to the rich ferment of community and trade-union-based experimentation and innovation. The women's health movement is a significant force not only for changing health care but also for the accelerated self-education of women in the biology of women. Trade union groups seeking, like the Lucas workers, for socially responsible products as a means to save jobs and produce something worthwhile similarly serve to release the creativity and self-learning of groups excluded from traditional ways of planning science and technology. Critically examining the experience of the radical local authorities in trying to make these links could provide us with the necessary knowledge to develop an alternative 'new blood' strategy which a Labour government could introduce on a nationwide scale. The hermetically sealed world of science and technology education and research, opened or closed by the selection of subjects at 16, could be perfused with such 'new blood'. Of course there would be resistance, but the remarkable way in which the sticks and carrots offered by a New Right government have forced education to the right suggest that an equally determined Labour government could, and with rather more popular support from within education, move it towards socialist objectives.

## Nothing Less than Half the Labs

It is not possible in any discussion of getting women into science and engineering – that is, to be satisfied with nothing less than half the labs – to think that this can be achieved without radical changes at a multiplicity of levels. It is the overwhelming strengths of great social movements that they do and can operate in this way. It is this creative strength which a Labour Party, if it is to capture office, let alone bring about change, must understand and work with. The strength and genius of the Labour movement was that it saw that in just social relations of production it could solve exploitation and want. Now feminism and ecology comprehend, more than most – not all – of the labour movement, that the central question for humanity is no longer production as the overwhelming priority, but necessarily, and with equal or even greater priority, reproduction in all its biological and social sense. Thus our hopes for the apparently modest reform of gender equality within the labs are unrealizable unless we understand and are willing to work simultaneously for the necessary changes in both the content and the form of science education and the content and the form of science and technology themselves. I think it was William Morris who observed that every serious social reformer was necessarily a revolutionary. This strikes me as an entirely reasonable position, and certainly an advance on the old dichotomy.[22] Thus the reforms, positive role models, sponsoring single-sex teaching, and a bunch of other innovations only work because even in these quite small ways they reach the evident desires of women and men for a different and safer society. The old manpower (*sic*) approach where the numbers of qualified scientists and engineers are totted up, and the captains of industry and the professors of engineering and biotechnology are looked to to produce an economically buoyant Britain, lacks the political – and economic – credibility it enjoyed in 1964.[23] Above all – for this book is concerned with 18+ education – such an approach shows little capacity to convince, let alone enthuse, young women and young men. It is to these young people socialists and feminists must listen, and these we have to convince and enthuse.

Opening science and technological education to serve new and more complex goals is no small task, and it is going to produce anxiety and resistance among educators who may well feel with some reason that they have something to lose. Restructuring scientific and technological education from the left cannot be carried out with the same indifference to the human costs as the ongoing restructuring carried out by the right. But we have to acknowledge that much of what presently passes for science and technology may prove unnecessary or unwanted and the training of scientists and engineers for these tasks quite inappropriate. Do we want aeronautical engineers or pharmacologists for instance, if our goals are those of – say – the development of methods and designs to convert a large part of the existing housing stock, obsolescent to the ways that women, men and children live now – into flexible homes that can accommodate new relations of domestic life?

To sum up, the present state of science and technology education is that of training predominantly men to enter into the unidimensional goals of science and technology for the growth of weaponry and profit. The declared goal of the Labour Party is to encourage men and women to enter a science and technology education designed to promote economic growth. While this is a welcome improvement on the present commitment to militaristic science, it must go beyond this to begin to respond to the demands both of the old labour movement and of the new social movements confronting the social and economic crisis of our time. We need science and technology for economic sufficiency *and social growth*, a science and technology education for women and men which will enable us to construct tools for conviviality and for the control and direction over our own lives. *Nothing less than half the labs* makes a good starting slogan.

### Notes

1 Alison Kelly, Judith Whyte and Barbara Smail, *Girls into Science and Technology: Final Report*, mimeo, University of Manchester, 1984.

2 Virginia Woolf, *Three Guineas* (1938), Penguin, 1977.

3 Despite the theoretical disagreements between radical and socialist feminists, both seek a radically different society – so I have called them 'transformative', as against the equal rights perspective.

4 Mrs Dicks was a biologist research worker, contesting her redundancy with the support of E.O.C. against the same university which was also discussing with the E.O.C. a conversion course to attract more arts women students into sciences.

5 *Annual Review on Government Funded Research and Development*, H.M.S.O., 1983.

6 *Eurostats*, 1983.

7 Audrey Leothard, *Inequalities in Health Care: Birth Control Provision in the U.K.*, paper given at Social Administration Association Conference, July 1984.

8 Hilary Rose and Steven Rose, 'The Incorporation of Science' in H. Rose and S. Rose (eds.), *The Political Economy of Science*, Macmillan, 1976.

9 Warnock, *Report of the Committee of Inquiry into Human Fertilization and Embryology*, Cmnd. 9314, H.M.S.O., 1984.

10  A. Schmidt, *The Concept of Nature in Marx*, New Left Books, 1973. A more popular account was that of W. Leiss, *The Domination of Nature*, George Braziller, N.Y., 1972.

11  Carolyn Merchant, *The Death of Nature*, Wildwood House, 1982.

12  Evelyn Keller, *A Feeling for the Organism*, Freeman & Co., San Francisco, 1983.

13  James Watson, *The Double Helix*, Weidenfeld & Nicolson, 1968.

14  J. D. Bernal was a crystallographer and a Marxist. The most influential book was *The Social Functions of Science*, Routledge & Kegan Paul, 1939, the catalyst both for the social relations of science movement and for the stress on productionism through science and technology described here.

15  New work on feminist epistemology explores these issues – see the collection edited by Sandra Harding and Merrill B. Hintikka, *Discovering Reality*, Reidel, Dordrecht, 1983.

16  The move to contest the objectivity and extreme reductionism of science comes from within science; see for example the writings of Fritjhof Capra, *The Turning Point; Science Society and the Rising Culture*, Bantam, 1983.
  Karl Pribram's – an erstwhile arch-reductionist – conversion to holism. Many of the papers gathered in the two volumes, *Towards a Liberatory Biology* and *Against Biological Determinism*, ed. Steven Rose *et al.*, Allison & Busby, 1982, and Helga Nowotny and Hilary Rose (eds.), *Counter-movements in Sciences*, Reidel, Dordrecht, 1979.

17  Hilary Rose, 'Hand, Brain and Heart: Towards a Feminist Epistemology for the Natural Sciences', *Signs: International Journal of Women in Culture and Society*, 9, 11, Autumn 1983.

18  Catherine Hakim, *Occupation Segregation*, Res. Paper No. 9, D.O.E., November 1979.

19  *Guardian*, 21 January 1984.

20  See Rosemary Deem, *Women and Schooling*, Routledge & Kegan Paul, 1978; (ed.) *Schooling for Women's Work*, Routledge & Kegan Paul, 1980. Jenny Shaw, 'Finishing School: some implications of sex-segregated education', in D. Leonard Barker and S. Allen (eds.), *Sexual Divisions and Society*, Tavistock, 1976, and 'Education and the individual: schooling for girls or mixed schooling – a mixed blessing?', in Deem (ed.), op. cit., 1980.
  The literature on girls and science education is expanding, and is important because of early specialization. See Alison Kelly, *Girls and Science: An International Study of Sex Differences in School Science Achievements*, Almquist and Wiksell, Stockholm, 1978; Alison Kelly (ed.), *The Missing Half*, Manchester University Press, 1981; R. Walden

and V. Walkerdine, *Girls and Maths: The Early Years*, Bedford Way Papers, 8, University of London, Institute of Education, 1981.

Since writing this paper I have learnt that Thameside Educational Authority is actively encouraging its women science teachers to develop a 'girls' science'.

21 And the sexual connotation of 'hard' and 'soft' remains acknow-ledged only at the level of jokes by malestream philosophy of science.

22 Of course The Redstockings Manifesto recognized this even more clearly: 'We will not ask what is "revolutionary", what is "reformist", only "what is good for women?" ' in Leslie B. Tanner (ed.), *Voices from Women's Liberation*, Signet, New American Library, 1971.

23 The resurrection of the 1964 programme, in 1984 with the A.S.T.M.S., A.U.T., etc. 'Alliance for Science' is bathetic. It fails to grasp the changed social, economic and technological conditions.

# Notes on Contributors

MICHAEL CUNNINGHAM has worked as a full-time trade union officer since 1975. Currently, as an officer of the National Union of Public Employees, he is the official responsible for N.U.P.E. members working in the university sector in London as manual and ancillary staff (porters, cleaners, catering workers, craft workers). He has worked extensively with his members on skills training, in association with London University, Camden Council and the G.L.C. His previous publications have been on health and safety at work, and on non-wage benefits, including educational leave.

ROSEMARY DEEM is a lecturer in the School of Education at the Open University. She has published widely on the topic of women and education. She has been a County Councillor in Buckinghamshire since 1982, and in 1982–5 was spokesperson on education for the Labour opposition group.

OLIVER FULTON is Director of the University of Lancaster's Institute for Research and Development in Post Compulsory Education. He has researched and published extensively in the areas of demand for and access to higher education. He was convenor of the S.R.H.E./Leverhulme seminar on demand and access, and edited its report *Access to Higher Education* (S.R.H.E., 1982).

GORDON LAWRENCE has recently retired. He has worked as a printmaker, sculptor and painter, and has held posts in art education both in schools and in the higher education sector. He has researched and published on art education policy, and has been active in promoting art education while serving as the chair of the Art and Design Committee of his trade union, A.T.T.I./N.A.T.F.H.E.

DAVID PAGE is a painter who has both exhibited his work and taught in higher education since 1959 in Germany and Britain. Until recently he taught at the North East London Polytechnic. He worked at Hornsey College of Art in the 1960s, and helped to produce and edit the book on the art school revolt of 1968, *The Hornsey Affair* (Penguin, 1969).

HILARY ROSE is Professor of Applied Social Studies at Bradford University. She has written, researched and been active in the politics of science since the sixties, initially within the radical science movement and, since the seventies, within the feminist movement. She has published widely on these issues. She also works as a member of the editorial group of *New Socialist*.

BILL SCHWARZ studied English and History at York University and subsequently became a research student at the Centre for Contemporary Cultural Studies, Birmingham. He now teaches cultural studies at the North East London Polytechnic. He has co-edited books on ideology, history and politics.

PETER SCOTT has been the editor of *The Times Higher Education Supplement* since 1976. He has also worked for *The Times*, and was a visiting scholar at the University of California, Berkeley, in 1973–4. He is the author of *The Crisis of the University* (Croom Helm, 1984).

JENNY SHAW has worked in higher education since 1966, in both the polytechnic and university sectors. Currently she works as a sociologist in the School of Social Sciences in the University of Sussex. She has published extensively on educational issues.

ALAN WHITE entered higher education as a mature student, after working in a camping shop and a children's home. He studied at the North East London Polytechnic and subsequently as a postgraduate at Leeds University, where he has been researching the formation of the nineteenth-century middle class. He is currently teaching sociology at the North East London Polytechnic.

BILL WILLIAMSON is a senior lecturer in sociology at the University of Durham and studied at Regent Street Polytechnic. His research interests and publications are in the fields of education, labour history and problems of educational development in the Third World. He is a member of the Labour Party and of the Association of University Teachers.

## MORE ABOUT PENGUINS, PELICANS, PEREGRINES AND PUFFINS

For further information about books available from Penguins please write to Dept EP, Penguin Books Ltd, Harmondsworth, Middlesex UB7 0DA.

*In the U.S.A.*: For a complete list of books available from Penguins in the United States write to Dept DG, Penguin Books, 299 Murray Hill Parkway, East Rutherford, New Jersey 07073.

*In Canada*: For a complete list of books available from Penguins in Canada write to Penguin Books Canada Ltd, 2801 John Street, Markham, Ontario L3R 1B4.

*In Australia*: For a complete list of books available from Penguins in Australia write to the Marketing Department, Penguin Books Australia Ltd, P.O. Box 257, Ringwood, Victoria 3134.

*In New Zealand*: For a complete list of books available from Penguins in New Zealand write to the Marketing Department, Penguin Books (N.Z.) Ltd, Private Bag, Takapuna, Auckland 9.

*In India*: For a complete list of books available from Penguins in India write to Penguin Overseas Ltd, 706 Eros Apartments, 56 Nehru Place, New Delhi 110019.

# A CHOICE OF
# PELICANS AND PEREGRINES

☐ **The Knight, the Lady and the Priest**
**Georges Duby** £6.95

The acclaimed study of the making of modern marriage in medieval France. 'He has traced this story – sometimes amusing, often horrifying, always startling – in a series of brilliant vignettes' – *Observer*

☐ **The Limits of Soviet Power** **Jonathan Steele** £3.95

The Kremlin's foreign policy – Brezhnev to Chernenko, is discussed in this informed, informative 'wholly invaluable and extraordinarily timely study' – *Guardian*

☐ **Understanding Organizations** **Charles B. Handy** £4.95

Third Edition. Designed as a practical source-book for managers, this Pelican looks at the concepts, key issues and current fashions in tackling organizational problems.

☐ **The Pelican Freud Library: Volume 12** £5.95

Containing the major essays: *Civilization, Society and Religion, Group Psychology* and *Civilization and Its Discontents*, plus other works.

☐ **Windows on the Mind** **Erich Harth** £4.95

Is there a physical explanation for the various phenomena that we call 'mind'? Professor Harth takes in age-old philosophers as well as the latest neuroscientific theories in his masterly study of memory, perception, free will, selfhood, sensation and other richly controversial fields.

☐ **The Pelican History of the World**
**J. M. Roberts** £5.95

'A stupendous achievement . . . This is the unrivalled World History for our day' – A. J. P. Taylor

# A CHOICE OF
# PELICANS AND PEREGRINES

☐ *A Question of Economics* **Peter Donaldson** £4.95

Twenty key issues – from the City and big business to trades unions –
clarified and discussed by Peter Donaldson, author of *10 × Economics* and one of our greatest popularizers of economics.

☐ *Inside the Inner City* **Paul Harrison** £4.95

A report on urban poverty and conflict by the author of *Inside the
Third World*. 'A major piece of evidence' – *Sunday Times*. 'A classic:
it tells us what it is really like to be poor, and why' – *Time Out*

☐ *What Philosophy Is* **Anthony O'Hear** £4.95

What are human beings? How should people act? How do our
thoughts and words relate to reality? Contemporary attitudes to
these age-old questions are discussed in this new study, an eloquent
and brilliant introduction to philosophy today.

☐ *The Arabs* **Peter Mansfield** £4.95

New Edition. 'Should be studied by anyone who wants to know
about the Arab world and how the Arabs have become what they are
today' – *Sunday Times*

☐ *Religion and the Rise of Capitalism*
  **R. H. Tawney** £3.95

The classic study of religious thought of social and economic issues
from the later middle ages to the early eighteenth century.

☐ *The Mathematical Experience*
  **Philip J. Davis and Reuben Hersh** £7.95

Not since *Gödel, Escher, Bach* has such an entertaining book been
written on the relationship of mathematics to the arts and sciences.
'It deserves to be read by everyone ... an instant classic' – *New
Scientist*

# A CHOICE OF
# PELICANS AND PEREGRINES

☐ *Crowds and Power* **Elias Canetti** £4.95

'Marvellous . . . an immensely interesting, often profound reflection about the nature of society, in particular the nature of violence' – Susan Sontag in *The New York Review of Books*

☐ *The Death and Life of Great American Cities*
**Jane Jacobs** £5.95

One of the most exciting and wittily written attacks on contemporary city planning to have appeared in recent years – thought-provoking reading and, as one critic noted, 'extremely apposite to conditions in the UK'.

☐ *Computer Power and Human Reason*
**Joseph Weizenbaum** £3.95

Internationally acclaimed by scientists and humanists alike: 'This is the best book I have read on the impact of computers on society, and on technology and on man's image of himself' – *Psychology Today*

---

These books should be available at all good bookshops or news-agents, but if you live in the UK or the Republic of Ireland and have difficulty in getting to a bookshop, they can be ordered by post. Please indicate the titles required and fill in the form below.

NAME_____BLOCK CAPITALS

ADDRESS_____

_____

_____

Enclose a cheque or postal order payable to The Penguin Bookshop to cover the total price of books ordered, plus 50p for postage. Readers in the Republic of Ireland should send £1 R equivalent to the sterling prices, plus 67p for postage. Send to: The Penguin Bookshop, 54/56 Bridlesmith Gate, Nottingham, NG1 2GP.

You can also order by phoning (0602) 599295, and quoting your Barclaycard or Access number.

Every effort is made to ensure the accuracy of the price and availability of books at the time of going to press, but it is sometimes necessary to increase prices and in these circumstances retail prices may be shown on the covers of books which may differ from the prices shown in this list or elsewhere. This list is not an offer to supply any book.

**This order service is only available to residents in the UK and the Republic of Ireland.**